The Politics of Inclusion and Exclusion

Assessing the limits of pluralism, this book examines different types of political inclusion and exclusion and their distinctive dimensions and dynamics. Why are particular social groups excluded from equal participation in political processes? How do these groups become more fully included as equal participants? Often, the critical issue is not *whether* a group is included but *how* it is included. Collectively, these essays elucidate a wide range of inclusion or exclusion: voting participation, representation in legislative assemblies, representation of group interests in processes of policy formation and implementation, and participation in discursive processes of policy framing.

Covering broad territory—from African Americans to Asian Americans, the transgendered to the disabled, and Latinos to Native Americans—this volume examines in depth the give and take between how policies shape politics and how politics shape policy. At a more fundamental level, Ericson and his contributors raise some traditional and some not-so-traditional issues about the nature of democratic politics in settings with a multitude of group identities.

David F. Ericson is a Professor in the Department of Public and International Affairs at George Mason University. His current research focuses on the centrality of slavery to the American experience.

The Politics of Inclusion and Exclusion

Identity Politics in Twenty-First Century America

Edited by
David F. Ericson

Routledge
Taylor & Francis Group

NEW YORK AND LONDON

First published 2011
by Routledge
605 Third Avenue, New York, NY 10017

Simultaneously published in the UK
by Routledge
4 Park Square, Milton Park, Abingdon, Oxon OX14 4RN

Routledge is an imprint of the Taylor & Francis Group, an informa business

Library of Congress Cataloging in Publication Data
The politics of inclusion and exclusion : identity politics in twenty-first century America / [edited by] David F. Ericson.
    p. cm.
    1. Minorities–Political activity–United States. 2. Identity politics–United States. I. Ericson, David F., 1950–
    E184.A1P645 2011
    323.5–dc22
                            2010028851

ISBN13: 978-0-415-87620-9 (pbk)
ISBN13: 978-0-203-85793-9 (ebk)

Contents

Tables

Contributors

Victor Asal joined the faculty of the Department of Political Science at the University at Albany, State University of New York, in fall 2003. He received his PhD from the University of Maryland in 2003 and his MA from Hebrew University, Israel, in 1996. Asal is a specialist in Comparative Politics and International Relations. His research focuses on the interaction of international relations and domestic politics, notably how this interaction influences ethnic conflict and terrorism. Asal's dissertation, "The Political Inclusion of Minorities at Risk, 1870–2000," was a broad global comparative study of the political inclusion of minorities at risk involving 300 groups over a 100-year period. In conjunction with the Minorities at Risk Project, Asal has overseen several ethnic conflict coding studies. His current research expands on the work in his dissertation, looking at the impact of political discrimination on political violence. Asal has also examined how a terrorist group's characteristics impact the group's behavior. He, finally, has done research on international crises and the impact of nuclear proliferation.

Jenna Basiliere is a PhD candidate in Gender Studies at Indiana University. Her research interests include gender justice activism, non-binary gender constructions, camp, drag performance, and rural sexuality studies. Her dissertation will be an ethnographic examination of the relationships between space, place, and camp forms of gender expression, focusing specifically on constructions of rurality. She recently published an article on the ramifications of the feminist sex wars in *Michigan Feminist Studies*.

José E. Cruz is an Associate Professor of Political Science and Latino Studies at the University at Albany, State University of New York. He is also director of the New York Latino Research and Resources Network (NYLARNet), a research consortium based at University at Albany, and of the Latino Political Barometer (LPB), an annual regional survey of political values, attitudes, and behavior of Latinos. His publications include *Identity and Power: Puerto Rican Politics and the Challenge of Ethnicity* (Temple University Press, 1998) and *Adiós Borinquen*

Querida: The Puerto Rican Diaspora, Its History and Contributions, with Edna Acosta-Belén *et al.* (CELAC, 2000). His paper, "Pluralism and Ethnicity in New York City Politics: The Case of Puerto Ricans," received the Best Faculty Paper Award from the New York State Political Science Association in 2009.

David F. Ericson is a term Associate Professor in the Department of Public and International Affairs at George Mason University. He received his BA from Wayne State University, MA from the University of Michigan, and PhD from the University of Chicago. His publications include *The Debate over Slavery: Antislavery and Proslavery Liberalism in Antebellum America* (New York University Press, 2001) and *The Shaping of American Liberalism: The Debates over Ratification, Nullification, and Slavery* (University of Chicago Press, 1993). He is currently working on a book manuscript, *Slavery in a House Divided: Following the Money Trail*, which is under contract with University Press of Kansas. His research focuses on the centrality of slavery to the American experience.

Sally Friedman is an Associate Professor of Political Science at the University at Albany, State University of New York. She is particularly interested in processes of legislative representation. Her book, *Dilemmas of Representation* (State University of New York Press, 2007), provides case studies exploring the balance of local and national elements that make up the home styles of current members of Congress. Her work has also centered around questions relating to the role of gender in Congress and the impact of a business background on legislative behavior. She teaches a variety of courses in American politics and methodology.

Pei-te Lien is a Professor of Political Science at the University of California, Santa Barbara. Her research focuses on race, ethnicity, gender, and the political participation and incorporation of Chinese and other Asian Americans. She is the author of four books and numerous other publications. Her latest book, *The Transnational Politics of Asian Americans* (Temple University Press, 2009), is co-edited with Chris Collet. She is currently working on a co-authored book on the changing multicultural political leadership in America.

Julie Novkov is a Professor of Political Science and Women's Studies at the University at Albany, State University of New York. Her research and teaching address the intersections of law, history, US political development, and subordinated identity. She is particularly interested in the way that the law defines and translates categories associated with identity, such as race, gender, and sexuality, and the ways that these categories transform and are transformed by legal discourse. She is the author of *Racial Union: Law, Intimacy, and the White State in Alabama 1865–1954* (Michigan, 2008), a co-recipient of APSA's Ralph Bunche Award in 2009. She has also published *Constituting Workers, Protecting*

Women (Michigan, 2001) and co-edited two volumes, *Race and American Political Development* (with Joseph Lowndes and Dorian Warren) and *Security Disarmed: Critical Perspectives on Gender, Race, and Militarization* (with Barbara Sutton and Sandra Morgen), as well as numerous peer-reviewed articles, book chapters, and shorter works. She is currently working on a book addressing the intersections of sexuality, race, and gender in times of military crisis as subordinated groups struggle for rights on the basis of their service to the nation.

William Roth is the Vincent O'Leary Professor Social Welfare and Public Policy in the University at Albany School of Social Welfare. His works include *Movement: A Memoir of Disability, Cancer, and the Holocaust* (McFarland, 2008) and *The Assault on Social Policy* (Columbia University Press, 2002). He co-edited the forthcoming volume, *Globalization, Social Justice, and the Helping Professions* (State University of New York Press, 2010).

Nadia Rubaii-Barrett is Associate Professor of Public Administration at Binghamton University, State University of New York. She is widely regarded as an expert on immigration issues at the local level, with an emphasis on the intergovernmental implications of national policies and the varied responses of local governments to immigrant influxes. In 2000–1, she was part of a four-member research team selected by the US–Mexico Border Counties Coalition and funded by a congressional earmark that examined the costs of illegal immigrants on the law enforcement, criminal justice, and emergency medical systems of counties along the border. In 2008, she was selected by the International City/County Management Association to prepare a White Paper documenting the implications of federal immigration policies on cities, counties, towns, and villages, and developing recommendations for policy change. She has spoken at state, regional, national, and international conferences on the subject of immigration, served as a consultant to local governments interested in immigrant integration, and is leading an effort to develop an interdisciplinary program of study in immigration at Binghamton.

Shannon Scotece is a doctoral candidate in the Department of Political Science at the University at Albany, with a BA from Allegheny College. She specializes in American Politics, particularly political behavior, parties and interest groups, the presidency, and Congress. Her research interests include the current state of youth political engagement and the intersection between religion and politics in the United States. Scotece's dissertation explores the political activism of religious organizations on behalf of progressive issues and the ways they mobilize faith communities.

Patricia Strach received a PhD in political science from University of Wisconsin at Madison in 2004 and is an Assistant Professor in the

Departments of Political Science and Public Administration and Policy at the University at Albany, State University of New York. Her research examines the relationship between social and political institutions in American public policy. Her book, *All in the Family: The Private Roots of American Public Policy* (Stanford, 2007), maps the role of family in the policy process and the consequences for policy when social practices change over time. Currently, she is working on a project that examines why organizations that wish to make a change turn to government (hence making public policy), why they take alternative strategies (fundraising, marketing), and the effect of these strategies on American public policy.

Kathleen Sullivan is an Associate Professor of Political Science at Ohio University in Athens, Ohio. Her research interests include constitutional interpretation and American political development. Her book, *Constitutional Context: Women and Rights Discourse in Nineteenth-Century America* (Johns Hopkins University Press, 2007), places women's struggles to liberate themselves from the common-law doctrine of coverture into the larger development of rights discourse in American politics and law. Her current research interests involve a study of race and the development of state and local police powers in the nineteenth century, as well as a study of the role of the non-state actors that the state employs in governance. She received her PhD in Government from the University of Texas at Austin, her MA from the University of Toronto, and her BA from Colgate University.

Acknowledgments

Most of the chapters in this volume were first presented at the "American Dilemmas: Historical and Comparative Perspectives on Diversity, Health Disparities, and Issues of Substance Abuse" conference at the University at Albany, State University of New York, 23 May 2007. Those authors would like to especially thank Katharine Briar-Lawson, Dean of the School of Social Welfare, for her extremely determined and generous support of the conference. They would also like to thank the following for helping to organize and fund the conference: Sandra Austin, Iris Berger, Manrong Chen, Thomas Church, Beth Elitzer, Glynne Griffith, Susan Herbst, Michael Hill, Pamela Laverty, Daniel Levy, Cathleen Lewandowski, Philip McCallion, Nancy Macy, Dikla Madera, New York Latino Research and Resources Network, Jacqueline Davis Ohwevwo, David Petite, Carole Roth, Leonard Slade, and Lynn Videka. We, finally, are very grateful to those who have since joined our "team," either as writers or editors: Mary Altman, Michael Kerns, Pei-te Lien, Tony Nixon, and Shannon Scotece.

1 Introduction

David F. Ericson

The essays in this volume explore the contemporary politics of inclusion and exclusion. Collectively, they attempt to answer two major questions. Why are particular social groups excluded from equal participation in particular political processes? How do those groups become more fully included as equal participants with other groups in those processes? The critical issue is often not whether a group is included but how it is included. Though most of the essays consider both processes of inclusion and exclusion, readers will be able to sort the essays in terms of whether they focus more on inclusion (Asal, Cruz, Friedman and Scotece, Lien, and Sullivan and Strach) or exclusion (Basiliere, Novkov, Roth, and Rubaii-Barrett).

Another way of distinguishing the volume essays is whether they focus more on how "politics determine policies" or "policies determine politics."[1] The Basiliere essay suggests a particular politics that the transgendered might pursue to create more favorable public policies, while the Friedman and Scotece essay shows how Latino members of Congress are attempting to do just that. The Rubaii-Barrett essay demonstrates how local political constellations are more or less conducive to the political inclusion of recent immigrants, while the Lien and Cruz essays detail how Asian Americans and New York Puerto Ricans, respectively, have included themselves. From the "policies determine politics" side, the Asal essay examines the factors that have led to the political incorporation of "minorities at risk" across the Americas.[2] On a more micro-level, the Roth essay argues that the Americans with Disabilities Act (ADA) has produced a disability politics in the United States dominated by bureaucrats and special interests to the exclusion of the disabled themselves. The Sullivan and Strach essay chronicles how "policies determine politics" through the concept of governance, in terms of how various federal policies require private agents to do the work of government.[3] The Novkov essay analyses both dynamics in explaining how race-conscious judicial decisions precipitated a "colorblind" conservative politics that is now producing a quite different set of decisions. Again, most of the essays in the volume consider both dynamics to some extent, despite their emphases on one or the other.

Relative to the current scholarship, the volume essays interrogate the limits of pluralism. In first presenting his pluralist model in the 1950s, Robert Dahl recognized that not every social group has equal access to the key processes of policy formation in the "American hybrid."[4] Since then, William Connolly, among others, has developed this social fact into a sweeping critique of the pluralist model.[5] Regardless of whether one views unequal access as a qualification to the pluralist model or as a refutation of the model, the fact remains that particular social groups are excluded from equal participation in a range of political processes in a range of ways in the United States and other nations around the world. Political inclusion and exclusion fall on a continuum; they are not dichotomous variables. They are also frequently process specific.[6] Still, as many of the essays in the volume remind us, some groups are excluded from equal participation in more political processes than other groups are, while other groups are excluded from any meaningful participation in all but the most trivial political processes in the nations in which they reside.

In total, the volume essays discuss five political processes in which particular social groups are more or less included: 1) voting participation (Lien); 2) representation in legislative assemblies (Friedman and Scotece); 3) representation of group interests, whether actually or virtually, in processes of policy formation (Basiliere, Cruz, Friedman and Scotece, Roth, and Rubaii-Barrett); 4) representation of group interests, again whether actually or virtually, in processes of policy implementation (Cruz, Roth, Rubaii-Barrett, and Sullivan and Strach); and 5) participation in discursive processes of policy framing (Basiliere and Novkov). Noticeably, several essays (Basiliere, Cruz, Friedman and Scotece, Roth, and Rubaii-Barrett) traverse multiple processes and policy domains.

The essays

Operating at a macro-level of analysis, the Asal essay compares the overall level of political inclusion across the Americas.[7] Asal uses an index of minimal political inclusion to measure whether minorities at risk in the nations of the Western hemisphere achieved, or failed to achieve, inclusion from 1870 to 2000. He tested a number of societal variables that might explain why previously excluded groups were included. His results were often counter-intuitive. He uncovered no spillover effects from the extension of the franchise to women or other measures of democratization to the rate of inclusion of politically marginal groups. Instead, he found that modernization variables had the most exploratory power. Using a comparative-historical method that is rarely used in studies of political inclusion, Asal establishes a baseline for studying specific cases of inclusion and exclusion, including, of course, in the United States.

The Lien essay documents the political participation of Asian Americans. As their percentage of the population rises in the United States, Asian

Americans have become a larger percentage of the electorate. In terms of voting and other forms of political participation, Lien argues that Asian Americans have not lagged behind other groups but it only seems that way because they are more recent immigrants and, therefore, have yet to hurdle the citizenship and voter registration barriers in the three-step voting process that is almost unique to the United States. Once Asian Americans have leaped those barriers, she shows that their voting rates are as high, or higher, than those of other recent immigrant groups.[8]

In modern democratic societies, a process of representation typically links voting to actual influence on public policy. Lien notes that the number of both elected Asian American and Latino officials has increased dramatically in the last decade. Still, both ethnic groups remain heavily disenfranchised in the United States and, consequently, under-represented in Congress.[9] The Friedman and Scotece essay takes a different tack on the congressional representation of Latinos by analyzing the "home styles" of seven Latino members of Congress from the Los Angeles area.[10] In an interesting twist on the "voting is symbolic" and "representation is substantive" assumptions of many social scientists, Friedman and Scotece demonstrate that the "home styles" of Latino members of Congress often emphasize the symbolic nature of representation, which may be particularly important for traditionally under-represented groups. Just as Lien's study is significant for the multiple ways it measures political participation, Friedman and Scotece's study is significant for the multiple ways it analyzes political representation.[11]

Political participation and congressional representation are the political processes that social scientists study most often in the United States. They are the most binary forms of political inclusion and, hence, the easiest to quantify.[12] The Cruz essay explores political participation more qualitatively within a particular social context. In overlapping narratives of the critical events that transformed the Puerto Rican community in New York during the 1960s, Cruz explains the many, often disparate ways that New York Puerto Ricans attempted to increase their political influence. Their most significant achievement was the "Puerto Rican Amendment" to the Voting Rights Act of 1965, which specifically barred voting discrimination against their community, but, in many ways, that victory was a hollow one.[13] The status of New York Puerto Ricans as partly inside and partly outside New York politics is the story that Cruz tells in rich historical detail. His lesson is the crucial role historical contingency, on the one hand, and political willfulness, on the other, play in the success of social movements.

Processes of policy formation may also include particular social groups by proxy or, in the vernacular, by virtual representation.[14] Public policies may then serve the interests of a particular group even when that group is disenfranchised and not actually represented in the processes by which the policies are made. The Sullivan and Strach essay starts from the presumption that governments often make policies without the participation of the social groups that are most directly affected by them. Yet, their focus is not on how those policies may or may not serve the interests of excluded groups but rather on how governments rely on individual group members to implement those very policies. Sullivan and Strach present four case studies of this process of governance: 1) (emerging) obesity policy; 2) Native American citizenship; 3) veterans' education benefits; and 4) tax expenditures. In each case, they show that private agents do much of the work that we traditionally associate with state actors. They thus locate political inclusion and exclusion within the processes of government, not outside those processes as either inputs or outputs.

The Nadia Rubaii-Barrett essay analyzes local immigration policies from a more traditional "virtual representation" perspective. She finds a wide variation in those policies. Some cities have funded day laborer centers to broker employment opportunities for undocumented immigrants, while other cities have imposed fines on landlords who rent living spaces to undocumented immigrants and on employers who hire them.

Policy-exclusion is then no more a dichotomous variable than process-inclusion is. Typically, however, the interests of social groups that are more adequately represented in the processes by which policies are made are better served by those policies than groups that are less adequately represented. This dynamic is one of the dynamics that Friedman and Scotece discuss in terms of Latino representation in Congress.[15] Cruz describes how New York Puerto Ricans demanded more adequate representation in the processes by which the delivery of social services were made in New York precisely because they believed that their interests were not being well served. Rubaii-Barrett demonstrates that this situation is the norm at the local level for politically marginal groups but she underscores the exceptions. Her essay does important work in developing a multidimensional model that explains this local variation in immigration policy better than existing unidimensional models. Her essay also does important work in reminding us that most public policy in the United States is made or at least implemented at the local level, not at the federal or state level.[16]

The Basiliere essay theorizes the complicated issues the transgendered confront in achieving the social and legal recognition that is a prerequisite to their political inclusion as a distinctive group of people. Writing in an advocacy mode and building on the scholarship of radical feminist, gay, and lesbian theorists, Basiliere calls for transcending binary gender distinctions. She notes that if feminist, gay, and lesbian politics, and for that matter racial politics, have taught us anything it is that binary distinctions distort a much more complex reality in which many people are neither one nor the other.[17] Those distinctions then function to oppress people who do not fit either category. The Basiliere essay breaks new ground in examining the politics of the transgendered community, outlining a two-pronged strategy for their inclusion within the now-dominant gender and development framework.

The Roth essay is the most similar to the Basiliere essay as a piece of advocacy but it is written in a more personal style.[18] Roth notes how the disabled, unlike the transgendered, have gained legal recognition through the ADA. At the same time, the disabled remain socially and politically marginalized. Roth details how the ADA actually further marginalized them by creating a "disabilities bureaucracy" that purports to virtually represent their interests but really does not. Yet even if it did, he argues that the disabled would still face a participation deficit in the implementation of the policies that most directly affect their lives, often literally so.

Roth explicitly raises the problem of citizen inclusion in administrative processes of policy implementation, a problem that the Sullivan and Strach essay also raises and the Cruz and Rubaii-Barrett essays raise more implicitly. Both the Roth and the Sullivan and Strach essays suggest that citizen inclusion in more formal democratic processes, such as voting and representation in legislative assemblies, is insufficient to democratic practice in modern administrative states.[19] Roth also suggests that the disabled exemplify the difficulties all people confront in building more democratic societies. Their supposed lack of physical ability to fully participate in democratic processes is a synecdoche for the other abilities other people supposedly lack for full democratic participation.

Finally, the Julie Novkov essay analyzes the processes by which public policies are culturally framed. This framing then acts as a boundary condition for future policy formation, either as a warrant for or a barrier to more inclusive policies. In a rich, historical mapping of the cultural framing of race-conscious judicial decisions as "colorblind," Novkov demonstrates how that framing left a large opening for conservative opponents of those decisions to turn the decisions against themselves. The recent Supreme Court ruling that local school districts can not use race as a factor in assigning children to public schools because it is not a "colorblind" policy perfectly illustrates this "backlash."[20] By focusing on legal discourse as a particularly important site for the cultural framing of public policies, Novkov offers a postmodern twist to the now-iconic adage that "policies determine politics."

The implications

All the essays in the volume discuss the controversies that either governments or groups face in either excluding or being excluded from equal participation in particular political processes. They also discuss the strategies governments and groups have developed to negotiate those controversies. Many of the essays in the volume weigh the advantages for politically marginal groups of pursuing coalition-building strategies as opposed to more purist strategies that emphasize their unique social identities. For example, the Cruz essay presents the various options New York Puerto Rican leaders confronted in attempting to define their community as separate from the African American community.[21] Some of the essays weigh the advantages for governments of de-linking the provision of social services from citizenship and other exclusionary statuses. The Rubaii-Barret essay describes how local governments have pursued quite different strategies on this "hot button" issue. Other essays look at both sides of the government–group equation, the Friedman essay in terms of symbolic representation, the Sullivan and Strach essay in terms of governance, and the Novkov essay in terms of litigation strategies.

At a more fundamental level, the essays in the volume raise some traditional and some not-so-traditional issues about the nature of democratic politics. What do we want the nature of democratic politics to be (Roth)? How do we best achieve democracy in multi-ethnic settings (Asal)? What is the status of immigrants in democratic societies (Lien)? How proactive should democratic governments be in incorporating immigrants (Rubaii-Barrett)? Is racial inequality an especially invidious form of inequality in a democracy (Novkov)? Is discrimination on the basis of sexual orientation antithetical to democratic practices (Basiliere)? How do we want to be governed in a democratic society (Sullivan and Strach)? What do we want representatives to do in a democratic government (Friedman and Scotece)? What role do radical politics play in democratic processes of policy formation (Cruz)? These are big issues but these are big essays.

Obviously, the volume is not itself inclusive of all the social groups that might be included in a volume on political inclusion and exclusion in the contemporary United States. The volume essays discuss a broad range of groups, African Americans, Asian Americans, the disabled, Latinos, Native Americans, Puerto Ricans, and the transgendered. Yet, our goal was not to attempt to cover as many groups as possible within the limits of one volume. Rather, it was to examine different processes of political inclusion and exclusion, and to explore the distinctive dimensions and dynamics of each process. In this sense, the essays in the volume are case studies of particular processes of political inclusion and exclusion.

Most of the authors in the volume are political scientists. But, as should be clear by now, all the essays are interdisciplinary. They draw on a variety of other disciplines, including African American studies, history, legal studies, philosophy, public administration, social work, sociology, US Latino studies, and women's studies, to address the two main questions of why particular social groups are excluded from equal participation in particular political processes and how do those groups become more fully included as equal participants with other groups in those processes. Individually, the essay authors offer uniformly provocative answers to these questions.

Notes

1 See Theodore J. Lowi, "American Business, Public Policy, Case-Studies, and Political Theory," *World Politics* 16, no. 4 (July 1964): 677–715; Theodore J. Lowi, "Four Systems of Policies, Politics, and Choice," *Public Administration Review* 32, no. 4 (July–August 1972): 298–310.

2 On the "minorities at risk" project, see Ted Robert Gurr, *People versus States: Minorities at Risk in the New Century* (Washington: United States Institute of Peace Press, 2000).

3 On the concept of governance, see Lester M. Salamon, ed., *The Tools of Government: A Guide to New Governance* (New York: Oxford University Press, 2002).

4 See Robert Dahl, *A Preface to Democratic Theory* (Chicago: University of Chicago Press, 1956), 145–47.

5 See William E. Connolly, *Pluralism* (Durham, NC: Duke University Press, 2005). For earlier critiques, see William E. Connolly, ed., *The Bias of Pluralism* (New York: Atherton Press, 1969), especially the Peter Bachrach and Morton S. Baratz essay, "The Two Faces of Power."

6 In addition, political inclusions and exclusions are not holistic. An individual may be excluded from equal participation in a particular political process on the basis of one identity (sexual orientation) and included on the basis of another (union member). Similarly, an individual may be excluded because he or she lacks resources but included on the basis of a group identity.

7 Asal restricted his comparison to the nations of the Western hemisphere because they have historically been socially diverse nations. They also have had distinctive historical experiences with racial slavery and the exploitation of indigenous populations.

8 Cf. Pei-te Lien, M. Margaret Conway, and Janelle Wong, *The Politics of Asian Americans: Diversity and Community* (New York: Routledge, 2004).

9 Compared with Asian Americans, a much larger percentage of Latinos are disenfranchised because of their undocumented status.

10 See Richard F. Fenno, *Home Style: House Members in Their Districts* (Boston: Little, Brown, 1978); Sally Friedman, *Dilemmas of Representation: Local Politics, National Factors, and the Home Styles of Modern US Congress Members* (Albany: State University of New York Press, 2007). All seven of these members of Congress represent majority-minority districts.

11 See Heinz Eulau and Paul D. Karps, "The Puzzle of Representation: Specifying Components of Responsiveness," in *The Politics of Representation: Continuities in Theory and Research*, eds Heinz Eulau and John C. Wahlke (Beverly Hills, CA: Sage Publications, 1978), 55–71.

12 None of the three preceding essays relies exclusively on such measures of political inclusion. For example, Asal used an index of minimal political inclusion that is explicitly not based on voting rights.

13 See Juan Cartagena, "Latinos and Section 5 of the Voting Rights Act: Beyond Black and White," *National Black Law Journal* 18, no. 2 (2005): 201–23.

14 See Hanna Fenichel Pitkin, *Representation* (New York: Atherton Press, 1969).

15 See Rodney Hero and Caroline Tolbert, "Latino and Substantive Representation in the U.S. House of Representatives: Direct, Indirect, or Nonexistent?" *American Journal of Political Science* 39, no. 3 (October 1995): 640–52; Brinck Kerr and Will Miller, "Latino Representation, It's Direct and Indirect," *American Journal of Political Science* 41, no. 3 (October 1997): 1066–71.

16 In fact, one of the dimensions Rubaii-Barrett analyzes is the congruence between local and national immigration policies.

17 See, for example, Judith Butler, *Undoing Gender* (New York: Routledge, 2004); Julie Novkov, *Racial Union: Law, Intimacy, and the White State of Alabama, 1865–1954* (Ann Arbor: University of Michigan Press, 2007).

18 Cf. William Roth, *The Assault on Social Policy* (New York: Columbia University Press, 2002).

19 See Benjamin Barber, *Strong Democracy: Participatory Politics for a New Age* (Berkeley: University of California Press, 1984).
20 The paired cases were: *Meredith v. Jefferson County Board of Education* and *School Parents Involved in Community Schools v. Seattle School District No. 1.*
21 In an earlier work, Cruz studied this issue in Hartford. See José E. Cruz, *Identity and Power: Puerto Rican Politics and the Challenge of Ethnicity* (Philadelphia: Temple University Press, 1998).

Part I

Politics of inclusion

2 Minimal Political Inclusion of Minorities at Risk

The Case of the Americas, 1870–2000

Victor Asal

Studies of political inclusion are not lacking. From Alexis de Tocqueville onward, students of democracy have examined political inclusion. Tocqueville himself argued that:

> The gradual progress of equality is something fated. The main features of this progress are the following: it is universal and permanent, it is daily passing beyond human control, and every event and every man helps it along. Is it wise to assume that a movement, which has been so long in train, could be halted by one generation? Does anyone imagine that democracy, which has destroyed the feudal system and vanquished kings, will fall back before the middle class and the rich? Will it stop now, when it has grown so strong and its adversaries so weak.[1]

Many of the researchers who have followed Tocqueville have, like him, been most interested in issues of class. From Seymour Martin Lipset through Dietrich Rueschemeyer to Ruth Berins Collier, the examination of inclusion has focused on the process by which the middle and working classes have become included in Western political systems.[2] Much of this research has focused on the impact of modernization and class alignment. Even Tocqueville, though, did not completely ignore the issue of ethnicity for he despaired of the inclusion of African and Native Americans in the US political system. Of the latter, he noted that "[f]rom whatever angle one regards the destinies of the North American natives, one sees nothing but irremediable ills."[3]

Until recently, cross-national investigation of the political inclusion of other excluded groups has not been a primary concern in the literature. The recent work that has begun to investigate the issue of the inclusion of previously excluded groups has focused on women and social movements, and on the specific issue of suffrage.[4] Our focus is different. Given the wide range of scholars who have identified the problem that ethnicity presents to democracy and the nation state as well as the evidence that this is indeed the case, we believe that a focus on Minorities at Risk (MAR) serves as a useful prism to examining the causes of Minimal Political

Inclusion (MPI) and particularly its relationship to democratic institutions and norms.[5] We should note that our concern is the removal of obstacles to inclusion as opposed to attempting to measure how proportionally represented a group might be in the political process.

In addition to their utility as a hard case in examining political inclusion, the treatment of MAR is an important topic because it is one of the primary causes of ethnic conflict.[6] Although ethnic conflict is on the decline, it is still the most frequent type of civil conflict around the world.[7] We focus specifically on the Americas because in the Americas there is such a large number of minorities who are indigenous and also because, unlike in other regions of the world, international war has not been a driving force in the political inclusion and exclusion of ethnic groups. Given the fact that political inclusion provides access to limited resources of power and material goods to a larger group of people, why would those who have power share it with those who do not? Thus the question of this chapter, why include the excluded?

Which inclusion?

When researchers have focused on political inclusion as an important variable in large cross-national studies of inclusion, they have usually focused on the granting of suffrage to women. Accordingly, they have used suffrage exclusively as a measure of political inclusion.[8] As Joe Foweraker and Todd Landman have pointed out, a focus on legal rights, while useful, does not comprehensively address the issue of inclusion for there is often an important difference between the rights in principle that people possess and the rights in practice that the state will allow them to use.[9] The right to inclusion is often restricted "extralegally."[10] African Americans, for example, had the right to vote in the 1840s in some of the northern United States but if they actually tried to vote, as Tocqueville found, "their lives are in danger."[11] Researchers who have focused on rights in practice or on other groups than women have often used comparative case studies, limiting the generalizations that have been possible.[12] Even in related research on repression and human rights, the focus is more on the phenomena than the target, such that the research loses the ability to analyze how specific minorities are treated.[13] The inclusion of women is important in its own right, but we cannot assume that the inclusion of minorities will develop in the same way as it has for women. Even where minorities have been the main focus, researchers have treated political inclusion or its absence for the most part as an independent variable and the focus has been on how their inclusion affects their behavior or, alternatively, the behavior of the state.[14] Finally, researchers that have focused on political rights for minorities as a dependent variable using statistical methods have looked mostly at Europe, which may have a very different explanatory structure than the Americas.[15]

Identifying the key actor

Before identifying possible explanations for the political inclusion of minorities, it is first critical to identify the agent who is being acted upon. In other words, which agent's behavior is being changed due to the independent variables? When explaining ethnopolitical inclusion, the key actor is the state or, more specifically, the groups that control the state and have a legitimate claim to compete for power. The number and size of these groups may vary widely depending on the form of the regime, a monarchy having fewer competing groups and a democratic regime having many more. But in either case they are the agents that will make the key decisions about inclusion. As Andrew Cortell and Susan Peterson suggest, when examining institutional and policy change we must explain the pressures on the groups that control the state, for "state officials ultimately control the reins of power within a state" that determine which policies will be implemented.[16] Our central concern then is not the mobilization of the excluded groups but rather the structure of the government and society within which those groups must mobilize.

Because we are focusing on the political inclusion of minorities, many of whom may have already mobilized, there might be a tendency to look at the excluded or newly included groups as the actors whose actions we need to explain. While this is the focus of many of the other chapters in this volume, it is not the focus of this chapter. Although we would expect demonstrations, riots, or guerilla wars to have an impact on the level of political inclusion a group possesses, we are not attempting to explain the actions of the excluded groups. Instead, we follow Charles Tilly's suggestion that in any state there are governments that control the means of coercion and those groups that are allowed to try to influence governments are contenders while those outside of the "political game" are challengers. Tilly's focus is on the struggles between contenders and challengers.[17] Our focus is on the struggles of the contenders, those groups that are already included in the political process. It is the decision of the included groups that determines when and if an excluded group will be included. Although the state and the previously included groups that control it may not be able to determine whether and when the struggle over inclusion will end, they can determine who is included in that struggle up to the point that revolution or secession takes the decision away from them.

Elite studies of democracy support the view that it is those groups who compete for political power who have the greatest impact on the level and type of democracy that a nation state achieves.[18] As John Dryzek pointed out, the imperatives of the state determine inclusion. He argued that "[i]rrespective of what interest groups seek, states must meet certain imperatives. ... Democratization of the state in the future is possible only to the extent that the imperatives of the state continue to change."[19] According to Dryzek, the state will include those groups who it makes sense to include depending on the imperatives that drive it. This way of framing the question is very useful for it focuses our attention on those factors that drive the state to include previously excluded groups. Inclusion itself is not a state imperative; nor will a state politically include a group unless it benefits from this action. Anthony Marx made a similar point in focusing on coalition building among white elites as the root cause of racial domination. He described nation building as coalition building among the most powerful groups of a society who will oppress other groups, especially racial and ethnic groups, within the society as a means to that end. If a group poses a threat to politically stability, it must be brought into the consensus and any means, including the exclusion of former allies who now represent less of a threat, is legitimate.[20]

Given that our key actors are the state and those groups that are legitimate contenders in the political game, we will use a structural approach to explore the factors that lead to the political inclusion of MAR groups.[21]

Hypotheses

The impact of democracy

Robert Dahl, Christian Davenport, Ted Gurr, Arend Liphart, and Harold Wilensky have all argued that the institutions of democracy lead to inclusion.[22] Much of the cross-national literature on political inclusion supports the contention that a democratic regime is likely to be more inclusive.

The literature has focused on the fact that democracies seem to manage inclusion better. As Gurr, Monty Marshall, and Deepa Khosla asserted, "when divisive ethnic and political issues do surface in democracies, they are usually expressed in protest rather then rebellion and often culminate in reformist policies."[23] This view begs the question of why this is so. Gurr has found that "democracy, state power, and institutional change help determine whether conflict takes the form of protest or rebellion" and lead to groups expressing themselves "nonviolently."[24] Nevertheless, conflict management is not the same as alleviating or ending discrimination and much of the current research that has taken political exclusion and inclusion into account has been much more interested in explaining the level of conflict, social unrest, and repression than in exploring the end of exclusion.[25]

It is interesting to note that there has been much more empirical exploration of the impact of democratic institutions on repression, protest, and social movements than there has been on their impact on political inclusion.[26] As recently as 1999, Davenport wrote of the related phenomena of human rights that "[a]utocratization is expected to worsen human rights conditions; democratization is frequently heralded as a means for improving them. Unfortunately, neither relationship has been subjected to

empirical investigation."[27] Given this lack of exploration of the relationship between democracy and inclusion, it is worth testing what that relationship actually is in the case of MAR groups. Because of the limitations
of the existing research, this study will draw justifications for this possible
relationship from the human rights and repression literature as well as
from the social movements literature.

Both literatures suggest that democracies work to include groups
because the institutions and practices of democracy create ways for groups
to influence the government without resorting to violence. There is also
less incentive on the part of the government to resort to violence to control
groups given that it possesses other mechanisms for influencing them.
Matthew Cleary claimed that

> [c]itizens are more likely to have institutional channels through which
> grievances can be made known to the regime, and regimes are more
> likely to be responsive to these grievances. Furthermore, insofar as
> many of these institutions involve public political activity, protest and
> public dissent come to be seen as legitimate and nonviolent political
> behavior may become the norm.[28]

The institutions that make a democracy what it is, researchers argue, are
the ones that encourage inclusion. Lipset thus insisted that

> a political system which supplies regular constitutional opportunities
> for changing the governing officials, and a social mechanism which
> permits the largest possible part of the population to influence major
> decisions by choosing among contenders for political office provides
> more room for protest and less incentive for the state to repress.[29]

In a more general context, Mark Lichbach contended that "inconsistent
values and institutions are not likely to persist."[30] Democracy is a regime
whose institutions are more inclusive than others and therefore we may
expect to see the kind of value–institution clash that leads to more inclusion. Does evidence support the conclusion that democracy will have the
effect these researchers suggest? For the ameliorative impact of democracy
on repression and human rights, we have a great deal of evidence.[31] But
repression is not inclusion. We need to test the relationship of democracy
to the political inclusion of minorities.

Hypothesis 1: Minimal Political Inclusion is positively related to
democracy.

The impact of including women

There is a fierce debate in the literature about the value of suffrage. Some
scholars argue that it is irrelevant, while others argue that it makes a

significant difference in political outcomes. Norberto Bobbio claimed that the spread of suffrage has had a transformative impact on the state.[32] We can not examine the relationship between suffrage for minority groups and their political inclusion because the first variable is an indicator of the second. We, however, can examine the relationship between women's suffrage and the inclusion of minority groups because they are not the same phenomena.

Quantitative research has linked women's suffrage to an improvement of their political and economic circumstances in both democracies and non-democracies.[33] It is possible that women's suffrage would have an impact on the political inclusion of minorities in a variety of ways. Besides creating a new possible coalition partner in political struggles, women's suffrage may serve as an important gain by what Gurr called a "reference group."[34] This measure of progress may spur minority groups to action, or it may clarify the problem of exclusion in a society as the number of groups that are formally included in the political system doubles as a result of the inclusion of women. Women's suffrage changes who the contenders are and includes a group that was previously excluded. It fundamentally changes the structure in which rights are awarded with possibly important ramifications for the groups that are still excluded. We thus test the following hypothesis.

Hypothesis 2: Minimal Political Inclusion is positively related to women's suffrage.

Modernization and political inclusion

There is broad support among researchers who study democratization that it is positively related to modernization. Lipset first made the argument that the more developed a country was in terms of wealth, industrialization, education, and urbanization, the more likely it was to be a democracy.[35] More than 30 years later, Evelyne Huber and John Stephens wrote that "there is no doubt that there is an affinity between capitalist development and democracy both diachronically, at least in the *longue durée*, and synchronically across countries at different levels of development."[36] Although most of the literature supports this relationship, there have been several important critiques. For example, Adam Przeworski, Michael Alvarez, Jose Antonio Cheibub, and Fernando Limongi, while not disputing that the relationship exists, claimed that it is not that rich countries become democracies but that once rich countries become democracies they rarely revert to dictatorships.[37] Despite this and other criticisms, the preponderance of the evidence supports the connection between modernization and democratization. This connection—at least theoretically—should apply to political inclusion as well. We then will also test the following relationships.

Hypothesis 3: Minimal Political Inclusion is positively related to urbanization per capita.

Hypothesis 4: Minimal Political Inclusion is positively related to energy consumption per capita.

Inclusion in the Americas

While all these factors theoretically should apply globally, the case of the Americas presents several interesting regional peculiarities. Unlike many other regions where ethnic minorities are long-term ethnic competitors or else relatively new immigrant groups, a large portion of the MAR groups in the Americas are either indigenous or descendants of the slave trade. Indeed, 44 percent of the MAR groups are indigenous groups. Unlike many other MAR groups, indigenous groups present an interesting challenge to dominant groups in the Americas from two perspectives. First, unlike many other MAR groups, indigenous groups have a prior claim to ownership and legitimacy.[38] Second, in some cases indigenous groups are very large minorities and, in a few cases, aggregating different MAR groups results in them being the largest type of ethnic group in the country. As a result, they represent a threat to the government in ways that other ethnic groups do not (with Afro-Brazilians as the clear exception).[39] Given the double-edged nature of this potential threat to both the legitimacy and the power of the state, we believe that indigenous groups are much less likely to be politically included, all else being equal.

Hypothesis 5: Minimal Political Inclusion is negatively related to a group's indigenous identity.

Research design

The independent variables were all operationalized using fairly standard measures in the field, including the use of urbanization and energy consumption as indices of modernization given that data for per capita GNP is not available for the whole 1870–2000 time period. Much more challenging was the operationalization of the dependent variable, which heretofore has not been explicitly coded cross-nationally.

In order to analyze the relationship between our independent variables and political inclusion we need to be clear about what we mean by political inclusion. Defining political inclusion is problematic because the requirements of inclusion can mean very different things to different people.[40] Some see it as the extension of equal rights of participation to all people within a state.[41] Others see full political inclusion as necessitating the setting of quotas in parliament so that all groups are represented.[42] Still others insist that inclusion for the historically excluded should include a right to veto policies related to them.[43] All of these viewpoints share the view that political inclusion involves certain formal rights and practices that allow groups or group members to have an impact on decision makers and to attempt to replace them if they can effectively do so within the existing political system. This common assumption is not shared by everyone. Some scholars dismiss the importance of formal inclusion altogether. As John Mueller pointed out, "the weight of an individual's vote on policymaking is so small that the act of voting is scarcely a rational use of one's time."[44]

Given the different viewpoints on what consequential political inclusion means, the task of deciding where to set the bar for its measurement is not an easy one. This task is especially difficult if the definition needs to be one that can be operationalized and applied to a wide range of groups over a fairly long historical period of time. Johan Galtung distinguished positive human rights (omission of the state) and negative human rights (commission of the state).[45] The upward bounds of positive political inclusion can stretch as high as Iris Marion Young's ideas of inclusion or Benjamin Barber's desire for what he calls "strong democracy."[46] While we do not question the normative worth of the goals they set, their definitions create a bar so high that any index of political inclusion could only measure various levels of political exclusion.

By excluding positive political inclusion from our analysis, we will also be able to focus on a very specific set of phenomena. For this preliminary empirical exploration of political inclusion in the Americas, we will focus on what we will call Minimal Political Inclusion (MPI). MPI is negative political inclusion, meaning that it signifies the absence of meaningful political exclusion. It means that individuals are not excluded from participating in the political systems of their countries by virtue of their identity as members of a particular group; nor is the group itself excluded. Identifying a group as possessing full MPI does not mean that it does not suffer any form of discrimination or that it does not have any grievances. It means that there are no significant barriers to that group pursuing its goals in the political arena if it chooses to do so and, furthermore, that it can overcome whatever non-political barriers to inclusion that may exist.

A restricted focus on this negative type of political inclusion has certain advantages. Theoretically, MPI allows us to sort out political inclusion clearly from democracy and examine their possible inter-relationship as well as the possibility of MPI in non-democracies. From a methodological standpoint, it makes the task of operationalizing the concept much easier than would be the case if it was necessary to measure successful positive inclusion. Moreover, the use of MPI allows us to tie our investigation into an established measurement, that of political discrimination used by the Minorities at Risk (MAR) Project. Since MPI is the absence of meaningful discrimination, we can adopt the standard and tested operationalizations of political discrimination used by the MAR Project as a basis for our analysis and compare our findings with those in the MAR dataset.

However, the question arises, if MPI is a minimal point where discrimination stops *preventing* political participation due to group identity, should it be measured at the point where the government stops discriminating or at the point where society stops discriminating? Focusing on proactive government discrimination in the form of legal statutes and stated governmental policies has coding advantages as well as a tighter focus. Such a focus, though, ignores the important fact that political exclusion is not always carried out by the state and that exclusionary practices are often unstated parts of official state policy. Frequently, society as a whole imposes levels of discrimination either with the encouragement or through the apathy of the government. This societal discrimination may make inclusion impossible even if the state has removed formal barriers to exclusion. Thus the conceptual dividing line we choose is the one that marks the point where widespread governmental or societal discrimination prevents effective participation by groups or group members based on their identity. Governmental and societal behavior is such that groups and group members can participate if they choose to and can also overcome other obstacles to their participation. To construct an index of MPI, then, we used the coding schema the MAR Project uses for political discrimination, where groups facing governmental or societal discrimination are coded as not possessing MPI and groups with any level of inclusion above that are coded as possessing MPI.

It is important to underline that our definition of Minimal Political Inclusion is not dependent on the democratic nature of the state. The level of MPI in a country will rise or fall depending on the amount of its adult population who are accepted as legitimate rivals for power with access to the political tools that allow them to participate politically. In a communist regime, if anyone can join the political game by joining the communist party and attempt to rise through its ranks in order to achieve political power, then the country may not be democratic but it would be inclusive.[47] In a monarchy, the key question would be if groups or group members are excluded from political positions and patronage because of their identity. It is also important to note that individuals may be excluded on a variety of different identities. If they are not excluded from political participation on ethnic criteria, they might still be excluded because of their gender or sexual orientation.

As mentioned in the introduction, we will use MAR groups as our population for analysis. The general MAR Project database includes 285 such groups and covers the period from 1950 to 2000. A National Science Foundation Dissertation Improvement grant allowed this researcher to gather data on the discrimination variable back to the year 1870. The analysis in this chapter draws from that data, focusing on the fifty-six MAR groups from the Americas. In coding for MPI, I drew on a variety of historical texts and used the same coding procedure that was used in the MAR Project for discrimination.

Method

Our data is pooled time series data covering fifty-six ethnic groups over the 1870–2000 period. Because our data is a pooled cross-sectional time series, we will use a generalized estimating equation (GEE) model.[48] The GEE model allows us to specify a first-order autoregressive correlation structure within each unit. We do this with the xtgee command with the logit link using Stata9. While the GEE model is very useful for dealing with pooled cross-sectional time series data, it cannot estimate on interrupted series, causing a prohibitive loss of data. To deal with this problem, we can either interpolate data or "force" Stata to include the missing observations in the estimation. We have chosen to use the latter option with the force command in Stata9.

Results and analysis

Using the GEE model, we found that all of our independent variables are significant (either one tailed or two tailed) and in the direction we expected (see Table 2.1). When we use the predict function in Stata9 to predict the probabilities of the different variables when holding all the other variables at their mean or their mode, we discovered that, while all the independent variables have an impact, their impacts are radically different (see Table 2.2). Women's suffrage has very little impact; there is almost no spillover effect. Even more surprisingly, democracy has little impact. At least in the case of the Americas, this study provides empirical evidence that contradicts many of the assumptions held about the inclusive power of democracy. Much of the literature assumes a similarity of causes for inclusion but focuses on class. Even if democracy works well to gradually include all economic classes, it does not seem to work as well to gradually include all ethnic groups. What instead seems to be driving

Table 2.1 Results of Generalized Estimated Equation using a logit link with an ar1 correlation assumption using force

MPI	Coef.	Stderr.	z	P>z
Democracy (Polity2)	0.0138	0.0057	2.43	0.015
Women's suffrage	0.0879	0.0515	1.7	0.088
Energy per capita	0.2394	0.0127	18.92	0
Indigenous ethnic group	−2.3331	0.1275	−18.3	0
Urbanization population per capita	1.4281	0.2775	5.15	0
Cons	−0.9392	0.0525	−17.88	0

Number of obs	4295
Number of groups	123
Obs per group: min.	4
Avg	34.9
Max.	56
Wald chi2(5)	3758.82
Prob > chi2	0

Table 2.2 Probability that a group will possess MPI holding all the other variables at their mean or mode

Mean or mode = .4605	Min. rest at mode or mean	Max. rest at mode or mean	Change from min. to max.
Democracy (Polity2)	0.393	0.4605	0.0675
Women's suffrage	0.4605	0.4824	0.0219
Energy per capita	0.3562	0.9018	0.5456
Indigenous ethnic group	0.4605	0.0764	-0.3841
Urbanization population per capita	0.4092	0.6173	0.2081

their political inclusion is modernization. Our findings support the argument that, at least in the Americas, modernization is an essential explanation of political inclusion. The more energy consumption per capita in a country and the more urbanized that country is, the more likely it is that an ethnic group will be politically included. Of equal interest is the fact that, while the political inclusion of minorities is quite high when all factors are held at their mean (.4605), the indigenous identity of some ethnic groups had a strong, negative effect on the likelihood that they will be politically included.

Conclusion

This study has been a preliminary investigation of political inclusion in the Americas. While further research would benefit from the addition of factors related to the mobilization of the groups themselves and by an analysis that goes beyond ethnic groups to include both gender and class, the current analysis does provide some very interesting findings related to the structural conditions for an increase in political inclusion.

First, this analysis suggests that democracy, which is often operationalized as being generally inclusive, should not be assumed to lead to or be strongly associated with certain kinds of inclusion. At least this assumption should not be made in the case of ethnic groups in the Americas.

Second, this analysis suggests that economic factors are dominant in determining the political inclusion of MAR groups but with a caveat. This finding jibes with many of the arguments about modernization but the caveat is an important one. Certain identities are seen as fundamentally dangerous to the state and make it much less likely that groups with those identifies will be included in the political system. In the Americas, state actors see indigenous groups as a greater threat than other MAR groups. This factor significantly decreases the possibility that they will be included in the political system. An important next step is for us to identify those factors that lead to the inclusion even of those groups that state actors see as such a threat.

Notes

1 See Alexis de Tocqueville, *Democracy in America* (New York: HarperCollins, 1988), 12.
2 See Ruth Berins Collier, *Paths Toward Democracy: Working Class and Elites in Western Europe and South America* (Cambridge, UK: Cambridge University Press, 1999); Seymour Martin Lipset, *Political Man: The Social Bases of Politics* (New York: Anchor, 1963); Dietrich Rueschemeyer, Evelyne Huber Stephens, and John D. Stephens, *Capitalist Development and Democracy* (Chicago: University of Chicago Press, 1992).
3 See Tocqueville, *Democracy in America*, 339.
4 See, for example, Lee Ann Banaszak, *Why Movements Succeed or Fail: Opportunity, Culture, and the Struggle for Woman Suffrage* (Princeton, NJ: Princeton University Press, 1996); Joe Foweraker and Todd Landman, *Citizenship Rights and Social Movements: A Comparative and Statistical Analysis* (Oxford: Oxford University Press, 1997); Douglas McAdam, Charles Tilly, and Sidney Tarrow, *Dynamics of Contention* (New York: Cambridge University Press, 2001); Francisco Ramirez, Yasemin Soysal, and Suzanne Shanahan, "The Changing Logic of Political Citizenship: Cross-National Acquisition of Women's Suffrage Rights, 1896–1990," *American Sociological Review* 62, no. 5 (October 1997): 735–45.
5 Prime examples of MAR would be, prior to the 1960s, African Americans in the United States and, more recently, Zapotecs in Mexico and Quechua in Peru.
6 See Ted Robert Gurr and Barbara Harff, *Ethnic Conflict in World Politics* (Boulder, CO: Westview Press, 1994).
7 See Ted Robert Gurr, Monty G. Marshall, and Deepa Khosla, *Peace and Conflict 2001: A Global Survey of Armed Conflicts, Self-Determination Movements, and Democracy* (College Park, MD: Center for International Development and Conflict Management, 2001).
8 See, for example, Pamela Paxton, "Women's Suffrage in the Measurement of Democracy: Problems of Operationalization," *Studies in Comparative International Development* 35, no. 3 (October 2000): 92–111; Ramirez, Soysal, and Shanahan, "Changing Logic of Citizenship."
9 See Foweraker and Landman, *Citizenship Rights*, 19.
10 See Harold F. Gosnell, *Democracy: The Threshold of Freedom* (New York: Ronald Press, 1948), 19.
11 See John L. Stanley, "Majority Tyranny in Tocqueville's America: The Failure of Negro Suffrage in 1846," *Political Science Quarterly* 84, no. 3 (September 1969): 415; quoting Tocqueville.
12 See, for example, Banaszak, *Why Movements Succeed*; Anthony Marx, *Making Race and Nation: A Comparison of South Africa, the United States and Brazil* (Cambridge, UK: Cambridge University Press, 1998).
13 See, for example, Christian Davenport, "Human Rights and the Democratic Proposition," *Journal of Conflict Resolution* 43, no. 1 (February 1999): 92–116; Steven C. Poe and C. Neal Tate, "Repression of Human Rights to Personal Integrity in the 1980s: A Global Analysis," *American Political Science Review* 88, no. 4 (December 1994): 853–900. For an overview of the human rights literature in comparative politics, see Todd Landman, "Comparative Politics and Human Rights" (University of Denver, Human Rights Institute Working Papers Series, no. 10, October 2000).
14 See, for example, Ted Robert Gurr, *Peoples versus States: Minorities at Risk in the New Century* (Washington: United States Institute of Peace Press, 2000); Rita Jalai and Seymour Martin Lipset, "Racial and Ethnic Conflicts: A Global Perspective," *Political Science Quarterly* 107, no. 4 (Winter 1992–93): 585–606; David A. Lake and Donald R. Rothchild, eds, *The International Spread of Ethnic Conflict: Fear, Diffusion, and*

Escalation (Princeton, NJ: Princeton University Press, 1998); Landman, "Comparative Politics and Human Rights."

15 See David L. Rousseau and Bruce Newsome, "Women and Minorities: The Impact of War Time Mobilization on Political Rights," paper presented at the annual meeting of the American Political Science Association, Atlanta, September 2–5, 1999.

16 See Andrew P. Cortell and Susan Peterson, "Agents, Structures, and Domestic Institutional Change," in *Altered States: International Relations, Domestic Politics, and Institutional Change*, eds Andrew P. Cortell and Susan Peterson (Lanham, MD: Lexington Books, 2002), 14.

17 See Charles Tilly, "Major Forms of Collective Action in Western Europe, 1600–1975," *Theory and Society* 3, no. 1 (January 1976): 365–75.

18 See John Higley, Jan Pakulski, and Wlodzimierz Wesolowski, "Introduction: Elite Change and Democratic Regimes in Eastern Europe," in *Postcommunist Elites and Democracy in Eastern Europe*, eds John Higley, Jan Pakulski, and Wlodzimierz Wesolowski (New York: St Martin's Press, 1998).

19 See John S. Dryzek, "Political Inclusion and the Dynamics of Democratization," *American Political Science Review* 90, no. 3 (September 1996): 475–87.

20 See Marx, *Making Race and Nation*, 269–77.

21 For such a structural approach, see Theda Skocpol, *States and Social Revolutions: A Comparative Analysis of France, Russia, and China* (Cambridge, UK: Cambridge University Press, 1979), 31.

22 See Robert A. Dahl, *Democracy and its Critics* (New Haven: Yale University, 1989); Davenport, "Human Rights"; Gurr, *Peoples versus States*; Arend Liphart, *Democracies* (New Haven, CT: Yale University Press, 1984); Harold L. Wilensky, *Rich Democracies: Political Economy, Public Policy, and Performance* (Berkeley: University of California Press, 2002).

23 See Gurr, Marshall, and Khosla, *Peace and Conflict*, 20.

24 See Ted Robert Gurr, *Minorities at Risk: A Global View of Ethnopolitical Conflict* (Washington: Institute of Peace Press, 1993): 161; Ted Robert Gurr, "Peoples against States: Ethnopolitical Conflict and the Changing World System," *International Studies Quarterly* 38, no. 3 (September 1994): 347–77.

25 See Davenport, "Human Rights," 94–95.

26 Gurr's *Peoples versus States* is the rare exception.

27 See Davenport, "Human Rights," 92.

28 See Matthew R. Cleary, "Democracy and Indigenous Rebellion in Latin America," *Comparative Political Studies* 33, no. 4 (November 2000): 1131.

29 See Lipset, *Political Man*, 27.

30 See Mark Lichbach, *Regime Change and the Coherence of European Governments* (Denver: University of Denver Press, 1984), 11.

31 See Davenport, "Human Rights," 96–99.

32 See Noberto Bobbio, *The Future of Democracy* (Cambridge, UK: Polity Press, 1987). For the opposing view, see Benjamin Barber, *Strong Democracy: Participatory Politics for a New Age* (Berkeley: University of California Press, 1984); John Mueller, "Democracy and Ralph's Pretty Good Grocer: Elections, Equality and the Minimal Human Being," *American Journal of Political Science* 36, no. 4 (November 1992): 983–1003.

33 See Lane Kenworthy and Melissa Malami, "Gender Inequality in Political Representation: A Worldwide Analysis," *Social Forces* 78, no. 1 (September 1999): 235–68.

34 See Ted Robert Gurr and James R. Scarritt, "Minorities Rights at Risk: A Global Survey," *Human Rights Quarterly* 11, no. 4 (1989): 375–405.

35 See Seymour Martin Lipset, "Some Social Requisites of Democracy: Economic Development and Political Legitimacy," *American Political Science Review* 53, no. 1 (March 1959): 76–77.

36 See Evelyne Huber and John D. Stephens, "The Bourgeoisie and Democracy: Historical and Contemporary Perspectives from Europe and Latin America," paper presented at

the annual meeting of the Latin American Studies Association, Guadalajara, Mexico, 17–19 April 1997, 1.

37 See Adam Przeworski, Michael Alvarez, Jose Antonio Cheibub, and Fernando Limongi, *Democracy and Development* (Cambridge, UK: Cambridge University Press, 2000).

38 See Chadwick Allen, *Blood Narrative: Indigenous Identity in American Indian and Maori Literary and Activist Texts* (Durham, NC: Duke University Press, 2002); Stephen Curry, *Indigenous Sovereignty and the Democratic Project* (Aldershot, UK: Ashgate, 2004).

39 On the Brazilian case, see Marx, *Making Race and Nation*, 158–77.

40 See Dryzek, "Political Inclusion," 476.

41 The other chapters in this volume also reflect a range of conceptions of political inclusion.

42 See Anne Phillips, *Democracy and Difference* (University Park: Penn State University Press, 1993).

43 See Iris Marion Young, "Polity and Group Difference: A Critique of the Ideal of Universal Citizenship," *Ethics: A Journal of Moral, Political and Legal Philosophy* 99, no. 2 (January 1989): 117–42.

44 See Mueller, "Ralph's Pretty Good Grocer," 985.

45 See Johan Galtung, *Human Rights in Another Key* (Cambridge, UK: Polity Press, 1994), 1–25.

46 See Barber, *Strong Democracy*; Young, "Polity and Group Difference."

47 For an exploration of political participation in closed regimes, see Tianjian Shi, *Political Participation in Beijing* (Cambridge, MA: Harvard University Press, 1997).

48 See Christopher Zorn, "Generalized Estimating Equation Models for Correlated Data: Review with Applications," *American Journal of Political Science* 45, no. 2 (April 2001): 470–90.

3 Race, Nativity, and the Political Participation of Asian and other Americans

Pei-te Lien

With the election of the first person of color to the White House in 2008, the United States has finally entered a century where being nonwhite is no longer a barrier to the ultimate prize of political participation. However, for most nonwhite Americans, the challenge of the twenty-first century may still be that of the color-line, except that the line has now been complicated by issues well beyond those dealing with blacks and whites. In fact, owing in no small part to the passage of two landmark pieces of legislation in 1965 that opened up opportunities for the equal participation of blacks and other nonwhites in the voting process as well as for equal rights to immigration of individuals from countries in Asia and Africa, the color-line in the American population has been transfigured by the border line or nativity factor. As a result, a defining difference between the America of 2011 and the one of W.E.B. Dubois over a century ago is that a significant and growing portion of the present-day population is foreign-born and nonwhite.[1] Between 1990 and 2000, the United States foreign-born population increased by 57 percent, while the growth rate of the general population was only 13 percent. A lofty 78 percent of the foreign-born were from either Latin America or Asia. In the latest American Community Survey (ACS) three-year estimates, more than four in ten voting-age nonwhites (43 percent) were born outside the United States.[2] These statistics are evidence of the growing presence of the foreign-born, not just among the American population in general but also among the nonwhite electorate in particular.

What is the significance of this demographic transformation for the immigrant nation's prospect of becoming a multicultural democracy? Who are the foreign-born at the dawn of the twenty-first century? To what extent have they been included in the American political process and with what effect? We begin to answer these questions by examining the increase in the foreign-born population in recent decades. We follow this examination with a comparison of the demographic characteristics of the foreign-born to the US-born in the latest United States census data. We then focus on international migration-related information to understand racial differences among Asian, Latino, black, and non-Hispanic white immigrants in terms of their resources for voting and other types of political participation.[3] Using the concept of voting as a three-step process, we discuss variations in citizenship, voting registration, and turnout by race and nativity, and discuss how Asian Americans fare in these areas as compared with Latinos, blacks, and non-Hispanic whites in recent elections. We are particularly interested in the question of whether there is a foreign-born disadvantage in voting participation. We also discuss the domain of political participation beyond voting, especially homeland-oriented political behavior, to help us understand if the foreign-born stock is a liability or an asset to the political inclusion of nonwhite communities. We conclude by looking at the likely impact of the foreign-born on the contours of the American electorate and electoral leadership.

Our key findings are that the foreign-born of the twenty-first century are far from the huddled masses of the previous centuries and that the myth of the foreign-born deficit in voting participation is largely dispelled if one takes into account the three-step voting process in the United States. We also found that the rapid growth of new immigrants from Asia and Latin America in the post-1965 era has contributed to a dramatic transformation of the American electorate and electoral leadership.

The rise and current composition of the foreign-born population

Compared with other major American racial and ethnic groups in the post-1965 era, the Asian American community is distinguished by the rapid growth and predominance of the foreign-born. From 1970 to 2000, US census data show that the foreign-born among Asians (including Pacific Islanders) increased twelve-fold or from half a million to more than 4.5 million.[4] By comparison, foreign-born blacks grew nine-fold and foreign-born Latinos slightly more than seven-fold during the same period. Whereas the foreign-born sector in both the African American and Latino communities also experienced phenomenal growth, only foreign-born Asians were able to transform their status in the community from a numerical minority into a majority in the post-1965 era. Foreign-born persons constituted 32 percent among Asians in 1960, 36 percent in 1970, 59 percent in 1980, and 63 percent in 1990. In the 2000 census, 8.2 million foreign-born residents in the United States identified themselves as from Asia, which accounts for a quarter (26 percent) of the nation's total foreign-born population.[5] At 69 percent of the total Asian (alone) population in 2000, as compared with 40 percent among Latinos, 20 percent among Native Hawaiians and Pacific Islanders, 6 percent among blacks, 5 percent among American Indians and Alaskan Natives, and 3 percent among non-Hispanic whites, foreign-born persons constitute a substantially larger share of the population among Asians than among any other major racial or ethnic group in the United States.[6]

Table 3.1a The 2006–8 ACS three-year estimates for the foreign-born and the US-born

	Foreign-born	US-born
Total N	37,679,592	263,558,111
% report two or more races	1.3	2.3
Median age	40.3	35.7
% speak other than English at home	84.3	9.7
% speak English less than "very well"	52.3	1.9
% bachelor's degree or more	26.9	27.5
% in labor force	67.6	64.8
% employed	63.6	60.1
% M/F in management/professional	25.4/30.6	32.9/39.1
Median family income[a]	52,314	60,066
Per capita income[a]	28,725	27,286
% in poverty (all people)	15.9	12.8

Note: [a]income in the past 12 months (in 2008 inflation-adjusted dollars).
Source: compiled by author from the US Census Bureau, the 2006–8 ACS three-year estimates.

Who are the foreign-born at the dawn of the twenty-first century? Table 3.1a reports key characteristics of the US foreign-born population using the three-year average data from the 2006–8 ACS. Compared with the US-born, the foreign-born are older in age, mostly speak a language other than English at home, and about half of them report not being able to speak English very well. They are slightly behind the US-born in educational achievement, are significantly less likely to be in managerial/professional occupations, and have lower median family incomes and higher poverty rates than the US-born. However, they are somewhat more likely to be in the labor force and to be employed than the US-born, and those who are employed earn a slightly higher per capita income than the US-born. Despite problems of social and workplace discrimination against immigrants and minorities, the characteristics presented above are certainly far from the "huddled masses" portrayal of immigrants from Europe who migrated between the late nineteenth and the early twentieth centuries.[7] As a collectivity, the foreign-born in the United States of the twenty-first century may be older in age, face greater challenges in English language proficiency, and are more likely to be declared poor, but a higher proportion of them are working and, for the individuals who work, their per capita income is actually higher than that of the US-born.

Focusing on migration-related information, one notes significant racial differences among the foreign-born in terms of their size and share of the population, time of entry, world region of origin, and language proficiency (Table 3.1b). Specifically, Latino immigrants constitute the largest share of the foreign-born population at 47.1 percent, followed distantly by Asians who were about a quarter of the immigrant population in 2006–8. However, the relationship between the two is reversed in terms of the share of

Table 3.1b Migration-related information among foreign-born persons in ACS 2006–8

	Asian	Latino	Black	White	All
Total N	9,008,810	17,753,901	3,129,939	7,713,238	37,679,592
% of all foreign-born	23.9	47.1	8.3	20.5	100
% of all persons w/n race	60.6	39.1	7.9	3.9	12.5
% entered in 2000 or later	27.3	29.5	30.3	21.8	27.6
% entered before 1990	43.4	39.4	40.3	52.8	43.1
% from Africa	1.0	*	32.7	4.0	3.7
% from Latin America	2.1	99.1	63.4	6.1	53.4
% from Asia	96.0	*	1.0	18.3	26.9
% from Europe	1.1	*	2.0	60.8	13.2
% speak other than English at home[a]	70.8	77.4	8.0	5.9	84.3
% speak English less than "very well"[a]	33.9	38.4	2.8	1.7	52.3
% naturalized	56.2	28.2	47.5	57.8	42.5

Notes: all persons in each race include those of mixed origin. [a]Entries for each race are percentages among persons age five and over, who may or may not be foreign-born.
Source: compiled by author from the US Census Bureau, the 2006–8 ACS three-year estimates.

the foreign-born within each race, where Asians lead the pack at 61 percent, followed distantly by Latinos at 39 percent. Both groups do not differ much in terms of the percentage of immigrants who entered since 2000 or before 1990. In contrast, white immigrants are most likely to have entered before 1990, while black immigrants are most likely to have entered in 2000 or later. Although it would not be surprising to see that almost all of the Asian and Latino immigrants were from Asia or Latin America, respectively, only a third of black immigrants were from Africa and nearly two in ten white immigrants were from Asia. More than three in four Latinos report using a language other than English at home; as many as four in ten report not being able to speak English "very well." The figures for Asians are similar but slightly lower. But less than one in ten black or white immigrants use a language other than English at home.

Voting participation as a three-step process

The fascinating growth of the foreign-born population in recent decades portends great potential to expand the American electorate and the promise of a multiracial democracy. Nevertheless, an immigrant's ability to participate fully in the electoral process needs to be understood as a three-step process.[8] In order to cast his or her ballot, an immigrant voter must engage in the process of becoming naturalized, becoming registered to vote, and actually voting (or mailing in a ballot) before or on Election Day. A set of barriers or costs is involved at each step of the process. Becoming a citizen requires, among other things: a minimum period of continuous residence and physical presence in the United States; an ability to read, write, and speak English; a knowledge and understanding of American history and government; and the ability to pay a continuously rising application fee, which jumped from $400 to $675 in July 2007.[9] For those immigrants who have survived the naturalization process, their franchise can be wasted by their failure to become registered to vote, which is a procedure foreign to many Asian immigrants who came from systems with government-initiated voter registration.[10] Registering to vote and casting a vote, either in person or by mail, require the acquisition and/or possession of information, time, skills, and other resources.[11] This step may be particularly onerous in a referendum-heavy state such as California, where an estimated 40 percent of the Asian American population lives. When one adds to the equation such unique factors as language barriers, lack of familiarity with the American system, social discrimination, and economic hardship for working-class immigrants, it comes as little surprise that Asian Americans have one of the lowest citizenship, voting registration, and turnout rates among voting-age persons. Nonetheless, because voting in the United States is a three-step process, it is premature to draw conclusions from these unadjusted statistics about the political aptitude and behavior of Asian Americans and other immigrant communities.

The latest naturalization rates among the foreign-born are shown in the bottom row of Table 3.1b. Non-Hispanic white immigrants are more likely than Asians, who, in turn, are more likely than blacks, to become naturalized. In line with prior research, Latino immigrants are a distant last in the rate of naturalization. Studies looking at the naturalization rates from long-term perspectives consistently find immigrants from Asia to have become naturalized at an earlier time and at rates higher than immigrants from Mexico and many other parts of the world.[12] Asian immigrants' exceptional speed of naturalization may be attributed to their greater use of early-naturalization procedures, which may, in turn, be related to a lack of proximity to their ethnic homeland, emigration driven more by political than economic motives, higher educational and/or occupational background, and the ability of US citizens to sponsor the immigration of family members.[13] However, because the acquisition of citizenship is influenced by the length of stay in the United States, white immigrants are advantaged by having the highest share of entry before 1990. They have the highest naturalization rates among all groups. Latino immigrants, especially those from Mexico, have the lowest naturalization rates, not only because of their proximity to their homeland and shorter tenure in the host country but also because of their relative disadvantage in English-language proficiency and lack of socioeconomic resources. These statistics, produced at the intersection of race and nativity, caution against treating all foreign-born persons as one unified group in the American political process.

How politically active are nonwhite immigrants in voting and registration?

To assess the current extent of political inclusion at the basic levels of formal citizenship, voting registration, and turnout for the nation's major racial and ethnic groups, Table 3.2 reports the percentage distribution among various eligibility groups by race and nativity in the November 2008 elections as reported in the US Census Current Population Survey (CPS) Voter Supplement data.[14] Reflecting the vast variations in the share of the foreign-born population as well as in the naturalization rates among the foreign-born for each racial group, there are substantial racial gaps in citizenship rates among the voting-age population (VAP), with whites having the highest rate (98 percent), followed by blacks (94 percent) and (distantly) Asians (69 percent) and Latinos (63 percent). Underscoring the central role of immigrants in Asian American political empowerment, more than half of the citizens among Asians acquired their citizenship through naturalization, a rate much higher than the 22 percent among Latinos and the single-digit figures among blacks and whites.

Because not all foreign-born persons at any given point in time are either eligible or able to successfully petition for naturalization, the racial disparities in nativity and citizenship directly impact the rates of voter registration. Less than four in ten voting-age Asians and Latinos were registered to vote, rates that were nearly half that among whites and 27 points behind the rate among blacks. A similar pattern is found in the rates

Table 3.2 CPS voting and registration rates by race, gender, and nativity in November 2008

	Asian	Latino	Black	White	All
% citizenship among VAP	69	63	94	98	91
% by naturalization	56	22	5	3	7
% registration among VAP	38	38	65	72	65
among citizens	56	59	70	72	71
{-} foreign-born	58	60	64	62	60.5
{-} US-born	53	59	70	74	72
% voting among VAP	33	32	61	65	58
among citizens	48	50	65	66	64
among the registered	86	84	93	90	89
{-} foreign-born	85	91	94	90	89
{-} US-born	86	84	92	89	90
N (x1000)	11,009	30,852	27,483	154,472	225,499

Note: VAP stands for voting-age persons.
Source: Compiled by author from U.S. Department of Commerce, Bureau of the Census. *Current Population Survey*, November 2008, Tables 2, 13.

of voting among voting-age persons. Yet, when voting and registration rates are examined among eligible persons (citizens for registration and registered voters for voting), more than half of Asian American citizens (56 percent) reported having registered and 86 percent of registered Asians reported having voted in November 2008. Although Asians are still at the bottom in terms of registration rates among eligible persons, the voting rate of registered Asians exceeds that of registered Latinos and is only a few percentage points less than the rate of registered whites. Perhaps because of the historic candidacy of Senator Barack Obama, black turnout among the registered scored a historic high of 93 percent. This exercise shows that for communities that have a majority (Asians) or plurality (Latinos) foreign-born population, the major source of their apparent deficit in voting participation lies in the first two steps of the voting process. Once those institutional barriers are crossed, racial gaps may be significantly reduced or sometimes removed, as we will see in the following section when we analyze the intersection of race and nativity in voting and registration.

Is there a foreign-born disadvantage in voting and registration?

Are immigrants inherently disadvantaged by their foreign-born status in voting participation? Foreign-born persons do not possess US citizenship except through naturalization.[15] They are more likely to face challenges in language barriers and social mobility. Not all foreign-born persons are ready, able, or willing to petition for naturalization even if they meet the length-of-residency requirement. Although recent research shows that as many as seven in ten Asian non-citizens expected to become US citizens in the next few years, only a fraction of the voting-age persons who are foreign-born may be eligible to become registered voters at any given point in time.[16] Nevertheless, one's foreign-born status may not necessarily be linked to a lower likelihood to participate in American elections. When voting and registration rates are calculated only among eligible persons, the results in Table 3.2 show that foreign-born Asians registered at a higher rate than US-born Asians and voted at the same rate as they did in 2008. Still compared with their white counterparts, the 21 percentage-point gap for US-born Asians is surprising and disturbing. More than 80 percent of registered voters of Asian descent, foreign-born or not, voted in 2008. Although this rate is significantly higher than the 33 percent voting rate among the VAP, foreign-born Asians are still 5 percentage points behind, and US-born Asians 3 percentage points behind, their white counterparts in turnout rates among registered voters. These statistics show that for US-born Asians who possess birthright citizenship becoming registered to vote is the biggest hurdle in the three-step voting process.

The myth of the foreign-born disadvantage also does not hold true for Latinos, but it has some truth for black and white immigrants. For naturalized Latino immigrants, they not only do not show a lower propensity to become registered voters than US-born Latinos, but also the reverse is true regarding their turnout rates. About six in ten Latino citizens, either by birth or naturalization, registered to vote in 2008. Slightly more than 90 percent of Latino immigrants who registered to vote turned out to vote, a rate significantly higher than the 84 percent turnout rate among registered US-born Latinos. The foreign-born sector of registered voters among blacks and whites also had a higher voting rate than the US-born sectors. Nevertheless, the US-born sectors of these two groups had a higher voter registration rate than their foreign-born counterparts.

These results show that the role of nativity in registration and voting varies by race. For communities where there are few immigrants, the foreign-born may be disadvantaged in learning how to become registered to vote. For communities with a foreign-born majority, one's foreign-born status not only does not form a natural barrier to voter registration but also the reverse may be true, especially in the case of Asian Americans. Among registered voters of all races, the foreign-born sectors voted at rates at least on par with their US-born counterparts.

How exceptional was the 2008 election cycle?

Was the 2008 election cycle the exception or the norm in terms of the effect of the foreign-born or nativity factor on voting? We answer this question by looking at the longitudinal data provided every other year in the CPS, which began asking questions about respondents' and their parents' country of birth in 1994. Table 3.3 reports the registration and voting rates among eligible persons by nativity for the four major racial groups in the eight election cycles between 1994 and 2008. Among Asian American citizens, the pattern of equal registration between the foreign- and US-born did not become apparent until the 2002 election. Prior to that, foreign-born citizens registered at lower rates than the US-born. Among Latinos, the disadvantage of foreign-born citizens in registration rates was apparent only before 2000 and in midterm elections. Nativity has been practically a non-factor in the registration rates among citizens since 2000. For Asians and Latinos, whenever US-born persons had an edge in registration rates, the gap was much smaller in presidential than in midterm elections. The heightened campaign stimuli in presidential elections might have helped close the registration gaps. Nonetheless, for both black and white immigrants who became naturalized citizens, foreign-born status was consistently linked to lower registration rates in all eight elections, except in 2006 among whites. The small share of the foreign-born population among those groups and the lack of immigrant-targeted voter registration drives may explain this persistent foreign-born disadvantage. These observed trends in voter registration rates suggest that the 2008 figures are part of a trend rather than a one-time phenomenon.

Table 3.3 Percentage distribution of voter registration and voting by race and nativity in November elections, 1994–2008

	Asian	Latino	Black	White
% registration among citizens				
1994 foreign-/US-born	48/59	47/54	51/61	67/70
1996 foreign-/US-born	**57/60**	**57/59**	**62/67**	**69/73**
1998 foreign-/US-born	45/57	51/57	55/64	64/69
2000 foreign-/US-born	**51/54**	**57/58**	**59/68**	**64/72**
2002 foreign-/US-born	49/50	52/54	58/63	63/69
2004 foreign-/US-born	**53/52**	**59/58**	**63/69**	**70/75**
2006 foreign-/US-born	52/46	51/51	53/62	61/61
2008 foreign-/US-born	**58/53**	**60/59**	**64/70**	**62/74**
% voting among the registered				
1994 foreign-/US-born	73/78	75/62	77/63	78/73
1996 foreign-/US-born	**79/80**	**86/72**	**87/80**	**84/83**
1998 foreign-/US-born	63/70	69/56	66/66	71/68
2000 foreign-/US-born	**84/81**	**85/76**	**93/84**	**88/86**
2002 foreign-/US-born	61/67	64/57	66/68	71/71
2004 foreign-/US-born	**85/85**	**87/80**	**90/87**	**91/89**
2006 foreign-/US-born	65/68	67/58	66/67	71/73
2008 foreign-/US-born	**85/86**	**91/84**	**94/92**	**90/89**

Note: all populations are of age 18 and over. Each racial category is mutually exclusive of each other. "White" stands for non-Hispanic whites. Entries in parenthesis for registration are rates among citizens; those for voting are rates among the registered. Entries in **bold** are for presidential election years.

Source: US Department of Commerce, Bureau of the Census. *Current Population Survey: Voter Supplement File*, 1994, 1996, 1998, 2000, 2002, 2004 [computer files]. ICPSR version. Washington, DC: US Department of Commerce, Bureau of the Census. Data for 2006 and 2008 elections are from US Bureau of the Census, Current Population Survey, November 2006 and 2008, respectively.

The lower half of Table 3.3 shows that the role of nativity in voting participation operated differently in influencing voting turnout than registration rates among eligible persons in the eight election cycles. Once foreign-born persons crossed the citizenship and self-registration hurdles, and became registered voters, they typically participated in elections at rates that were either equal to or higher than their US-born counterparts. This trend was particularly true among Latinos, where the foreign-born consistently outvoted the US-born. It was also true for black and white registered voters, except for the small reverse gap in 2006 among whites. For Asians, the observed pattern of foreign-born advantage in voting turnout only applies to one election cycle (2000). In midterm elections, foreign-born Asians consistently voted less than US-born Asians. Nevertheless, in presidential elections, foreign-born Asians did not vote much differently than their US-born counterparts. Thus, we may reject notions of an absolute foreign-born disadvantage in voter turnout even among Asians. The longitudinal analysis also allows us to conclude that, despite the Obama phenomenon, the 2008 findings on voter turnout are within the norm set in previous presidential elections.

How unique is the foreign-born factor in voting registration and turnout?

To assess the unique role of the foreign-born factor in voting participation, we need to understand and sort out the significance of other factors that may influence participation. We begin with four sets of factors based on well-established theories of political participation.[17] In general, voting participation can be influenced by *socioeconomic* factors, such as education and income. It can also be influenced by *socialization* factors, such as gender and age, and the degree of *social connectedness,* as indicated by residential mobility, marital status, employment status, and union membership. In addition, voting registration and turnout—particularly the latter—can be affected by the amount of campaign stimuli in the *political mobilization context,* as shaped by media coverage, candidate and party evaluation, significance of office, issue salience, certainty of outcome, election type, and regional political culture.[18] On top of these traditional theoretical frameworks, some researchers argue for the inclusion of factors related to *international migration,* such as nativity (foreign- or US-born) and length of stay in the United States (as a percentage of political life in the country), which may affect adult (re-)socialization as well as the related institutional constraints of citizenship and registration requirements.[19]

Previous research on the applicability of these theories to predicting the voter registration and turnout rates of Asians have not generated consistent findings, in part because of the variation in data source and methodology. Because of the substantive differences in major population characteristics between Asians and non-Asian groups, it seems increasingly clear that the conventional indicators of voting participation, such as socioeconomic class and group- and family-based social ties (gender, union membership, employment status, and marital status), may be relatively less significant for Asians than for whites and, to some extent, blacks and Latinos.[20] Nevertheless, US census-based research focusing on Asians as a whole shows that some of the conventional indicators, such as education, income, age, length of residence, and length of stay in the United States, are useful predictors of the voting participation of Asians.[21] Greater length of stay in the United States as a percentage of political life in the country may have a positive effect because of its relationship to immigrant political socialization.[22]

Research using the 2000 election data finds that, after controlling for differences in a variety of conditions, including the percentage of time spent in the United States, naturalized foreign-born citizens as a whole have a higher tendency to become registered voters than their US-born counterparts, while foreign-born registered voters as a whole do not have a significantly different voting tendency than their US-born counterparts.[23]

Everything else being equal, foreign-born Latinos are more likely both to become registered once naturalized and to vote once registered, foreign-born blacks are more likely to vote but not more likely to become registered than US-born blacks, and the reverse is true with respect to foreign-born Asian Americans, who are more likely to become registered but are not more likely to vote than US-born Asians. Although multivariate analysis of combined CPS data for the four election cycles between 1994 and 2000 shows that a foreign-born status is a greater hurdle for Asians than Latinos to become registered to vote, once they jump the registration hurdle nativity has no significant net effect on their propensity to vote.[24]

Geopolitical context may have an effect in that the heightened levels of participation for Asian Americans in Hawaii and California may reflect the greater elite incorporation and participation of Asians in the electoral processes in those two western states.[25] However, the net effect of mobilization context may differ according to the acts of political participation. It may be less significant in shaping voting registration than turnout. In the former process, individual characteristics may matter more. Seung-Jin Jang's analysis of the CPS 2000 data found that individual Latinos and Asian Americans are more likely to vote in places where there is a significant presence of a co-racial population, possibly because they are more likely to perceive the group-level benefits of voting.[26] Another recent study of the political participation of Asian Americans considered the racial-context effects in the sense of racial linked fate and experience of discrimination.[27] The author analyzed the Pilot National Asian American Political Survey (PNAAPS) and found that respondents' voting participation in both Hawaii and mainland states were not influenced by their perception of the racial context.[28] Nonetheless, in the acts of participation beyond voting, such as contacting officials, donating money, attending rallies, signing petitions, or working with others to solve a community problem, both racial linked fate and experience of discrimination had a positive effect for mainland Asian Americans, while neither had a significant effect for Asians residing in Hawaii.

How active are the foreign-born in other means of participation?

So far, our research shows that foreign-born naturalized citizens may not be disadvantaged in the voting process by their foreign-born status. Rather, their immigrant backgrounds may sometimes provide an extra incentive for them to seek greater political incorporation. This effect can happen when immigrants sense a hostile political environment that threatens to deprive themselves or their friends, relatives, and immigrant children in general of access to education, health care, and other governmental services associated with US citizenship.[29] Immigrants may also seek greater political incorporation out of concern about the people and status of the ethnic homeland.[30] Voting participation, however, is only one of the indicators of political engagement and one that is restricted to citizens and registered voters. Legend has it that Asian Americans, because of their affluence and immigrant background, prefer to participate in the American electoral process through other means than voting.[31] How active are foreign-born Asians in non-electoral activities that do not require US citizenship? And is a foreign-born status a positive or negative factor for participation in these other political activities?

The PNAAPS data provides an unprecedented opportunity to empirically examine participation beyond voting by nativity among Asians. Participation beyond voting is gauged by responses to a question asking whether respondents had participated in a range of political activities in their communities during the past four years. Lien, Conway, and Wong found that, compared with voter registration and voting, few Asian Americans participated in activities such as working with others in the community to solve a problem (21 percent), signing a petition for a political cause (16 percent), attending a public meeting, political rally or fundraiser (14 percent), donating to a campaign (12 percent), or writing or phoning a government official (11 percent).[32] Still fewer participated through taking part in a protest or demonstration (7 percent), contacting an editor of a newspaper, magazine, or television station (7 percent), serving on a governmental board or commission (2 percent), or working on a political campaign or other electoral activities (2 percent). Ethnic communities differ in their favored modes of participation beyond voting. In the PNAAPS, a higher percentage of South Asians than other Asians report having worked with others to solve a community problem (36 percent), written or phoned a government official (at 17 percent they were tied with Filipinos), or contacted media (14 percent). A higher percentage of Japanese signed a petition (24 percent), attended political gatherings (22 percent), or donated money to political campaigns (20 percent). Finally, a higher percentage of Vietnamese participated in a political protest or demonstration (14 percent) than other Asian American groups.

Comparing the US-born to the foreign-born samples, it is clear that in most cases the US-born were more likely to participate across all activities than the foreign-born. For example, 30 percent of the US-born sample stated that they had worked with others in their community to solve a problem as opposed to 18 percent of the foreign-born sample. More of the US-born (18 percent) also reported writing or phoning a government official than the foreign-born (9 percent). However, differences between the US- and foreign-born are less pronounced when one examines taking part in a protest (10 percent to 7 percent, respectively). When differences in socioeconomic status, political engagement, civic involvement and mobilization, acculturation and racial group concerns, and migration-related variables are controlled, multivariate results show that a foreign-born status is associated with lower participation in non-electoral activities. Among the foreign-born sample, the results show that neither citizenship status nor ethnic origin indicators are significant in predicting the likelihood of participation in non-electoral activities, but having received an education mostly outside of the United States is associated with a lower likelihood of participation.

Does involvement in homeland politics lessen interest in American elections?

The foreign-born sector of the US population often suffers suspicion and doubts about their "foreign attachments."[33] This suspicion is especially directed at Asian Americans, who have received the most amount of scrutiny in the popular media and mainstream politics regarding their loyalty and citizenship as well as their ability to become socially, culturally, and politically "assimilated."[34] Because of their foreign-born status and the continuing influx of new immigrants from Asia, Asian Americans may have a greater interest in politics related to their homeland than to their host country. How much do immigrants show concern over and get involved with people and the government of their home country? And how do these attitudes affect their participation in American politics, both electoral and non-electoral?

More than half of the PNAAPS respondents (56 percent) reported paying very close or fairly close attention to news events happening in Asia. But respondents were just as likely or even more likely to follow news events about Asian Americans as they were to keep up with stories about events in Asia. Most of the immigrant respondents also maintained strong social ties with people in their countries of origin. A large majority of them reported having contacted individuals in their country of origin at least once a month. However, when asked if they had ever participated in any activity dealing with the politics of their home countries after arriving in the United States, a lofty 94 percent answered "no" to the question. Lien and Wong found that the incidence of participation in homeland politics after an immigrant's arrival in the United States does not have a significant relationship to his or her acquisition of US citizenship or voting.[35] An immigrant's political activism prior to emigration also does not have a significant relationship to his or her rate of naturalization, voting, or participation beyond voting. Nevertheless, an immigrant's participation in homeland politics after arriving in the United States has a positive and significant relationship to his or her incidence of participation in politics beyond voting, as well as to his or her participation in ethnic community organizations or related activities in the United States. This last set of relationships does not change when we controlled for an assortment of factors related to transnational political participation, such as transnational social, cultural, and political ties, degree of social and political incorporation, and personal skills and resources related to international migration. Thus, everything else being equal, an immigrant's engagement in homeland politics is associated with a greater, not lower, likelihood to participate in non-electoral activities in the United States, while it has no impact on voter registration and voting.[36] These results clearly show not only that an immigrant's connections with his or her country of origin do not take place at the expense of his or her voting participation in the United States but also that there may even be a complementary relationship to political activities beyond voting.

Prospects of transforming the electorate and electoral leadership

Last but not least, we gauge the likely political impact of the continuing influx of the foreign-born population on the contours of the American electorate and its elected leadership. Table 3.4 reports the results of a trend analysis of CPS voting data during the eight most recent election cycles. It shows that, of the four major US racial and ethnic groups that were examined, Asians had the highest growth rate in terms of the size and share of both the VAP and the entire electorate between 1994 and 2008. In those fourteen years, the Asian American community has more than doubled its size of the VAP, growing from 2.5 percent in 1994 to 4.9 percent in 2008. Its 131 percent growth rate is far ahead of the second place occupied by Latinos, who grew from a 9.2 percent share of the VAP in 1994 to 13.7 percent in 2008. With a growth rate of 28 percent, blacks fell far behind Asians and Latinos but remained significantly ahead of non-Latino whites in their share of the VAP. Although the black share of the VAP grew by less than 1 percent in this fourteen-year span, it actually fared much better than the white share of the VAP, which experienced a significant decline from 76 percent to 68 percent between 1994 and 2008. The Asian American and Latino increase is inconceivable without the rapid growth of new migration from Asia and Latin America.

To a similar but more moderate extent, we observe an increase from 1.2 percent to 2.8 percent share of the electorate for Asian Americans between 1994 and 2008. Their growth rate of 81 percent was the highest of all four groups. The Latino share of the electorate grew from 4.2 percent to 7.4 percent, or a growth rate of 64 percent. Black voters increased their share of the electorate from 9.4 percent to 12.7 percent, or a growth rate of 31 percent. While white voters saw a decrease in their share of the electorate from 84.7 percent to 76.3 percent, they still experienced a growth rate of 12 percent. Between 2006 and 2008, both Latinos and blacks had a significant jump in their share of the electorate, but whites had a significant decline, most likely due to the historic Obama candidacy in the 2008 election cycle.

Corresponding to the dramatic growth in their share of the VAP and electorate, there has been a dramatic growth in the number of Asian American and Latino elected officials at state and local level offices in

Table 3.4 Percentage share of the voting-age persons and voters by race in November elections, 1994–2008

	Asian	*Latino*	*Black*	*White*
Share of voting-age persons				
1994	2.5%	9.2%	11.3%	76.4%
1996	3.4	9.5	11.3	75.1
1998	3.7	10.3	11.4	73.9
2000	3.9	10.7	11.6	73.1
2002	4.0	11.1	11.6	72.5
2004	4.5	12.5	11.4	70.8
2006	4.7	13.1	12.0	69.4
2008	4.9	13.7	12.2	68.5
N in 1994 (x1000)	4772	17,476	21,514	145,027
N in 2008 (x1000)	11,009	30,852	27,483	154,472
% change 94{-}08	+131	+76	+28	+6
Share of the electorate				
1994	1.2%	4.2%	9.4%	84.7%
1996	1.7	4.8	10.5	82.4
1998	1.7	4.9	10.9	81.9
2000	1.9	5.8	11.7	80.0
2002	2.0	6.1	11.2	80.0
2004	2.4	6.0	11.2	79.9
2006	2.4	5.8	10.6	80.4
2008	2.8	7.4	12.7	76.3
N in 1994 (x1000)	2003	5934	12,749	89,468
N in 2008 (x1000)	3627	9745	16,674	100,042
% change 94{-}08	+81	+64	+31	+12

Note: all populations are of age 18 and over. Each racial category is mutually exclusive of each other. "White" stands for non-Hispanic whites.
Source: US Department of Commerce, Bureau of the Census. *Current Population Survey: Voter Supplement File*, 1994, 1996, 1998, 2000, 2002, 2004 [computer files]. ICPSR version. Washington, DC: US Department of Commerce, Bureau of the Census. Data for 2006 and 2008 elections are from US Bureau of the Census, Current Population Survey, November 2006 and 2008, respectively.

recent decades.[37] For example, the total number of Asian American elected officials grew from 120 in 1978 to 346 in 2004. Their growth rate was particularly sharp at the local level, where the change was from 52 to 260 during this 26-year period. In 2004, 35 percent served at the school board level, 31 percent at the municipal level, and 23 percent at the state legislative level. An even more dramatic change occurred among Latino elected officials. Their total number rose from 3147 in 1985 to 5205 in 2000, or a growth rate of 65 percent. The number of Latino federal and state legislators steadily grew from 129 in 1985 to 253 in 2004, or 96 percent. The number of Latino county and municipal officials grew from 1316 to 2059, or 56 percent. The number of Latino education/school board officials grew the fastest, from 1185 in 1985 to 2682 in 2000, or

125 percent. Whereas black elected officials reached a historic high of 9101 in 2001, a 2003 report from the Joint Center for Political and Economic Studies showed a decline in the number of black male elected officials between 1999 and 2001, with black women accounting for all of the growth during that period.[38]

More importantly, first-generation immigrants constituted 42 percent of Asian Americans holding state and local elective office, according to a recent, first-ever nationwide survey of state and local nonwhite elected officials.[39] In comparison, only 8 percent of Latino and 1 percent of black elected officials in the survey were foreign-born. Second-generation Americans or those who are US-born but with foreign-born parents were 26 percent among Asians, 28 percent among Latinos, and 1 percent among blacks. Third-generation respondents who themselves and their parents are US-born but not their grandparents were 24 percent among Asians, 22 percent among Latinos, and 3 percent among blacks. These statistics show that Asian American elective leaders have a much closer and more personal experience with immigration than their Latino and black colleagues. Defying the myth of assimilation over generations, first-generation immigrants from Asia not only have become voters but also candidates and elected officials, and they have contributed more to their community's growth of electoral leadership than immigrants in other demographic groups.[40] Breaking the traditional Japanese and Chinese dominance in electoral leadership and adding ethnic diversity to this arena, immigrant elected officials increasingly have South Asian, Korean, and Southeast Asian backgrounds.[41]

Conclusion

This study shows not only that the nation's foreign-born population from Asia and Latin America is rapidly growing but also that it has the potential to reinvigorate the political process. For those immigrants who are in the majority or plurality of their respective communities, their foreign-born status not only is not a liability to political participation but also may be an asset to the empowerment of their minority communities. At both aggregate and individual levels, Asian American and Latino immigrants have shown strong inclinations to become politically incorporated through the acquisition of US citizenship. They have also registered to vote and voted once eligible, often at equal or higher rates than their US-born counterparts. They may compensate for their relative disadvantages in participation resources due to language and socialization barriers compared with the US-born by a greater concern over issues dealing with immigration and by their transnational ties to their ethnic homeland. Their foreign-born status may well be a source of political mobilization, for getting citizenship and becoming voters are seen as safeguards against the loss of jobs and benefits related to anti-immigrant initiatives or legislation, such as California Proposition 187 in 1994, the 1996 Illegal Immigration Reform and Immigrant Responsibility Act, and the 2005 Border Protection, Antiterrorism, and Illegal Immigration Control Act. A foreign-born status is associated with a lower likelihood to participate in activities beyond voting, including making campaign donations, contacting public officials and the media, and working with others to solve community problems. Yet, contrary to popular perceptions, their transnational ties and homeland concerns do not inhibit their political incorporation into the host country and may actually help motivate them to participate in non-electoral activities in their new communities.

The foreign-born population is critical to the growth and vitality of a multiracial democracy in the United States. To help deliver its full potential, we need to support and maintain a thriving, immigrant-friendly civil society. Civil society organizations, such as labor unions, worker centers, religious institutions, community-based nonprofits, and ethnic voluntary associations, have taken the lead in turning new Asian and Latino immigrants into citizens and voters, and to engage them in other political activities.[42] These organizations have taken the lead because political parties have not committed themselves to incorporating nonwhite immigrant communities *en masse* into the political system as they did white European immigrants during the second half of the nineteenth and early part of the twentieth centuries.[43] Today's political parties have neither the capacity nor the will to incorporate the new, mostly nonwhite immigrants into the political system because of weakened local party structures, changing campaign tactics, selective mobilization strategies that maintain the existing, white-dominant party coalitions, and wrongful assumptions about the political apathy of immigrants. Because political parties are strategic institutions created to win elections, they seek to mobilize not voters in general but supporters in particular. Previous research has found that racial and ethnic minorities, especially small, emergent political communities, are exposed to substantially lower levels of campaign mobilization efforts than are traditional white voters.[44] Community-based civic organizations may also be better able to incorporate immigrants than political parties because they have stronger and closer connections to the immigrants they serve. Nevertheless, they have limited resources and often have other priorities and goals than political mobilization. Both national and local party organizations therefore should be urged to construct and invest in issue-based coalitions with immigrant communities by adopting a long-term approach "through regular mass voter-registration drives, voter-education programs, and the establishment of a stronger presence in immigrant communities."[45] Finally, we need to proactively protect the voting rights of foreign-born and non-native-speaking Americans by ensuring them equal access to citizenship, voter registration materials, and ballots printed both in English and the vernacular languages of their ethnic communities.

Notes

1 See W.E.B. Dubois, *The Souls of Black Folk* (Chicago: McClurg, 1903).
2 The ACS is an annual national survey that provides the most current economic, social, demographic, and housing information on the American population. It uses a series of monthly samples to produce annually updated data for the same small areas (census tracts and block groups) formerly surveyed by the decennial census long-form sample. Each year approximately 3 million housing unit addresses in the United States and Puerto Rico are selected for participation in the ACS. The 2006–8 ACS three-year estimates are based on data collected between January 2006 and December 2008. They represent the average characteristics over that three-year period, and thus are based on a larger sample size than the one-year estimates but are also less current.
3 For practical purposes, the term "immigrants" is used interchangeably with the "foreign-born" in this chapter. In reality, "foreign-born" is a broader term than "immigrants." According to the Census Bureau, a foreign-born person is anyone who is not a US citizen at birth. The foreign-born population in the United States includes naturalized citizens, lawful permanent residents (immigrants), temporary migrants (such as foreign students), humanitarian migrants (such as refugees), and people illegally present in the United States. See www.census.gov/population/www/socdemo/immigration.html.
4 See Campbell J. Gibson and Emily Lennon, *Historical Census Statistics on the Foreign-born Population of the United States: 1850–1990* (Washington: Bureau of the Census, Population Division Working Paper No. 29, 1999); Dianne Schimdley, *Profile of the Foreign-Born Population in the United States: 2000* (Washington: Bureau of the Census, Current Population Reports, Series P23–206, 2001).
5 See Nolan Malone, Kaari Baluja, Joseph Constanzo, and Cynthia Davis, *The Foreign-born Population, 2000* (Washington, DC: Bureau of the Census, Census 2000 Brief, 2003).
6 See Pei-te Lien, "The Voting Rights Act and Its Implications for Three Nonblack Minorities," in *The Voting Rights Act: Securing the Ballot* (Washington: CQ Press, 2006), 129–44 (Table 8–1). This table is based on an analysis of the Census 2000 Summary File 3, the 1-in-6 sample, race-alone data. Direct comparison of racial figures between the 2000 census and earlier censuses is difficult because of the addition of a mixed-race category in the 2000 census.
7 See Ki-Taek Chun and Nadia Zalokar, *Civil Rights Issues Facing Asian Americans in the 1990s* (Washington: US Commission on Civil Rights, 1992); Debra Woo, *Glass Ceiling and Asian Americans: The New Face of Workplace Barriers* (Walnut Creek, CA: AltaMira Press, 2000).
8 See Pei-te Lien, Christian Collet, Janelle Wong, and Karthick Ramakrishnan, "Asian Pacific American Politics Symposium: Public Opinion and Political Participation," *PS: Political Science & Politics* 34, no. 3 (September 2001): 625–30.
9 See the US Citizenship and Immigration Services website at www.uscis.gov for the latest set of requirements and changes.
10 Most countries, except the United States and some Latin American countries, have automatic voter registration. See Thomas Mackie and Richard Rose, *International Almanac of Electoral History*, 3rd edn (Washington: Congressional Quarterly, 1991).
11 See Sidney Verba, Kay Schlozman, and Henry Brady, *Voice and Equality: Civic Voluntarism in American Politics* (Cambridge, MA: Harvard University Press, 1995).
12 See Bryan C. Baker, "Fact Sheet: Trends in Naturalization Rates" (Office of Immigration Statistics, US Department of Homeland Security, 2007); John Simanski, "Annual Flow Report: Naturalization in the United States 2006," (Office of Immigration Statistics, US Department of Homeland Security, 2007).
13 See Guillermina Jasso and Mark R. Rosenzweig, *The New Chosen People: Immigrants in the United States* (New York: Russell Sage Foundation, 1990); Alejandro Portes and Rafael Mozo, "Political Adaptation Process of Cubans and Other Ethnic Minorities in the United States: A Preliminary Analysis," *International Migration Review* 19 (1985): 35–63.

14 The Current Population Survey (CPS) is a monthly survey of about 56,000 households conducted by the Census Bureau for the Bureau of Labor Statistics. The November data consist of responses to two sets of questions, the basic labor force questions given every month and the supplemental questions on voting and registration asked every other November after the general elections. The universe of this data series consists of all adult persons in the civilian, non-institutional population of the United States living in households in all 50 states and the District of Columbia. A major redesign in 1994 added new questions on nativity and place of birth, permitting a rare but limited opportunity for this researcher to analyze the effects of nativity, place of birth, and ancestral origin on the voting registration and turnout rates of voting-age persons of Asian (including mixed racial) descent. Another major revision in 2004, which began to phase out the 1990 sample and phase in the 2000 sample, may improve data quality and add confidence to the results reported for elections in 2004 and beyond. However, the adoption of a new question format on race that permits the reporting of mixed origins has complicated the comparison of results between the post-2004 elections and earlier ones. To maximize comparability, I used a definition of race that includes persons who report more than one race on the census form.

15 The exception is biological or adopted children of US citizens who were born abroad and did not acquire US citizenship at birth. In 2000, Congress passed the Child Citizenship Act, which allows any child under the age of 18 who is adopted by a US citizen and emigrates to the United States to acquire immediate citizenship. The law became effective on 27 February 2001.

16 See Pei-te Lien, M. Margaret Conway, and Janelle Wong, *The Politics of Asian Americans: Diversity and Community* (New York: Routledge, 2004).

17 See M. Margaret Conway, *Political Participation in the United States*, 2nd edn (Washington: Congressional Quarterly, 1991); Jan E. Leighley, *Strength in Numbers? The Political Mobilization of Racial and Ethnic Minorities* (Princeton, NJ: Princeton University Press, 2001); Steven J. Rosenstone and John M. Hansen, *Mobilization, Participation, and Democracy in America* (New York: Macmillan, 1993); Sidney Verba and Norman H. Nie, *Participation in America* (New York: Harper & Row, 1972); Sidney Verba, Kay Schlozman, and Henry Brady, *Voice and Equality*; Paul Abramson, John Aldrich, and David Rohde, *Change and Continuity in the 1996 Elections* (Washington: Congressional Quarterly, 1998); Raymond E. Wolfinger and Steven J. Rosenstone, *Who Votes?* (New Haven, CT: Yale University Press, 1980).

18 See Robert A. Jackson, "A Reassessment of Voter Mobilization," *Political Research Quarterly* 49 (1996): 331–49.

19 See Pei-te Lien, "Asian Americans and Voting Participation: Comparing Racial and Ethnic Differences in Recent U.S. Elections," *International Migration Review* 38 (2004): 493–517; Lien, Conway, and Wong, *Politics of Asian Americans*; Janelle Wong, Pei-te Lien, and M. Margaret Conway, "Group-Based Resources and Political Participation among Asian Americans," *American Politics Research* 33 (2005): 545–76.

20 See Wendy Tam Cho, "Naturalization, Socialization, and Participation: Immigrants and (Non-)Voting," *Journal of Politics* 61 (1999): 1140–55; Lien, "Asian Americans and Voting Participation"; Pei-te Lien, "Does the Gender Gap in Political Attitudes and Behavior Vary across Racial Groups? Comparing Asians to Whites, Blacks, and Latinos," *Political Research Quarterly* 51 (1998): 869–94; Pei-te Lien, *The Making of Asian America through Political Participation* (Philadelphia: Temple University Press, 2001); Pei-te Lien, *The Political Participation of Asian Americans: Voting Behavior in Southern California* (New York: Garland, 1997); Pei-te Lien, "Who Votes in Multiracial America? An Analysis of Voting and Registration by Race and Ethnicity, 1990–96," in *Black and Multiracial Politics in America*, eds Yvette Alex-Assensoh and Lawrence Hanks (New York: New York University Press, 2000); Don Nakanishi, "The Next Swing Vote? Asian Pacific Americans and California Politics," in *Racial and Ethnic Politics in California,* eds

Byran O. Jackson and Michael B. Preston (Berkeley: IGS Press, 1991); Jun Xu, "Why Do Minorities Participate Less? The Effects of Immigration, Education, and Electoral Process on Asian American Voter Registration and Turnout," *Social Science Research* 34 (2005): 682–702.

21 See Lien, "Asian Americans and Voting Participation"; Pei-te Lien, "Comparing the Voting Participation of Chinese to Other Asian Americans in U.S. Elections," *Chinese America: History and Perspectives* 17 (2003): 1–13; Lien, *Making of Asian America*; Lien, "Who Votes in Multiracial America?"; Paul Ong and Don T. Nakanishi, "Becoming Citizens, Becoming Voters: The Naturalization and Political Participation of Asian Pacific Immigrants," in *Reframing the Immigration Debate,* eds Bill Ong Hing and Ronald Lee (Los Angeles: LEAP Asian Pacific American Public Policy Institute and UCLA Asian American Studies Center, 1996): 275–30.

22 See Cho, "Naturalization, Socialization, and Participation"; Janelle S. Wong, "The Effects of Age and Political Exposure on the Development of Party Identification among Asian American and Latino Immigrants in the U.S," *Political Behavior* 22 (2001): 341–71.

23 See Lien, "Asian Americans and Voting Participation."

24 See Xu, "Why Do Minorities Participate Less?"

25 See James Lai, "The Recruitment of Asian Pacific American Elected Officials and Their Impact on Group Political Mobilization," Ph.D. diss., University of Southern California, 2000; Lien, "Asian Americans and Voting Participation"; Lien, *Making of Asian America.*

26 See Seung-Jin Jang, "Get Out on Behalf of Your Group: Electoral Participation of Latinos and Asian Americans," *Political Behavior* 31 (2009): 511–35.

27 See Kathy H. Kim, "Racial Context Effects and the Political Participation of Asian Americans," *American Politics Research* 37 (July 2009): 569–92.

28 The PNAAPS is the first multi-city, multi-ethnic, and multi-lingual sample survey of the political attitudes and opinions of Asian Americans. A total of 1218 adults in the six largest Asian ethnic groups residing in the nation's five major population hubs of Asians were surveyed by phone between 16 November 2000 and 28 January 2001. The survey was sponsored by a research grant from the National Science Foundation (SES 9973435) and supplemented by a community grant from KSCI-TV of Los Angeles. I am the principal investigator.

29 See Matt A. Barreto, "Latino Immigrants at the Polls: Foreign-Born Voter Turnout in the 2002 Election," *Political Research Quarterly* 58 (2005): 79–86; Lisa Bedolla García, *Fluid Borders: Latino Power, Identity, and Politics in Los Angeles* (Berkeley: University of California Press, 2005); Adrian D. Pantoja, Ricardo Ramirez, and Gary M. Segura, "Citizens by Choice, Voters by Necessity: Patterns in Political Mobilization by Naturalized Latinos," *Political Research Quarterly* 54 (2001): 729–50; Adrian D. Pantoja and Gary M. Segura, "Fear and Loathing in California: Contextual Threat and Political Sophistication among Latino Voters," *Political Behavior* 25 (2003): 265–86; S. Karthick Ramakrishnan, *Democracy in Immigrant America: Changing Demographics and Political Participation* (Stanford, CA: Stanford University Press, 2005).

30 See Lina Basch, Nina Glick Schiller, and Cristina Szanton Blanc, *Nations Unbound* (New York: Routledge, 1994); Louis DeSipio, "Transnational Politics and Civic Engagement: Do Home-Country Political Ties Limit Latino Immigrant Pursuit of U.S. Civic Engagement and Citizenship?" in *Transforming Politics, Transforming America: The Political and Civic Incorporation of Immigrants in the United State,* eds Taeku Lee, S. Karthick Ramakrishnan, and Ricardo Ramirez (Charlottesville: University of Virginia Press, 2006), 106–26; Anna Karpathakis, "Home Society Politics and Immigrant Political Incorporation: The Case of Greek Immigrants in New York City," *International Migration Review* 33 (1999): 55–78; Pei-te Lien, "Transnational Homeland Concerns and Participation in U.S. Politics: A Comparison among Immigrants from China, Taiwan, and Hong Kong," *Journal of Chinese Overseas* 2 (2006): 56–78; Reuel Rogers, *Afro-Caribbean*

Immigrants and the Politics of Incorporation: Ethnicity, Exception, or Exit (Cambridge, MA: Cambridge University Press, 2006).

31 See Steven P. Erie and Harold Brackman, "Paths to Political Incorporation for Latinos and Asian Pacifics in California," paper presented at the California Policy Seminar, University of California, Berkeley, 1993.

32 See Lien, Conway, and Wong, *Politics of Asian Americans*.

33 See Tony Smith, *Foreign Attachments: The Power of Ethnic Groups in the Making of US Foreign Policy* (Cambridge, MA: Harvard University Press, 2000).

34 See Neil Gotanda, "Citizenship Nullification: The Impossibility of Asian American Politics," in *Asian Americans and Politics: Perspectives, Experiences, Prospects*, ed. Gordon Chang (Washington: Woodrow Wilson Center Press, 2001), 79–101; Ling-chi Wang, "Race, Class, Citizenship, and Extraterritoriality: Asian Americans and the 1996 Campaign Finance Scandal," *Amerasia Journal* 24 (1998): 1–21; Frank Wu, *Yellow: Race in America beyond Black and White* (New York: Basic Books, 2002).

35 See Pei-te Lien and Janelle Wong, "Like Latinos? Explaining the Transnational Political Behavior of Asian Americans," in *The Transnational Asian American Politics*, eds Chris Collet and Pei-te Lien (Philadelphia: Temple University Press, 2009), 137–98.

36 Lien, Conway, and Wong, *Politics of Asian Americans*.

37 See Lien, "Voting Rights Act."

38 See David A. Bositis, *Black Elected Officials: A Statistical Summary 2001* (Washington: Joint Center for Political and Economic Studies, 2001).

39 The Gender and Multicultual Leadership Survey, 2006–7. Principal investigators are Christine Sierra, Carol Hardy-Fanta, Pei-te Lien, and Dianne Pinderhughes. Details of the survey methodology and findings are available at www.gmcl.org.

40 See Robert Dahl, *Who Governs? Democracy and Power in an American City* (New Haven, CT: Yale University Press, 1961).

41 See James Lai, Wendy Cho, Thomas Kim, and Okiyoshi Takeda, "Asian Pacific American Campaigns, Elections, and Elected Officials," *PS: Political Science and Politics* 34, no. 3 (September 2001): 611–17.

42 The Rubaii-Barrett chapter in this volume discusses how some local governments have also taken the lead in the political inclusion of immigrants.

43 See Janelle Wong, *Democracy's Promise: Immigrants and American Civic Institutions* (Ann Arbor: University of Michigan Press, 2006).

44 See Leighley, *Strength in Numbers*.

45 See Wong, *Democracy's Promise*, 175.

4 The Home Styles of California Latino Representatives

Policy, Constituency, and Symbolic Representation

Sally Friedman and Shannon Scotece[1]

It is well known that Latinos are the fastest growing minority in the United States.[2] They accounted for 6.4 percent of the American population in the 1980 census, 9 percent in 1990 and 12.5 percent in 2000. Currently, they outnumber African Americans as the nation's largest minority group and are projected to outnumber white Americans in perhaps the not so distant future. Latinos have clearly expanded their presence in terms of simple physical number of people that must be served and their relative percentages as a potential electoral bloc. So, too, the descriptive representation of Latinos—the number serving in political office at all levels of government—has dramatically increased. In Congress, this number has risen from a handful of members in the 1960s and 1970s to twenty-six in the 110th Congress, the highest number of Hispanics serving in US history.[3]

What do these trends mean for the substantive representation of Latinos? Studies of the representation of minorities in Congress have demonstrated a linkage between a member's race or ethnicity and his/her policy decisions. For instance, African American representatives are more likely to support policies in Congress that primarily benefit African American citizens. As Kenny Whitby and George Krause assert, African American representatives "vote in a unified manner that is consistent with a common race-group consciousness grounded in both common political goals and subjective policy interests as uncovered in public opinion surveys."[4] A relationship appears to exist between the race and ethnicity of legislators and the decision to pursue policies that help particular groups.[5]

Thus, when we highlight the substantive representation of Latino members of Congress, we rightly begin with policy representation and a Washington focus. Examining the seven Democratic Latino legislators serving in and around the Los Angeles area, this chapter takes a step toward broadening our understanding of substantive representation from policy representation inside the legislature to a consideration of how members of Congress portray themselves to constituents. Building on the work of Richard Fenno on home styles, we will examine substantive policy representation over and above the roll-call voting stage and place that representation in the context of the wider set of legislative activities taking place in congressional districts. Appreciating what legislators do in their districts reminds us that activities such as constituency service, obtaining federal funding, and symbolic activity can be as critical as speaking out on national policy issues, especially for constituents who are generally under-served.

Literature

The starting points for this study are the scholarship analyzing the roll-call voting behavior of Latino representatives as well as the broader literature on congressional representation.

An examination of the roll-call literature yields several findings of relevance to this project. First, that literature generally finds a fairly high degree of cohesion among Latino legislators at least as compared with non-Latinos.[6]

Additionally, research has begun to highlight, albeit sometimes with more debate than one might expect, the constituency and legislator background factors that explain variation in voting behavior. Thus, constituency characteristics, generally measured by the percent Hispanic in a legislative district, are thought to impact roll-call voting, though sometimes this effect occurs in interaction with a legislator's party, ethnicity, or other circumstances.[7]

But what factors account for any differences among Latinos themselves? Using data from the 101st–108th Congresses, Michael Rocca, Gabriel Sanchez, and Joseph Uscinski conducted statistical analyses attempting to sort out, after controlling for a variety of constituency and institutional variables, which of a number of "descriptive attributes" might help explain variation among Latino legislators themselves. Depending on the model specification, "national origin" of the legislator matters, as does level and type of education, generation, and gender of the representative.[8]

Other studies have also highlighted variation among Latino (and other minority) legislators. Examining cases of conflicting positions between the positions of the Democratic Party vs. the Congressional Hispanic Caucus (CHC), Rodolfo Espino argued that, "A representative's ethnicity instead of the makeup of their constituency appears to be a stronger determinant of one's level of support of the CHC's position against the Democratic Party's position."[9]

Studies by James Wilson, Richard Fenno, and David Canon also point out variation in the styles of minority (for them, African American) legislators more generally.[10] Among other dimensions, legislators must choose between an insider or an outsider style (Wilson) and between representing through highlighting "commonalities" (among their minority group and other constituents) or to emphasize "difference" (Canon). We would expect such variations to describe Latino legislative styles as well.

Regardless, at the same time as a substantial degree of voting cohesion exists among Latino legislators, a certain degree of variation, explained at least in a general way by their constituencies and background characteristics, is also apparent.

A broader literature on congressional representation reminds us that there is more to policy representation than roll-call voting, and that much of what representatives do is focused on their constituencies rather than on Washington.[11] In this regard, Heinz Eulau and Paul Karps have broadly characterized representation-oriented activities into policy (congruence between district policy positions and legislator decisions on policy issues), service (non-legislative work to help particular constituent groups), allocation (federally funded projects benefiting the local economy), and symbolic representation (where a legislator focuses on policies bringing non-tangible benefits to constituents).[12] Service and allocation matter, and symbolic representation is relevant for this paper as we explore the work done by members that would likely appeal to constituents and help generate feelings of trust and support.

All this brings us to Fenno's work on the home styles of legislators.[13] As is well known in the Congress literature, through extensively traveling with members of Congress and "soaking and poking" through member activities, Fenno has provided in-depth and comprehensive descriptions of the presentational styles of legislators. In addition to finding some policy representation, his work highlights the importance of the kinds of constituency-oriented activities described above. Most legislators have strong roots in their districts, travel frequently between Washington and home, and engage in substantial amounts of the service and allocation activities highlighted by Eulau and Karps.

Study design

Therefore, building on the work of Fenno and others, this chapter takes a cut at going beyond a policy focus in our understanding of Latino representation. We provide detailed descriptions of the activities of the seven Latino legislators currently representing the area in and around Los Angeles.[14] We focused on the state of California since this state has such a high number of registered Latino voters (3,270,228, up 18 percent since 2006), making the question of whether Latino legislators substantively represent their Latino constituents particularly important.[15] These representatives were chosen because their "large" number made comparison possible, particularly when they share a similar representational context. All represent largely Latino constituencies, where the constituents also are significantly less well off and less well educated than the average California resident.[16]

To conduct this research, public record sources—an appropriate alternative to in-depth interviews because so much information is available—were employed.[17] These included legislator websites,[18] articles from (mostly Californian) newspapers,[19] and descriptions of the legislators by expert analysts (in *The Almanac of American Politics* and *Politics in America*).[20] While newspaper articles and district profiles provide an objective account of legislators' representational styles, websites differ because they are constructed by the legislator. The sites allow members of Congress to communicate with their constituents, who can also represent the interests of their district by choosing which materials to post.[21] The fact that somewhat more information is available for some of these members than others should be noted but does not impact the quality of the profiles or the "success" of the legislator.

Because of space limitations and because comparisons of legislative styles are critical to this work, for each legislator we have limited our discussion to key elements of his or her home style.

In the profiles below, we focus first on varying styles of policy representation and then move to a discussion of explicitly constituency-oriented activity. A final section brings the material together by highlighting, on the one hand, the high degree of Latino-oriented activities in which these legislators engage and, on the other, the alternative ways by which these legislators have come to be included in the legislative process. Policy representation matters but so do service, allocation, and symbolic representation.

Policy and partisan representation

An examination of indicators, including website activity (as measured by press releases and home pages) and bills sponsored, shows that for the most part these legislators focus on Latino concerns (Table 4.1). That said, the profiles below explore the variation in the styles these legislators utilize to advocate for these issues.

Xavier Becerra: Latino issues insider style

Described as having a "pleasant and businesslike manner" (Almanac), Rep. Becerra appears to be an effective spokesperson inside Congress, using his party and committee positions to advocate for Latino as well as other concerns.

A graduate of Stanford, prior to entering Congress Becerra worked as a community activist for the mentally ill and served in the California state attorney general's office and as a staffer for a state senator. Though "he never envisioned a life in politics" (PIA), he was nonetheless recruited to run for the California State Assembly and then for the US Congress.

For political and personal reasons—as a child, he travelled across the border many times to visit family (PIA)—immigration issues have been

Table 4.1 Latino-oriented activities of legislators, 2007–8

District	Rep.	Website in Spanish?	Press releases	Percent	Latino legislation	Percent	Home page mentions Latino interests	Minority legislation	Percent	DW-nominate scores	National Council of La Raza
43	Baca	No	7 out of 44	16	3 out of 21	14	Yes	2 out of 21	10	-.336	100
31	Becerra	No	14 out of 34	41	3 out of 8	38	Yes	2 out of 8	25	-.443	100
38	Napolitano	No	4 out of 38	11	0 out of 2	0	Yes	0 out of 2	0	-.452	100
34	Roybal-Allard	Yes	29 out of 223	13	0 out of 6	0	No	2 out of 6	33	-.428	100
39	Sanchez, Linda	Yes	7 out of 63	11	2 out of 11	18	Yes	2 out of 11	18	-.501	100
47	Sanchez, Loretta	Yes	4 out of 38	11	0 out of 14	0	No	1 out of 14	7	-.37	100
32	Solis	Yes	35 out of 136	26	9 out of 19	47	Yes	8 out of 19	42	-.509	100
35	Waters	No	3 out of 158	2	0 out of 33	0	No	8 out of 33	24	-.637	100
51	Filner	Yes	No PR		3 out of 42	7	Yes	2 out of 42	5	-.642	100
28	Berman	Yes	3 out of 80	4	0 out of 8	0	Yes	1 out of 8	13	-.362	100
20	Costa	Yes	0 out of 26	6	0 out of 10	0	Yes	1 out of 10	10	-.197	100

important to Becerra. He made them central to his work on the House Judiciary Committee, so "when he left the panel ... Hispanic leaders worried they'd lost an effective advocate on the issue" (PIA).

Currently, Becerra is the first Latino to sit on the prestigious Ways and Means Committee, thus receiving an assignment showing he has the respect and trust of his party leadership. As a committee member, he can express his version of Latino/minority interests by weighing in on issues, including social security and free trade. For example, as a member of Congress who was opposed to the privatization of retirement accounts,

> Becerra noted in 2004 that three in four Latinos who receive Social Security benefits depend on them for half their income. "When we talk about Social Security, we need to be talking about how to protect this indispensable benefit, not about how to radically change a program that has worked and provided a guaranteed monthly check for our nation's neediest families," he told the *Inland Daily Valley Bulletin* (PIA).

He also "objected when Ways and Means chairman Bill Thomas suggested race or gender could be among the factors used for determining future Social Security benefits" (Almanac). Opposing a free-trade agreement with several Central American nations, "Becerra said 'he believed in a CAFTA but not this CAFTA' because the legal protections for workers were not as strong as those for products and intellectual property. 'I learned from NAFTA that good intentions are no substitute' for enforceable rules, Becerra told *The Los Angeles Times* in 2004" (PIA).

Becerra has also weighed in on other Latino issues, for instance expressing concern that declaring English as an official language "sends a message of intolerance for those trying to learn English" and opposing restrictions on bilingual education (Almanac). He is a former chair of the Congressional Hispanic Caucus, has presented the Labor Day Weekend National Hispanic Radio Address (PR 9/2/06) and his endorsement has been sought by Californian politicians courting the Latino vote (*San Francisco Chronicle* 2/16/98). In an effort to bring attention to issues that uniquely affect Latino youth, Becerra also participated in an MTV-sponsored forum to address the impact immigration has on young Latinos and their families.[22] Over a period of years, Becerra, along with Rep. Ileana Ros-Lehtinen (R-FL),

> has been a staunch advocate for the creation of a National Museum of the American Latino. He says the "country ought to have a museum dedicated to the nation's 38 million Hispanic Americans," and he introduced legislation in the 108th Congress to authorize $3.2 million and the creation of a bipartisan 23-member commission to plan the new museum (PIA).

The bill was enacted in 2008, and the museum will be located on the National Mall as part of the Smithsonian Institute.[23]

His insider advocacy style has led to a seat at the party leadership table. He was asked by party leaders to deliver the Democratic response in Spanish to President Bush's 2007 "State of the Union" address,[24] and more importantly he was named as "Assistant to the Speaker [where] Rep. Becerra wields a strong voice in House Leadership, helping to set priorities and drive the legislative decision making process" (bio).[25]

Becerra even worked with the consummate insider, former senator Ted Kennedy, to propose ways to help law enforcement keep track of guns used in violent crimes (PR 2/7/08).

Thus, viewing advocacy as a long-term process, Rep. Becerra has supported the interests of Latinos largely through the traditional congressional structures of committee and party.

Joe Baca: Latino advocate with a maverick slant

In terms of his overall record on issues and mostly in terms of his representational style, Rep. Baca appears to be something of a political maverick. Most of the time, it's not hard to figure out where he stands.

Born in New Mexico to a family of fourteen siblings "in a house where little English was spoken ... with single-minded ambition, Baca took himself from hardscrabble beginnings—to the California Assembly—to Congress ... 'I'm a fighter because I know what it's like to struggle'" (PIA).[26]

Having served as Chair of the Congressional Hispanic Caucus, he has advocated for more diversity in corporate boardrooms—"Part of our responsibility is to make sure that we look at corporate America, that its face looks like the way America looks like" (*Sacramento Bee* 9/15/05). He has also advocated for more recognition of Latino leaders—even as we celebrate Martin Luther King Day, "we should give recognition also to Cesar Chavez, an American hero and role model" (PR 1/18/07).

More specifically, he has championed the interests of Latino farm workers and immigrants. "Angered by the dangerous working conditions, excessive payroll deductions and primitive living arrangements endured by the migrant work force," he has publicized abuses of Latino forest workers (*Sacramento Bee* 12/31/05), and as chair of the Agricultural Subcommittee on Department Operations, Oversight, Nutrition, and Forestry, he sought "greater opportunities for socially disadvantaged farmers" and improved access for minority farmers to government services (Almanac).

In terms of immigration, Rep. Baca held a forum that addressed the concerns of immigrant families who risk being split apart due to the deportation of an undocumented family member. He asserted that this disruption to immigrant families is one sign that America's immigration system is "broken" (*Press Enterprise* 3/5/09). He has also supported "provisions in the education overhaul of 2002 that expanded bilingual education, directed more money to migrant education, and created a dropout prevention program" (PIA).

Not mincing words, he lets constituents know where he stands on minority issues more generally: "Haven't we learned it's wrong to treat our Native American brothers and sisters as second-class citizens?" (*San Francisco Chronicle* 6/11/03); "'We all need to be aware of what's going on and the impact it's having,' Baca said, pointing to cuts in education as moves that will hurt everyone. 'Feeding the hungry is a biblical imperative and an expression of Americans' compassion; a tax cut for rich folks is neither,' he said" (*Press Enterprise* 3/14/06);[27] "'People have to know how terrible, anti-immigration and anti-American it is,' Baca said of the bill by Rep. James Sensenbrenner (R-WI), 'It doesn't do anything to unify families or to make America stronger or better'" (*Atlanta Journal-Constitution* 1/10/06).

However, at the same time, the stands Baca takes are not always in line with our stereotypes about what Latinos, or for that matter Democrats, are assumed to believe. A member of the Blue Dog coalition of conservative Democrats (bio), he has supported gun owners' rights. As a state legislator, "he [also] worked to reduce welfare rolls, lower taxes on middle-income earners and increase penalties for drug dealers" (Almanac). While supporting some environmental legislation, he tempers this support with a concern for job loss. On the basis of that argument—jobs come first—he broke with the Democratic Party to support President Bush's proposals for drilling in the Alaskan Arctic. Even more, "[a]t a 2004 committee hearing in his district ... Baca called the Endangered Species Act a 'broken law,' and said it was costing communities millions of dollars in lost development and new jobs" (PIA).[28]

So, in addition to the substance of his positions, it is Baca's outspoken style that sets him apart. Thus, as a California state legislator, "[h]e earned a reputation as a hard worker ... but his aggressiveness rubbed some colleagues the wrong way" (Almanac), and, unlike Rep. Becerra, he has had difficulty obtaining from party leadership an assignment on a prestige committee (PIA). In a much publicized 2007 incident, he was involved in a personality clash with Rep. Loretta Sanchez, who, to be blunt, accused him of calling her a "whore."[29] Regardless of the merits of the claims of both sides—and the incident appears to have served as a wake-up call for some restructuring of the Congressional Hispanic Caucus—Baca, who denies the charge, has never apologized. More to the point, politicians with a more moderate bent would perhaps not be as likely in the first place to be caught in such a situation.[30]

But is such outspokenness always a bad thing? Perhaps when you start out in a family of fifteen and perhaps when you represent minority constituents, including marginalized migrant workers lacking political voice, maybe a little outspokenness, especially when you have been voted by

Latino magazine one of the most influential Latino leaders in the nation
(PR 7/15/09), serves as the best way to get your views across.

Linda Sanchez: the "liberal/labor" side of Latino issues

As is true for many of these Latino legislators, Rep. Linda Sanchez
is described as "one of the most liberal members of the House" who "sees
herself as a defender of working-class Americans" (PIA). Her activities
encompass work on Latino issues directly, as on immigration, but also
indirectly, as on education, labor, and gender equity. "I work hard in
Congress to uphold the everyday civil rights and liberties of all Americans"
(PR 3/22/06).

The sixth of seven children of immigrant parents (a laborer and machi-
nist), she learned early on the importance of political advocacy, initially in
the context of gender relations within her immediate family. "There was a
very clear distinction between what boys could do and what girls could
do. ... Boys were served first and girls served them" (PIA). Sanchez
acknowledges the influence of her mother, who suggested she go to law
school and helped her "on this path of wanting to empower women" (*The
Hill* 9/19/06).[31] She also credits her mother's advocacy efforts as a bilingual education aide: "I would often accompany her to meetings of teachers
and administrators and parents to help these kids. So I sort of saw her
being political in an activist sense" (*The Hill* 7/13/05).

These experiences have motivated Sanchez's congressional activity. Specifically requesting a seat on the House Judiciary Committee for the purpose
of working on immigration (bio), her perspective is clearly personal. "If
you are not very far removed from the immigrant experience of your
ancestors, you understand and you see the dedication and the sacrifice"
(*The Hill* 7/13/05). In terms of policy, she opposed President Bush's guest
worker program because she saw it as failing to help people become permanent residents or citizens (PIA). In the 110th Congress, she sponsored
an amendment to the Immigration and Nationality Act to "provide for
compensation to States incarcerating undocumented aliens charged with a
felony or two or more misdemeanors" (bills sponsored).

But as she expressed in a public statement, suspending her membership
in the Congressional Hispanic Caucus in the context of the power struggles involving her sister (see above), she explains her work as dealing with
issues certainly impacting the Latino community but also affecting a wider
set of Americans: "Since joining Congress, I have worked to address the
challenges facing the Latino community and all Americans" (PR 4/19/07).

Beginning with the economy, she centers her efforts in a broader context. She has gotten involved in advocating for an increased minimum
wage: "'No one who works full time for a living should live in poverty,'
said Sanchez, who grew up in working-class Anaheim wearing clothes
handmade by her mother" (PIA). She was "co-founder of the Labor and

Working Families Caucus" (bio), and has recently sponsored a resolution to recognize America's labor movement and clearly stands up for unions ("Corporate Executives Exploit Bankruptcy Laws to Reap Huge Benefits at Employee Expense," PR 4/17/07; "Rep. Linda Sanchez Applauds Passage of Employee Free Choice Act," PR 3/1/07).

Sanchez also continues her advocacy for gender equality. For instance, she was among those commemorating Equal Pay Day, noting that "[s]o long as we tolerate pay based on gender and not on performance, our overall economic strength will suffer" (PR 4/24/07). Nor did she mince words as to the impact a recent Supreme Court decision restricting partial-birth abortions would have on women's lives: "The Court, by the narrowest of margins, has upheld this bad law that would force medical decisions to be made for political reasons" (PR 4/19/07). Clearly a supporter of women's health issues, she has worked to end the disparities in health insurance costs between women and men (PR 5/21/09). As a gesture towards her efforts to improve the status of women, she even joined the "all male roster" of the annual partisan baseball game, wearing IX (for Title IX) on her jersey (PIA).

Finally, Sanchez has focused on issues of tangible benefit to her constituents. She is committed to ensuring the 39th district receives necessary funds to improve the economy, enhance education opportunities, and reduce crime ("Small Business and Infrastructure Job Creation Bill Includes Sanchez Provision," PR 3/17/2010; "Feb. 4–8 To Be 'National School Counseling Week' After Passage of Sanchez Resolution," PR 1/22/08; "Rep. Linda Sanchez Welcomes Passage of Hastings–Sanchez Anti-Gang Amendment," PR 2/7/08).

For Rep. Sanchez, then, her advocacy blends work on concerns relevant to Latinos with an effort to represent the needs of a lower-income California constituency more generally.

Hilda Solis: Latino generalist with an environmental slant

The political style of Rep. Hilda Solis incorporates insider and outsider strategies within her party and within Congress to advocate on behalf of a broad range of policy concerns. What distinguishes her policy representation is her style as a policy generalist, the nature of some of the issues she has highlighted, and the success she has achieved, culminating of course in her 2009 appointment as President Obama's Secretary of Labor.

Viewed from the outside, Solis's background certainly appeared to point her in directions fairly far from politics. She grew up in a tract home, which her parents still own, helping to raise six younger siblings while her immigrant parents worked (*Los Angeles Times* 1/20/09). Nevertheless, her interest in public service developed early, and she took advantage of opportunities. Through their stress on education and equity along with their own advocacy work within their unions, perhaps her factory worker parents set the standard as role models. By taking the family to local parks,[32] they also contributed to her concern for the environment— "It's part of me, part of my soul" (PIA).

In turn, Solis took advantage of scholarships to attend the California State Polytechnic University in Pomona and, as part of her Public Administration Masters degree program, "wrote dozens of letters" resulting in an internship with the Office of Hispanic Affairs in the Carter White House.[33] She challenged an incumbent to obtain her first political position with a seat on the Rio Hondo Community College Board of Trustees. The first Latina to serve in the California Senate and the youngest member serving at the time, she has led the way in supporting environmental justice on behalf of minorities. For these reasons, and for being "a politician who 'hasn't shied away from challenging the old boy network both within and without the Latino community,' she became the first woman to receive the prestigious Profile in Courage Award from the John F. Kennedy Library Foundation."[34] Thus, upon her entry into the US Congress, "*National Journal* magazine named her one of its Ten Freshmen to Watch."[35]

This description would appear to be accurate—Solis rose rapidly through the ranks of the Democratic Party to advocate on behalf of a variety of issues of relevance to the Latino community and larger interests. "Liberal, energetic and outspoken," Solis is a regular participant in Democratic presentations to the news media on topics ranging from the environment to immigration and from health insurance to domestic violence. In the 109th Congress, she was chosen by her Democratic colleagues as a regional whip, and she was named co-chairwoman of the Congressional Women's Caucus (PIA). "Her loyalty to Pelosi and her aggressive fundraising for the Democratic Congressional Campaign Committee earned her a spot as one of two vice chairmen of the Democratic Steering and Policy Committee" (PIA) as well as a slot on the coveted Energy and Commerce Committee.[36]

It was this committee work that served as the platform for her continuing work on the environment and environmental justice. She "enacted a bill for the Interior Department to restore the water flow of the San Gabriel River and study ways to create more green space and urban recreation areas" (Almanac). In 2008, Solis introduced a bill in the House that addressed the different effects of pollution and environmental damage on low-income and minority communities by allowing individual citizens to pursue civil rights cases (PR 4/24/08). Solis even joined Speaker Pelosi and other members of Congress in Mumbai to discuss global efforts to combat climate change (PR 3/24/08).[37]

A variety of other issues—immigration, education, women's concerns, and, not surprisingly in light of her subsequent cabinet appointment, labor matters—have also been on Solis's agenda. "She was among the early sponsors of the bill to give citizenship eligibility to immigrants who have served a year [lessened from three years] in the military" (Almanac), and she urged constituents to attend workshops that assist individuals in applying for citizenship (PR 6/30/06). In the area of education, she was so upset about a proposal to combine "minority serving institutions with special education programs" that she mobilized the network of college presidents she had cultivated during her days working on the Rio Hondo Board of trustees.[38] With respect to gender, Solis was the co-chair of the Congressional Caucus for Women's Issues, where she was an "outspoken advocate for issues of importance to women and families" (bio). She was a "leader in efforts to end the murders of women in Guatemala and the U.S. border town of Ciudad Juárez, Mexico, and played a key role in the reauthorization of the Violence Against Women Act in 2006" (bio).

Perhaps her work in support of labor can best be summarized as follows:

> I rise in support of H.R. 800, the Employee Free Choice Act. As the daughter of union family—my father was a Teamster and my mother worked tirelessly for twenty five years—I know that my seven siblings and I would not be where we are today without the wages, health coverage and retirement benefits my parents received (PR 3/1/07).

Thus, Solis's policy and party interests are wide ranging. Nonetheless, as is also clear from the above, she doesn't hesitate to add in a "minority" voice ("Solis: FCC Must Do More to Expand Diversity in Ownership, Ensure Minority and Low-Income Communities Not Left Behind," PR 3/14/07). And to mark International Women's Day, she reminds us to recognize the achievements of not only women we as "outsiders" know, but also women more connected with a particular community: "I am inspired by women like Dolores Huerta, who helped found the United Farmworkers, Gloria Molina, the first Latina elected to the Los Angeles County Board of Supervisors, and Speaker Nancy Pelosi, who became the first woman Speaker of the House in January" (PR 3/9/07).

In sum, focusing on a wide array of policies, Rep. Solis has served as a spokesperson on behalf of the Democratic Party even while she worked within that party as an advocate for minority concerns.

Accessibility, allocation and service: alternative styles

As with most other members of Congress, the electoral connection is alive and well for these representatives. Five were born in or around the areas they currently represent, and several attended college and often graduate school in California. Several served as local officials or state legislators, or were simply active in their communities before even beginning a political career. A detailed look at the constituency-oriented activities of three of these members puts a human face on their local efforts and also demonstrates some of the variety in their presentations of self.

Lucille Roybal-Allard: policy interests and constituency service

Representing California's 34th congressional district since 1992, Lucille Roybal-Allard certainly highlights key policy issues–under-age drinking, domestic violence, immigration. At the same time, constituency service, including considerable "symbolic" activity, is another strategy she utilizes to empower her constituents.

The daughter of pioneer Latino representative Edward Roybal, the first Latino elected to Congress from California since 1879,[39] Lucille was clearly influenced by her early life. "When I think you have a role model like both my father and my mother who have really dedicated their lives to the community and have taught human values and understand the value of people, it really has an impact on one's life."[40]

While it took Roybal-Allard some time to begin a political career in her own right,[41] she served in the California Assembly from 1987 to 1992 prior to being elected to Congress. As such, rising through the ranks to hold positions on key committees including Appropriations, she has earned a reputation as a consensus builder. "People may be your enemies today on one issue, but they may be your allies tomorrow on another issue."[42]

In Congress, Roybal-Allard has stressed such issues as the abuses of child labor. "It is unacceptable that children who work in agriculture, one of this country's most dangerous occupations, are less protected under U.S. law than juveniles working in other occupations" (PR 9/15/09). She has also emphasized health concerns, such as better screening for newborns (PR 2/26/09) and helping victims of domestic violence receive unemployment insurance (PIA). Other issue stances have included promoting legislation to help children of illegal immigrants get in-state tuition rates for public universities and opposing building a border fence between the United States and Mexico.[43]

Finally, "in Congress, she has focused much of her legislative energy on fighting underage drinking," including promoting efforts to promote public advertising campaigns, advocating that government agencies coordinate their efforts, and bringing the issue home to her constituents by expressing concern about Cinco de Mayo ("On Cinco de Mayo, We Must Caution Our Nation's Youth about the Dangers of Turning the Cultural Celebration into 'Drinko de Mayo'," PR 5/5/06).

Policy concerns notwithstanding, it appears to be the roots and connections she has with her community that most touch her. "Congresswoman Roybal-Allard enjoys every aspect of her job, but she especially enjoys hearing from residents of the district and serving them" (bio). "People often don't know how their lives are impacted by what's going on in Sacramento or Washington, D.C. People can take control of their lives. They can be involved in the political process and make a difference."[44]

Thus, "[w]hen at home in Los Angeles, the congresswoman spends much of her time meeting with residents and community leaders to discuss ways to improve the quality of life in the 34th Congressional District" (bio; "Congresswoman Roybal-Allard Attends Japanese American Cultural & Community Center's 29th Anniversary Celebration Town Hall Meeting," PR 3/13/09; "Roybal-Allard convened a breakfast meeting with city council members and city managers," PR 3/19/08"). In addition to these personal interactions, she helps bring funding to improve the quality of life for residents, acquiring congressional approval for a national education center in the district (PR 12/19/09) and an award for the Boyle Heights Coalition for a Safe and Drug-Free Community (PR 9/19/08).

> Back home, in her office at the Edward R. Roybal Federal Building, Roybal-Allard sponsors health fairs and workshops on home buying and U.S. citizenship. She wants to revive downtown's former Red Car trolley line, a five-mile loop that would include Staples Center and Chinatown, with possible expansion to USC to the south and Echo Park to the north (Almanac).

If Roybal-Allard learned the importance of "human values" from her politically active parents, she has herself remained true to community roots. Her own gloss on a successful campaign during her tenure in the state legislature to prevent the building of a prison in the community provides a nice summation of the importance of advocating for district interests: "This community was once viewed as powerless. However, the Mothers of East Los Angeles and other community groups have served notice to the state's powerbrokers that ignoring the desires of the East Los Angeles community will no longer be accepted."[45]

Grace Napolitano: district interests prominent in home style

While Rep. Napolitano is a former chair of the Congressional Hispanic Caucus and has stressed some Latino issues such as mental health, she also focuses her attention on bringing government assistance to her constituents and to Southern California. In so doing, she appears to be a good consensus builder, adept at problem-solving and bringing together the interests of diverse groups.

In addition to interacting with citizens ("I love hearing from constituents in the 38th District"),

> the Congresswoman has been a member of the House Committee on Natural Resources since the 106th Congress. ... She has always been an avid promoter of conservation, water recycling, desalination, and sound groundwater management and storage to address Southern California's need for adequate water quality and supply (bio).

As such, she has worked on issues including developing a water management plan for the area, the Bay-Delta ecosystem, and efforts to remove a "10.5 million ton uranium tailings pile at the banks of the Colorado in Moab, Utah," which could impact the health of people in seven western states (bio). "'The key to solving California's water problems is in building partnerships, working together and bringing all parties to the table,' she said when the measure [the Bay-Delta allocation program] was passed" (Almanac).

In part because of the experience she developed as a member of the California Assembly, Napolitano has also been appointed to the House Transportation Committee. She has used this post to advocate

> on behalf of the transportation needs faced in the eastern half of Los Angeles County, which lacks mass transit and has the most congested and underserved transportation system in the country. She will also continue advancing and promoting the ideas of minorities, including the many Hispanic Americans who not only design and build our transportation systems, but use mass transit in greater proportion (bio).

More generally, Napolitano views her role as serving the needs of her district. For instance, she has instituted an annual tradition of taking her staff on a tour of the district, which Napolitano believes improves her office's ability to serve constituents. On a recent tour of the "largest Buddhist temple in the Western hemisphere" located in her district, she reflected on this practice, saying "by understanding them and their culture, we are more able to understand their needs" (*San Gabriel Valley Tribune* 2/16/2010).

Napolitano also shows her constituents how federal policies will impact the area. For example, she used data from the House Committee on Energy and Commerce to show how health care reform would specifically benefit the 38th district, noting that a lack of insurance is a problem that is "especially acute in California" (PR 3/19/2010).

Thus, "[t]he Congresswoman is committed to 'constituent service' and to the economic revitalization of her district. She works aggressively with federal, state and local officials to bring in new businesses, higher wage jobs and training funds to the district" (bio). Napolitano has organized community task forces on health and manufacturing (bio), and has been involved in projects to obtain funds to train "local young people to work in green industries" so they are prepared for the new job market (PR 11/18/09). She has used federal money to improve the wellbeing of her community ("Rep. Napolitano Welcomes Funding for Local Water Projects," PR 7/15/09; "Freeway Widening Project Kicks Off," *Whittier Daily News* 4/5/07; "Politicians Seek Solution to Gang Problem," *Inland Valley Daily Bulletin* 1/14/07; "Napolitano Secures $2 Million for the 38th District in Defense Appropriations Bill," PR 9/26/06).

In sum, Napolitano works hard to be visible in the district and to solicit federal funds to enhance the quality of life for her constituents. In so doing, it seems important to her to work with community leaders and to bring all parties to the political table.

Loretta Sanchez: constituency accessibility with a Latino flair

Not surprisingly for a politician who pulled off the upset victory of 1996 by defeating well-known conservative Robert Dornan, district-centered activity is a central element of the home style of Loretta Sanchez.[46] "'I'm in a tough district,' said Rep. Loretta Sanchez, 'I don't get elected because I go out in the streets and march. I get elected because I go door-to-door. ... If I went out and marched all day, I wouldn't get any votes'" (PR 5/2/06).

As her website biography describes, "Loretta is known for two things: accessibility and collaboration." Her activities appear to back up this claim. She travels weekly from Washington back to her district, has "hosted hundreds of community events," "visited every school in the district," and "regularly hosts 'Community Office Hours,' a grassroots approach to generating community interest in and accessibility to their Congressional representative" (bio).

She has thus been extremely active around the district: "Rep. Loretta Sanchez Urges Constituents to Serve Their Community on Cesar Chavez Day" (PR 3/31/10); "Rep. Loretta Sanchez Announces Health Care Town Hall in Anaheim" (PR 7/17/09); "Sanchez Pays Visit to St. Anselm's Citizenship Class" (PR 8/9/06); "Sanchez Joins Arab American Community for Annual Festival" (PR 9/9/06).

A reporter's description corroborates the material on Sanchez's website:

> On a recent Saturday, after she shook hands at the Tet Festival, Sanchez again donned the red knit suit and headed to the Veterans Affairs hospital in Long Beach before attending a formal event in her district. As Sanchez chatted with a patient about his mother's enchiladas and planted a kiss on his forehead, a hospital staffer whispered that the congresswoman shows up far more often than other politicians (*Los Angeles Times* 3/5/07).

Apparently she also shows up with considerable style. "A close talker with a penchant for patting arms and gripping shoulders, Sanchez has a style that some label friendly and others flirtatious" (*Los Angeles Times* 3/5/07). As Sanchez sees it, "I think that traditionally what the public has seen as far as a woman in politics is someone that dresses a certain way and has a certain demeanor and is always very serious, because that's what it took to break through." Sanchez said, "I think you're seeing a whole new set of women ... feeling much more comfortable about being themselves vs. being some blob that will blend in" (*Los Angeles Times* 3/5/07).

Capitalizing on her public image, Sanchez has also hosted a monthly cable-access television show in which she discusses controversial issues. With topics selected in part based on constituent letters, Sanchez can educate voters about what goes on in Washington. "It's all about bringing a little bit of the beltway to Orange County viewers, Sanchez noted" (*Orange County Register*, 4/26/07).

She has additionally taken this flair to Washington.

> Last month, as President Bush entered the House of Representatives to give his State of the Union speech, Sanchez smooshed herself against a railing in her bright blue dress. ... Bush smiled, shook her hand and said, "Hola, chica." Sanchez replied, "Hello, George." Asked later about the encounter, Sanchez told the *Orange County Business Journal*'s Rick Reiff, "That's the kind of relationship we have. ... Usually we hug and kiss. He knows the Latino thing" (*Orange County Weekly* 3/1/07).

Conclusion

To place the policy representation of Latino members of Congress into a broader context, we have examined aspects of their home styles in Washington and in the district. Consistent with the literature suggesting that minority legislators will highlight "minority" issues, our findings show that for these representatives the focus on Latino issues is considerable. In general, these legislators engage in policy representation and share the common goal of advancing their perspectives on Latino interests.

Yet, our findings also remind us that for Latino legislators, as for others, there is more to representation than a policy focus. Eulau and Karps are correct to additionally highlight symbolic, service, and allocation activities, each of which has particular meaning for under-served communities.

For instance, a surprising amount of even the policy-oriented material gathered for this study points to the importance of symbolic activity: advocating for a Latino museum (Becerra), seeking to recognize the work of Cesar Chavez with a national holiday (Baca), or reminding constituents not to over-drink as they celebrate on Cinco de Mayo (Roybal-Allard). While such activities may not in themselves change national policy, they certainly can legitimize the concerns of constituents historically excluded from the political process, in turn raising the awareness of outsiders. Even the sometimes controversial in-your-face style of Rep. Loretta Sanchez might serve as a way to break down barriers, thus getting people's attention and promoting inclusion.

Both the constituency-oriented activities of these legislators and their visibility within their districts place them in positions as role models to their communities. Because many of their activities center on the promotion of tangible concerns, such as promoting minority businesses or citizenship forums, even these "usual" electoral-oriented activities take on additional significance, potentially making a real difference in the quality of life of these communities.

What is additionally striking is how each of these representatives places his/her individual slant on Latino concerns. As the Congress literature would suggest, it becomes clear that these representatives do have notably different home styles, styles varying on dimensions including insider (Becerra) vs. outsider (Baca), commonality (Linda Sanchez) vs. difference (Baca), and a generalist (Solis) vs. a specific (Napolitano) focus. While not necessarily indicative of the universe of ways Latinos might be represented in Congress, the variation in styles even among this small number of legislators is noteworthy.

Our findings reiterate the importance of descriptive representation; more Latinos in office change not only the political agenda but also how we think about Latino concerns. Our findings also raise the question of which style of advancing Latino interests works best. Is it the insider style of Becerra, the more in-your-face styles of Baca (on issues), or Loretta Sanchez (on personal interactions), or the Linda Sanchez model of advocating for policies important to Latinos but policies with implications beyond the Latino community as well? Are there other, better representational styles that minority legislators might adopt?

While full answers to these questions are beyond the scope of this project, one potential style seems absent from this case study, that of a legislator who makes minority concerns his/her sole focus. As is true for other legislators, Latino legislators must respond to the partisanship of their times, the issues of the day, and the needs of individual constituents. The styles of the legislators we have discussed indicate that all of them had to incorporate their Latino advocacy into a broader political context.

A final set of questions–and also questions worthy of future research– remain. How do these home styles of a group of minority legislators compare with those of other members of Congress? We found in the self-presentations of these legislators many elements generic to home styles, such as constituency-oriented activities, issue advocacy, and partisanship. Are these legislators different above and beyond their concerns for a particular set of policies?

These minority representatives stand out in at least two ways. First, they are breaking new ground; all in their own way highlight that they are the "first" to do some part of their job. They clearly (and rightly) want their constituents to appreciate the significance of their place in Congress. Obviously, other representatives share less in this kind of claim. Second, these representatives focus on issues with ramifications beyond the borders of their districts. The possibilities for "surrogate" representation are apparent and, at least in an informal way, have received documentation in our findings.[47] Finally, a more detailed classification of the impact of constituency characteristics (such as majority vs. less-than-majority Latino) and legislator ethnicity (Latino vs. non-Latino heritage) on how legislators represent constituents could be a next step in understanding the variation in home styles among Latino legislators.

Looking to the future, the substantive representation of Latinos in Congress, such as their work to reform immigration policy, will surely increase as their descriptive representation increases. But it is clear from our study that this substantive representation will take many different forms depending on the home styles of individual Latino legislators.

Notes

1 We want to thank David Eisenstein for research assistance on early drafts of this chapter and Eric J. Juenke for helpful comments.
2 Though, as the Lien chapter showed, Asian Americans are the fastest growing minority relative to their percent of the population.
3 See Greg Giroux, "Democratic-Led 110th Congress is Old Boys' Club with a Twist, as Women, Blacks Gain Clout," *New York Times*, February 26, 2007, www.nytimes.com/cq/2007/02/26/cq_2328.html?pagewanted=1 [accessed May 10, 2010].
4 See Kenny J. Whitby and George A. Krause, "Race, Issue Heterogeneity and Public Policy: The Republican Revolution in the 104th US Congress and the Representation of African-American Policy Interests," *British Journal of Political Science* 31 (2001): 571.
5 Also, African American and Latino legislators tend to intervene more frequently in committee hearings on racial policies. See Michael D. Minta, "Legislative Oversight and the Substantive Representation of Latino Interests in Congress," *Legislative Studies Quarterly* 34 (2009): 193–218.
6 See Rodney Hero and Caroline Tolbert, "Latinos and Substantive Representation in the U.S. House of Representatives: Direct, Indirect, or Nonexistent?" *American Journal of Political Science* 39 (1995): 640–52; Brinck Kerr and Will Miller, "Latino Representation, It's Direct and Indirect," *American Journal of Political Science* 41 (1997): 1066–71; David Ian Lublin, *The Paradox of Representation: Racial Gerrymandering and Minority Interests in Congress* (Princeton: Princeton University Press, 1997); James W. Endersby and Charles E. Menifield, "Representation, Ethnicity and Congress: Black and Hispanic Representatives and Constituencies," in *Black and Multiracial Politics in America*, eds Yvette M. Alex-Assensoh and Lawrence J. Hanks (New York: New York University Press, 2000).
7 See Susan Welch and John R. Hibbing, "Hispanic Representation in the U.S. Congress," *Social Science Quarterly* 65 (1984): 328–35; Kerr and Miller, "Latino Representation"; Endersby and Menifield, "Representation, Ethnicity and Congress"; Lublin, *Paradox of Representation*.
8 See Michael S. Rocca, Gabriel R. Sanchez, and Joseph Uscinski, "Personal Attributes and Latino Voting Behavior in Congress," *Social Science Quarterly* 89 (2008): 392–405.
9 See Rodolfo Espino, "Minority Interests, Majority Rules: Representation of Latinos in the U.S. Congress," Ph.D. diss., University of Wisconsin, 2004. Similarly, James B. Johnson and Philip E. Secret's application of role theory to members of the Congressional Black and Hispanic Caucuses highlighted variation among the legislators but also pointed to the commitment of most of them to representational styles that sometimes focused beyond the borders of their individual districts. See James B. Johnson and Philip E. Secret, "Focus and Style: Representational Roles of Congressional Black and Hispanic Caucus Members," *Journal of Black Studies* 26 (1996): 245–73. See also Susan J. Carroll, "Representing Women: Congresswomen's Perceptions of Their Representational Roles," in *Women Transforming Congress*, ed. Cindy Simon Rosenthal (Norman: University of Oklahoma Press), 50–68; Carol Swain, *Black Faces, Black Interests* (Cambridge, MA: Harvard University Press, 1995).

10 See James Q. Wilson, "Two Negro Politicians: An Interpretation," *Midwest Journal of Political Science* 4 (1960): 346–69; Richard Fenno, *Going Home: Black Representatives and Their Constituents* (Chicago: University of Chicago Press, 2003); David T. Canon, *Race, Redistricting, and Representation: The Unintended Consequences of Black Majority Districts* (Chicago: University of Chicago Press, 1999).

11 See David R. Mayhew, *Congress: The Electoral Connection* (New Haven, CT: Yale University Press, 1974); Heinz Eulau and Paul D. Karps, "The Puzzle of Representation: Specifying Components of Responsiveness," in *The Politics of Representation: Continuities in Theory and Research* (Beverly Hills, CA: Sage Publications, 1978), 55–71; Richard Fenno, *Home Style: House Members in their Districts* (Boston: Little Brown, 1978); Morris P. Fiorina, *Congress: Keystone of the Washington Establishment* (New Haven, CT: Yale University Press, 1989).

12 See Eulau and Karps, "Puzzle of Representation," 241–42.

13 See Fenno, *Home Style*, 31–131.

14 At the time when this study began, all seven legislators discussed in the profiles were current members of Congress. In 2009, Hilda Solis left Congress to become the Secretary of Labor in the Obama Administration.

15 See Antonio Gonzalez and Steven Ochoa, "The Latino Vote in 2008: Trends and Characteristics," William C. Velasquez Institute (Los Angeles) report, www.wcvi.org/data/election/wcvi_nov2008nationalanalysis_121808.pdf [accessed April 25, 2010].

16 Data on the specifics of the constituency and background characteristics of these legislators are available upon request from the authors.

17 See Sally Friedman, *Dilemmas of Representation: Local Politics, National Issues and the Home Styles of New York State Representatives* (Albany: SUNY Press, 2007).

18 Information taken from legislators' websites includes press release, bills sponsored, home page content, and biographical material. References to press releases will be made parenthetically with the abbreviation "PR" and the date. References to legislators' home pages, bills sponsored, and biographies will be made parenthetically with the abbreviations "bio," "bills sponsored," and "home page." The online content was accessed in March–April 2010 and in the spring of 2007.

19 References to newspaper articles will be made parenthetically, including the name of the newspaper and the date of the article.

20 See Michael Barone and Richard E. Cohen, *The Almanac of American Politics* (Washington: National Journal Group, 2005); Jackie Koszczuk and H. Amy Stern, *Politics in America* (Washington: CQ Press, 2005). References to these works will be made parenthetically (Almanac) and (PIA) and are taken from these editions unless otherwise noted.

21 See Walter Wilson, "Latino Representation on Congressional Websites," *Legislative Studies Quarterly* 34 (2009): 427–48.

22 See "Residente of Calle 13, Malverde and U.S. Congressman Xavier Becerra are Among Students, Politicians, Activists and Artists Who Gather for 'Beyond Borders: An MTV Tr3ìs Immigration Forum,'" *Hispanic PR Wire* (September 25, 2007), www.hispanicprwire.com/news.php?l=in&id=9581&cha=7 [accessed March 15, 2010].

23 See Michael Barone, Richard E. Cohen, and Jackie Koszczuk, *The Almanac of American Politics* (Washington: National Journal Group, 2010).

24 See "Becerra to Deliver the Democratic Response to the President's State of the Union Address in Spanish," *PR Newswire* (January 16, 2007), www.prnewswire.com/news-releases/becerra-to-deliver-the-democratic-response-to-the-presidents-state-of-the-union-address-in-spanish-53549277.html [accessed March 15, 2010].

25 In November 2008, with the support of Speaker Pelosi, Becerra was elected vice chairman of the Democratic Caucus, and he served as Obama's "campaign liaison to the Hispanic community" (*PR Newswire*, January 16, 2007).

26 Baca was a railroad worker, army paratrooper (though he never saw combat), community relations officer for GTE, and California state assemblyman before he entered Congress.

27 Baca's interest in the relevance of federal education policy to Latinos was also evident in his stand on the 2002 education overhaul bill.

28 Baca has also taken a notably conservative position on media decency standards. "The Founder of Sex and Violence in the Media Caucus, Baca has called for more enforcement of decency standards on Spanish-language broadcast media, and he wants controls on video games that depict nudity, sexual conduct or other content deemed harmful to minors" (Almanac).

29 See Chuck McCutcheon and Christina L. Lyons, *Politics in America* (Washington: CQ Press, 2009).

30 See McCutcheon and Lyons, *Politics in America*.

31 After law school, Sanchez "practiced law as a civil rights and employment attorney, then as a union lawyer. Soon she became the secretary-treasurer for the Orange County AFL-CIO" (*The Hill* 7/13/05).

32 See "Hilda Solis for Congress," www.hildasolis.org/index.php?submenu=Home& src [accessed May 26, 2010].

33 See McCutcheon and Lyons, *Politics in America*.

34 See Emily Rodriguez. "Hilda Solis: Profile in Courage," *California Journal* (December 1, 2001), www.house.gov/apps/list/press/ca32_solis/morenews4/cajournal.html [accessed April 1, 2010].

35 See Rodriguez, "Hilda Solis."

36 See Barone, *et al.*, *Almanac of American Politics*.

37 Solis has advocated for environmental issues on numerous occasions ("GAO: Underground Storage Tanks Threaten Public Health," PR 2/22/07; "Solis: EPA's Budget Ignores Core Public Health and Environment Needs—Time to Invest in Our Communities, not Polluters," PR 3/8/07).

38 See Barone, *et al.*, *Almanac of American Politics*.

39 See "Hispanic Americans in Congress," *Library of Congress,* www.loc.gov/rr/hispanic/congress/ [accessed April 18, 2010].

40 See "Lucille Roybal-Allard," www.answers.com/topic/lucille-roybal-allard [accessed April 10, 2010].

41 She raised a family and held jobs in the nonprofit sector, including working for an alcoholism council, before running for the state legislature.

42 See "Lucille Roybal-Allard."

43 See McCutcheon and Lyons, *Politics in America*.

44 See "Lucille Roybal-Allard."

45 See "Lucille Roybal-Allard."

46 In addition to constituency service, Rep. Sanchez is active in particular policy areas, including homeland security.

47 See Jane Mansbridge, "Should Blacks Represent Blacks and Women Represent Women? A Contingent 'Yes'," *Journal of Politics* 61 (1999): 628–57. See also Carroll, "Representing Women"; Espino, "Minority Interests."

5 Puerto Rican Politics in New York City during the 1960s

Structural Ideation, Contingency, and Power

José E. Cruz

This chapter is a historical collage of Puerto Rican political participation in New York City from 1960 to 1970. It focuses on the role Puerto Rican political elites and groups played within New York City politics, seeking insights into the process of access to power and its exercise. The chapter first places Puerto Rican political participation in context by briefly outlining the demographic and socioeconomic characteristics of the community during the 1960s. Next, it offers a description of three types of political participation at the elite and group level: electoral, community, and radical politics. Based on this account, the chapter concludes with a comment on the consequences of Puerto Rican political participation for the community and for city politics, along with a reflection on the nature and character of access to and exercise of political power that favors a willful and contingent style of thinking and action.

Demographic context and socioeconomic characteristics

New York City has long been the city of largest settlement of Puerto Ricans outside the island. While the city was a magnet for Puerto Ricans prior to the Great Migration of the 1950s, it is in the post-World War II period that the size of the Puerto Rican population became an increasing and significant fraction of the city's total population. The initial migration flow of Puerto Ricans outside the island in the 1950s was truly monumental, particularly in light of the island's population at the time.[1]

During the 1950s, nearly a quarter of the island's labor force migrated to the United States, predominantly to New York City. While birth and mortality rates declined dramatically on the island, the demographic transition Puerto Rico experienced during that time was due mostly to migration. It was primarily an agricultural labor force that was being dislocated from the island and gradually moved into the low-skill–low-wage echelons of the New York City labor market and occupational hierarchy.

During the 1960s, net migration from Puerto Rico to the United States declined relative to the earlier decade. While the net immigration flow was still in the direction of New York City, return migration patterns

were already being felt, thus reducing the rate of growth of the Puerto
Rican population in the city compared with the 1950s.[2] By 1970, the
Puerto Rican population comprised approximately 11 percent of the
city's population (844,303 people), a proportion that declined a bit to
10.5 percent by 1990 (887,573 people) and to 9.8 percent by 2000
(789,172 people).[3]

In 1960, the socioeconomic status of Puerto Ricans was mixed. They
were at the lower end of the income scale and at the higher end of the
unemployment rate. The median income for second-generation and island-
born men, for example, was $3325 and $2884, respectively, compared
with $4780 for all men in New York. Puerto Rican students did not
receive full-time educational services and their classes were offered by
inexperienced teachers in run-down buildings, often with no textbooks.
Puerto Ricans born in New York did better than Puerto Ricans born on
the island but this was small consolation. Unlike second-generation men,
second-generation women were earning a little over the average for all
women in the metropolitan area. School enrollment figures were at the
74 percent mark for 16- and 17-year-old Puerto Ricans born in New
York. Puerto Rican women born in the city had completed eleven years of
school and most had white-collar jobs. Residential mobility, however, was
high, with 30 percent of the 5-years-old and older not having changed
their address between 1955 and 1960, compared with 58 percent for the
city as a whole. Thus, as the 1960s began, 70 percent of Puerto Ricans
were newcomers to the city, their neighborhoods, or both, compared with
42 percent for the city's total population. Despite these statistics, many
assessed the community's status and prospects in positive terms. "The
Puerto Rican community here has been quietly engaged in its own
Operation Bootstrap," reads a report, "residents are making important
advances, overcoming differences in language and cultural background."[4]
Not everyone agreed with this assessment but key observers concurred
that Puerto Ricans had options to address poverty, exploitation, and
disfranchisement through labor activism, electoral politics, and socialist
agitation.[5]

Electoral and community politics

Puerto Rican organizations during the early 1960s in New York City
emerged in a context in which participatory, grassroots democracy was
normatively juxtaposed to representative government. Never before in the
twentieth century had the suspicion of political elites and the rejection of
political hierarchies been stronger than during this period of intense normative dissent. Emerging Puerto Rican leaders were not only shaped by
this *Zeitgeist* but also, in addition, saw themselves as distinct and even
alienated from the community leadership residing at the Migration Division
of the Department of Labor of the Commonwealth of Puerto Rico. They

saw this leadership as traditional, island-centered, and divorced from the people. In this context, what began as resentment of "an arm of the Puerto Rican government attempting to represent Puerto Ricans in New York" transformed itself into a general anti-establishment attitude.[6] This attitude led the new Puerto Rican leadership away from traditional political avenues and strategies. According to Josephine Nieves, the emerging leadership wanted to use their education and skills to assist the community. In her view, the desire to break away from the older set of leaders and organizations did not reflect condemnation but rather a preference for a new style of organization and tactics.[7]

During the Kennedy–Johnson administration loads of money began to flow to New York City to fight juvenile delinquency and poverty. Among Puerto Rican organizations, the Puerto Rican Forum became the main recipient of funds. It used the funds to set up day-care services and the Puerto Rican Family Institute, among other initiatives. The basic assumption behind this strategic path was that traditional party and electoral politics was a poor choice for Puerto Ricans. The leaders that espoused this view did not question the legitimacy of the political system and were not interested in radical, systemic change. The poverty of politics was apparent to them but their choice was never "exit." To them "loyalty" was not even an issue except to the extent they felt compelled by circumstances to prove they were not alienated foreigners. The third option, "voice," simply required a new strategy.[8]

The 1960 presidential campaign was a source of political opportunities for Puerto Ricans in New York. Herman Badillo, one of the most prominent Puerto Rican political leaders during this period, got his start in politics as part of this campaign. Through the John F. Kennedy political club, he became head of the Kennedy campaign for president in East Harlem. This campaign made Badillo a household name in the Puerto Rican community and gave him visibility beyond El Barrio.[9]

Badillo was elected to Congress in 1970 but he was not the first to try. Running against incumbent Democrat Alfred Santangelo in 1960, Faustino Luis García was the first Puerto Rican to run for Congress during the 1960s. Santangelo represented District 18 in Manhattan and he defeated García by almost 41,000 votes.[10] The following year, Puerto Ricans began a campaign to dethrone the "Italian mafia" in El Barrio, focusing on Santangelo because his district was fundamentally Puerto Rican. Badillo ran against Santangelo for district leader but he lost by seventy-five votes.[11]

Badillo did not have to worry about literacy requirements to participate in the electoral process; other Puerto Ricans did. To fight in US wars, an editorial in *El Diario-La Prensa* declared, Puerto Ricans were not required to learn English; to exercise their right to vote English was a must. This discrepancy made them "citizens of convenience"; good for their blood but not for their vote. The argument that literacy tests were beneficial because they forced Puerto Ricans to learn English, which was considered essential for social and political integration, was decried in the editorial as a "bare-faced deception."[12]

Attorney Gene Crescenzi initiated the fight against the voter literacy requirements on behalf of José Camacho, a Puerto Rican businessman.[13] Winning this battle took a while. In 1965, the test was abolished and the provision that made it possible came to be known as the Puerto Rican Amendment to the Voting Rights Act.[14]

But rather than wait for a court decision on the literacy test, a number of Puerto Rican groups, led by the Migration Division and the League of Women Voters, decided to register voters.[15] In addition, the community organization program run by the Migration Division focused on promoting self-help efforts and inter-ethnic alliances within the community. The program sought to make Puerto Ricans active in the civic and social life of their neighborhoods, to create an environment of mutual understanding and acceptance among ethnic groups, to assist them in creating their own organizations, to advocate for social services, and to promote new leaders.[16]

Reportedly, in 1964 alone, no less than 700,000 pieces of educational material on registration and voting were distributed nationally, the bulk of which was distributed in the city. The Bustelo coffee corporation, for example, distributed 225,000 pamphlets produced by the Migration Division along routes covering Puerto Rican and Hispanic bodegas. Of the 191 meetings dealing with voting and registration sponsored by the Division nationally, thirty-seven were in New York. One voter registration campaign in particular included collaboration with a city-sponsored campaign in which fire departments were used as registration sites during the summer months. Further, a group of mayors from the island toured New York's five counties exhorting Puerto Ricans to register and vote.[17] The new Office of Economic Opportunity and the burgeoning civil rights movement provided much of the impetus for these and other social and legislative activities.[18]

The fight against literacy requirements and voter registration campaigns took place alongside other types of social action. On February 3, 1964, for example, Puerto Ricans joined African Americans and others in a one-day boycott of the city's schools, demanding an end to Jim Crow in education. The boycott, organized by a joint Puerto Rican and black leadership and directed by Bayard Rustin, drew nearly half a million children in what was termed "the biggest civil rights demonstration in the nation's history." One school in the Bedford-Stuyvesant area of Brooklyn, PS 129, illustrated dramatically the level of segregation prevalent throughout the city's schools. Out of an enrollment of 1400, only one student was white and twenty-five were Puerto Rican.[19]

Two weeks after the boycott, the police gave Puerto Ricans a new reason to demonstrate. On February 18, Francisco Rodríguez, an 18-year-old who had been selected 1962 Boy of the Year for the New York State Region by the Boys Club of America, was shot in the back of the head by an off-duty policeman. After the killing, more than 250 people picketed the 23rd precinct, chanting "Assassins!" and demanding an end to police brutality. The following day a silent march took place involving more than 300 persons, mostly Puerto Ricans.[20]

Puerto Ricans also protested the "stop and frisk" and "no knock" laws passed by the state legislature. These laws gave the police unprecedented and sweeping search powers. At a rally in Brooklyn, Puerto Rican community leader Gilberto Gerena Valentín warned that the "stop and frisk" and "no knock" laws would be applied mostly to blacks and Puerto Ricans, and urged the crowd to remain unified in the fight for first-class citizenship. Other Puerto Rican leaders present were: Joseph Monserrat, from the Migration Division; Irma Vidal Santaella, who Mayor Robert Wagner had appointed Deputy Commissioner of Corrections; Assemblyman Carlos Ríos; and the Rev. Pablo Cotto. In his address to the marchers, Monserrat declared: "Today we Puerto Ricans are really proud of being Puerto Ricans. Demonstrations are a new concept to Puerto Ricans. This is a beginning."[21]

Second-class citizenship and police brutality could have led Puerto Ricans into a state of muffled discontent. Instead, these conditions promoted protest and organization. According to reporter Mike Davidow, protesting and organizing meant "that the Civil Rights Revolution has finally swept the Puerto Rican Community into its orbit."[22] Voter registration campaigns were conducted by the Voters Club in the Bronx, the Young Democrats for Johnson in Brooklyn, the Ponce De León Democratic Club, headed by Iván J. Vice, and the Seneca Democratic Club, headed by George Swetnick.[23] One of the participants, the Legion of Voters, decided to become a permanent organization "concerned with all problems relating to the right to vote of every Spanish speaking citizen."[24]

Alongside these electoral initiatives, a coalition of Puerto Rican, African American, social work, and church groups supported other organizations calling for unity across race, class, religion, and nationality. One such organization, Mobilization For Youth, was under attack on suspicion of communist infiltration. "Communism is not the issue," declared Gerena Valentín, in reference to the charge. "Tell those who want to use McCarthyistic tactics that it died with him," he continued, "Tell those Democrats who are hiding that we won't wait any longer for them."[25]

In Puerto Rican circles, there was also a great deal of excitement over the 1964 candidacy of Attorney Manuel Roque for a congressional seat. According to *El Tiempo*, a sign of the level of interest in Roque's candidacy was the number of women that had called the newspaper expressing their hope that Roque would be elected as the first Puerto Rican congressman. "Tiene que ir a Washington a luchar por nosotros," the callers declared, "que estamos desamparados sin representación." (He has to go to Washington to fight for us; we are neglected because we have no representation.) Some of the callers offered to hold "novenas" (prayer sessions) to help him win.[26] The claims of *El Tiempo* notwithstanding, Roque's candidacy never ignited.[27] Its main significance is that, along with García's 1960 candidacy, it shows a pattern of repeated attempts by Puerto Ricans to win representation at the national level.

In 1965, the most significant electoral process for Puerto Ricans was Badillo's effort to become Bronx Borough president running against Joseph Perricone. "I met with Charlie Buckley who was a congressman and who was a head of the county leaders," Badillo recalled, "and I told him I wanted his support for Bronx Borough president. He talked to me and said 'stand up.' So I stood up and he said 'I am not going to support you because you are too tall and too smart. If I'm going to support a Puerto Rican for Borough President it's got to be somebody who's short and dark and cannot speak English very well.' Well, I'm gonna beat you anyhow," Badillo replied.[28]

Badillo had to contend with some opposition from Puerto Ricans and he had to win a primary against an African American candidate, State Senator Ivan Warner. The Puerto Ricans who opposed him did not actually campaign against him and did not have much of an impact. His African American rival was simply "a tool of the regular organization who was willing to do anything the organization wanted." No one thought Badillo could win the primary because he had no money. But he campaigned hard from 6:00 a.m. to 11:00 p.m., shaking hands with thousands of people. "There wasn't much of a Puerto Rican vote in the Bronx in those days, maybe 10 percent, and not that much of a black vote either." Nevertheless, Badillo won. "I carried basically the Puerto Rican community, the black community, and the Jewish community. Those were then the more liberal communities."[29]

Badillo's success was considered a victory for the black–reform–labor coalition seeking entry into the Democratic Party. In addition, it signaled the possibility of Puerto Rican representation on the city council. Incredibly, one at-large seat was contested by twenty-seven Puerto Rican primary candidates. Only one, former Assemblyman Carlos Ríos, was considered a likely winner.[30] The city council seat was considered critical since Puerto Ricans had no council representation despite being almost 10 percent of the city's population and about 25 percent of the population of Manhattan.[31] The *New York Times* endorsed Badillo and Ríos as well as Gilberto Ramírez for the Brooklyn 50th Assembly District, Robert García for the Bronx 83rd Assembly District, José Ramos-López for the Bronx 75th Assembly District, and José Fuentes for the Manhattan 67th Assembly District.[32] According to the *Times*, Badillo was worthy of support because of his record as Commissioner of Relocation and "his willingness to fight bossism in an area that has been machine-run for as long as most people can remember."[33]

In the November election, Badillo won the race for Bronx Borough president with the support of Puerto Ricans and other groups. Ríos was also elected as councilman at-large. Ríos was the first Puerto Rican elected to the council. Ramírez, García, and Ramos-López were elected to the State Assembly. Ramírez served only for one year, Ramos-López served until 1967, and García served until he moved to the State Senate in 1968. José Fuentes lost. At the Migration Division, jubilation was mixed with concern that Badillo may lose his seat as a result of a federal court decision that Congress had exceeded its constitutional powers in passing the so-called Puerto Rican Amendment to the Voting Rights Act. According to the records of the Division, 8107 Puerto Ricans had registered under the provisions of the amendment. Badillo's margin of victory was 2086 votes, hence the Division's concern. Badillo's victory, however, went unchallenged.[34] It was the first time a Puerto Rican was elected a borough president in the history of the city.

Along with Badillo, New Yorkers elected a Republican mayor. John V. Lindsay courted the Puerto Rican vote and during his administration, between 1965 and 1970, a succession of mayoral appointments and reappointments took place bringing Puerto Ricans into such positions as: Director of Business and Employment; Special Consultant for Puerto Rican Affairs; Assistant Deputy Administrator, Community Relations, Human Resources Administration; and Commissioner, Addiction Services Agency, Human Resources Administration. Puerto Ricans were also appointed to the Commission of Human Rights, the New York City Youth Board, and the Board of Higher Education.

In contrast, the community organization program at the Migration Division suffered a staff reduction of 66 percent during fiscal year 1966–67. Nevertheless, the office reportedly assisted thirty groups seeking funding from Great Society programs during that year. Of 113 proposals submitted, thirty were funded, which, according to the Division, meant that Puerto Rican organizations would receive about 20 percent of the $7 million the federal government had assigned to the city.[35] The Migration Division also continued to carry out periodic voter registration campaigns as well as to work with numerous community groups.[36]

After Badillo's election, four Puerto Ricans sought a congressional seat. They failed in part because they all vied for the same position, the 22nd Congressional District.[37] Simultaneously, the National Association for Puerto Rican Civil Rights fought provisions in the jury selection law that discriminated against individuals without property, young people, and racial minorities.[38] Puerto Ricans also continued to show an interest in homeland politics. A mail-in survey conducted by *El Diario-La Prensa* in 1966 revealed that 91 percent of Puerto Rican respondents living in New York were in favor of participating in the plebiscite on the commonwealth's status scheduled for 1967 in Puerto Rico. A tiny minority agreed with the position taken by Puerto Rico's governor Roberto Sánchez Vilella. In his view, Puerto Ricans in New York were not sufficiently informed to vote intelligently in matters pertaining to the island.[39]

As far as mainstream electoral and community politics is concerned, 1966 and 1967 were milestone years. Documents from the Office of the Commonwealth of Puerto Rico indicate that in the 1966 November elections five Puerto Ricans, unnamed in the documents, were elected to the State Assembly and Senate.[40] Also in 1966 Mayor Lindsay agreed to the establishment of a seven-member police review board that included Puerto Rican Manuel Díaz, Jr., then a consultant and acting executive director of the Puerto Rican Community Development Project.[41] His appointment was a major accomplishment. So was the celebration early in 1967 of a conference dedicated to exploring issues and identifying needs of importance to Puerto Ricans in the city. The conference provided Lindsay with a comprehensive policy agenda. Some proposals came to fruition, such as the decision to provide written notifications in English and Spanish to welfare recipients of their right to a fair hearing after any budgetary changes made by the Department of Social Services.[42] Another important outcome of the conference was the decision to build a new housing development at 201–5 West 93rd Street, on the corner of Amsterdam Avenue in Manhattan, and to have it bear the name of Puerto Rican intellectual and anti-colonial activist Eugenio María de Hostos. It was the first time in the city's history that a housing development was named in recognition of the Puerto Rican community.[43]

A signal event in 1967 was the July 23rd riot in El Barrio prompted by the police shooting of Reinaldo Rodríguez on the corner of 111th Street and Third Avenue. Disorder and violence prevailed for five days, forcing the intervention of the police's Tactical Patrol Force, a group also known as the "Riot Squadron." Demonstrators tossed bottles, bricks, and beer cans, hitting three policemen who suffered minor injures to their heads or backs. The hostilities ended with four arrests and two Puerto Ricans dead.[44] After the riots, in what seemed a sign of exasperation, the mayor reminded his subordinates that the follow-up process to the Puerto Rican issues conference "was to begin immediately!" He requested a detailed report, including actions taken, "by August 7, 1967, 9 a.m."[45]

But the big event of 1967 was the consideration of a new state constitution in November. The process was controversial. Republicans were strongly opposed to some of the fiscal provisions of the constitution and wanted each article to be voted upon separately. They lost that battle. The new constitution was ready at the end of September and it included a provision giving the power of redistricting to a bi-partisan commission of five citizens. Badillo, along with community leaders Antonia Pantoja, John Carro, Gilberto Ramírez, and a businessman named Joaquín Rivera, represented Puerto Ricans at the convention. Among other things, Badillo championed successfully a resolution relaxing the religious provisions for adoption of children in the state. Robert Kennedy, then in the US Senate, thought the new constitution was excellent and promised to campaign for its approval. Badillo agreed. In his view, the new constitution provided the tools to resolve most of the problems of Spanish-speaking people in New York.

On November 7, however, the front page of *El Diario-La Prensa* read: VOTE 'NO' SOBRE LA PROPUESTA CONSTITUCION POR SU PROPIO BIEN. (VOTE 'NO' ON THE PROPOSED CONSTITUTION FOR YOUR OWN GOOD.) "The bitterness created by the dispute is deep and could spillover into next year's election," wrote journalist Kirtland King. Several community organizations joined the newspaper in rejecting the proposed document. Low-income renters were warned that, if approved, the constitution would result in rent increases.[46] Badillo did well as a delegate but the final product was not as well regarded. Voters rejected the proposed constitution and *El Diario-La Prensa* rejoiced. "We welcome this 2 1/2 to 1 rejection, which saved all of us from a possible 80 per cent increase in state taxes within the next ten years."[47]

The following year, the key educational battle in the city was over community control of local schools. The main event of this battle was the 55-day strike led by the United Federation of Teachers over the job rights of its members. Puerto Ricans figured prominently alongside blacks in this battle. For example, in November, a group of Puerto Rican parents and teachers organized the Puerto Rican Inter-American Dynamic Educational Foundation, Inc. (PRIDE) to promote a boycott of the pubic schools until decentralization took effect. PRIDE wanted guarantees that a strike would not again disrupt the school system. In a letter written from the point of view of a student, PRIDE called for the boycott "until Lindsay, Donovan, Allen and Shanker decentralize all city schools, define the rights and duties of teachers, and promise that we will never be thrown out of school again."[48] At the conclusion of the strike in November, there was a protest outside the headquarters of the state education department involving about fifty Puerto Rican supporters of ousted principal Luis Fuentes, the first Puerto Rican principal in the New York Public School System. There were also sit-ins at PS 144, 155, and 271, predominantly black and Puerto Rican schools, protesting the reassignment of their principals to other schools. Other protests occurred on November 30 and December 2, but Puerto Ricans were not directly involved. The immediate outcome of these protests was the Board of Education's formal school decentralization proposal.

The decade came to a close with an electoral reversal of fortune for Puerto Ricans. Badillo ran for mayor for the first time in 1969 but he was not able to make it past the June primary. Then in November he lost the borough presidency to Robert Abrams. The two Puerto Rican councilmen were unseated as well. The losses at the city council had been forecast. No one was surprised but everyone was extremely unhappy.[49]

Radical politics

In 1960, the FBI actively sought to undermine New York political organizations seeking independence for Puerto Rico. This effort was part of a program of domestic counterintelligence dubbed COINTELPRO that the bureau ran from 1956 to 1971. The Puerto Rican component was added in 1960 and it was the most extensive of the five initiated that year. That may sound ominous but, truth be told, the program consisted of only thirty-seven actions over a period of eleven years. These actions included the publication of misleading articles and the mailing of anonymous letters seeking to cause dissension within the ranks of *independentista* organizations or to discredit their leaders.[50]

The FBI was not worried about the numerical strength of pro-independence groups but it believed that numbers were not the sole or best indicator of the potential of groups seeking to accomplish their goals by any means necessary. The bureau was worried about communist tendencies within the pro-independence movement. Thus, it considered the disruption of pro-communist organizations essential. An important tactic used in that effort was the development of

> intimate detailed knowledge of the more influential leaders as individuals. ... We should ... delve deeply into that part of their lives which do not show on the surface. ... We must have information concerning their weaknesses, morals, criminal records, spouses, children, family life, educational qualifications and personal activities other than independence activities.[51]

How dangerous was the radical element within Puerto Rican politics during the 1960s? The FBI saw a danger that had to be nipped in the bud. But, by the end of November 1960, the New York office of the FBI informed the director of the bureau that there was no need to develop a counterintelligence effort against the pro-independence movement "because the movement was doing a good job of disrupting itself, without outside help." The field office concluded its report by noting that it would continue its surveillance and intelligence activities, and would engage in counterintelligence actions when necessary.[52]

Subsequent assessments described the radical movement in the city as "woefully split," "dormant," "of a limited scope," and "crumbling." Even the group that was considered a moving force, the Movimiento Pro Independencia (MPI), was "not too active."[53] At the end of January 1964, the New York office of the FBI concluded that the pro-independence movement in the city was "in a chaotic condition." Acción Patriótica Unitaria, a nationalist group, was defunct, the Nationalist Party was torn apart, and the MPI was being challenged by the Movimiento Libertador de Puerto Rico, a group that the FBI described as of "doubtful importance" but whose continuous attacks on the MPI the bureau found extremely helpful. "The movement is its worst enemy," the report declared. "It is felt that the counterintelligence program is constantly being served by the power struggles, the name calling and the unpredictable antics of the members of the various groups. It is doubtful, under present conditions, that any counterintelligence measures could be more disruptive."[54]

In October 1964, the New York office of the FBI still held to the notion that the pro-independence movement in the city was its own worst enemy. In the case of the MPI, it hoped that a factional struggle between nationalists and communists would lead to the recruitment of informants among the anti-communist faction of the organization. It considered intervening in the dispute to further dissension but ruled against it after determining that a counterintelligence measure would be of doubtful value.[55]

During the mid-1960s, nationalist activities within the community often clashed with the initiatives of other Puerto Rican organizations. One key example is the 1966 dispute between the Migration Division and the MPI over relations between the community and the police. In July 1966, the Migration Division and the police department co-sponsored a series of conferences to promote cooperation between Puerto Ricans and the police in the wake of an outbreak of violence between the two in the Bedford-Stuyvesant section of Brooklyn.[56] In an open letter to the Brooklyn Puerto Rican community the MPI declared:

> This conference, compatriots, is another deception of the community. On the one hand, you have American politicians trying to secure the electoral support of Puerto Ricans on the next election. On the other hand, you have Puerto Rican politicians trying to secure positions for themselves at the expense of the sincere efforts and hopes of the community. This is just a ploy and we should not fall for it.[57]

Another example was the effort of the MPI to use the Puerto Rican Parade as a platform for the denunciation of the colonial rule of Puerto Rico by the United States. In April 1967 the organization circulated a letter among its members informing them that after a "heated struggle within the Puerto Rican Parade's organizing committee," the MPI had secured the participation of its spokesman, Pedro Juan Rúa, in the parade as a speaker. The parade was scheduled for April 15. According to the letter, the conservatives within the committee that opposed the MPI's inclusion were defeated thanks to the support of representatives from black and progressive organizations. "We have not ever needed your participation in an event as much as now," reads the letter. "A strong independentista contingent at the Parade will secure our participation in future and larger events. We must attend to help the MPI achieve independence for Puerto Rico and to show our support for the glorious Vietnamese people."[58] Supporting the people of Vietnam was the last thing the organizers of the parade wanted to do.

In May 1967, representatives of two Puerto Rican groups joined several other groups to protest the Vietnam War and to express their opposition to the draft. Dixie Bayó, from the MPI, and Flora Sánchez, from Tenants in Action, joined representatives of the Students for a Democratic Society, the Southern Conference Educational Fund, and the Student Non-Violent Coordinating Committee, among others, to occupy the offices of the army induction center at 39 Whitehall Street in Manhattan. "Our boyfriends, brothers, husbands and sons are being sent to die in an immoral war," said Nancy Ryan, one of the organizers of the event, to a reporter. "Isn't that enough for us to be mad about this war?"[59]

During the summer of 1967, the leadership of the MPI admitted privately that the work of the organization was deficient in many areas and that many members were irresponsible and lacked enthusiasm. In a letter dated June 27, the leadership of the organization declared: "We have concluded that an assessment of our work must take place. All members should air their grievances as they see fit. This discussion will take place on Friday June 30. At that meeting there should be no personal attacks. The discussion should proceed in a spirit of cooperation and solidarity." Members were also reminded to attend a talk on the situation of the Puerto Rican migrant worker. This event was part of the effort on the part of the MPI to develop links between the movement and Puerto Rican workers in New York.[60]

A year later, during the weekend of June 15, 1968, the MPI held a series of activities dealing with the organizational development of the group. During a seminar for members, they discussed questions related to mass political action within the community, support for independence for Puerto Rico by Puerto Ricans in the United States, and the relationship between the Puerto Rican movement and the American left. In separate activities, political leaders Juan Mari Brás, César Andreu Iglesias, and Lorenzo Piñero discussed the relationship between the struggle for democratic rights in the United States and the struggle for independence in Puerto Rico, as well as the justifications for ending colonialism in Puerto Rico.[61]

Later on, during the winter of 1968–69, a group of five or six people organized the Sociedad Pedro Albizu Campus at the Old Westbury campus of the State University of New York. This group was committed to a political agenda centering on Puerto Rican issues and needs in New York. Around that time, the Black Panthers, whose work had caught the attention of some of the members of the Sociedad, published an article about a group of Puerto Ricans in Chicago known as the Young Lords Organization (YLO). Some of the members of the Sociedad drove to Chicago, met with the leader of the YLO, Cha Cha Jiménez, and came back to New York committed to start an east coast branch of the YLO. Sociedad members contacted a gang on the Lower East Side and effected a merger that became the Young Lords Organization, New York City Chapter. There were some women involved at this stage, but the leadership of the newly founded organization was all-male. At the founding meeting the only woman present was Sonia Ivany, a New York University student at the time. The five-member Central Committee consisted of: Felipe Luciano, chairman; Juan González, minister of education; Pablo "Yoruba" Guzmán, minister of information; David Pérez, minister of defense; and Juan "Fi" Ortíz, minister of finance.[62]

On July 26, 1969, at a demonstration at Tompkins Square Park commemorating the anniversary of the dramatic attack on Cuartel Moncada by Fidel Castro and a band of Cuban revolutionaries, Felipe Luciano announced that the YLO had been established to "serve and protect the best interests of the Puerto Rican community." Luciano and his fellow partisans were certain that the community needed a revolution but admitted they had no idea how to bring it about.[63] The Cuban Revolution and the struggle of the Vietnamese for self-determination influenced the YLO. The work of some YLO members with War on Poverty programs contributed to their disillusionment with liberal reforms, leading to a more militant posture and membership. YLO members used the newspaper *Pa'Lante* as their calling card. Their community organizing revolved around a thirteen-point program, modeled after the platform of the Black Panthers, with whom YLO members worked closely.[64]

According to Richie Pérez, the social base and membership of the YLO was college students, college dropouts, and high school students and dropouts of working-class background. But "as time would pass, many of the leadership were coopted into the middle class and into the bourgeois superstructure, into media, into law." As far as the connection between the YLO and other Puerto Rican groups in the city, "the official relationship was not good." There were individual supporters within many of the same groups that rejected the YLO, like Evelina Antonetty, who was the director of the community-based organization United Bronx Parents, and Gilberto Gerena Valentín. But the slogan that guided the YLO's policy towards others was "no alliances with capitalists or traitors." A traitor was anyone who was perceived as conservative or took money from corporations or worked with military recruiters. The result of this attitude was that "many people who were potential allies we categorized immediately as enemies."[65]

Ultimately, the organization was, in the words of Pérez,

> a young movement without much continuity or ties to the past, theoretically very underdeveloped, eclectic in our study, not having a real clear sense of what we wanted or the kind of organization that we needed to bring about that transformation but nevertheless even with all of those things which are objective factors, it became a beacon for young Puerto Ricans, especially Puerto Ricans who were raised and had ghetto consciousness of life in America, it was speaking to our reality, and speaking very articulately to that kind of reality.[66]

The YLO strategy of providing basic social services was driven by the conviction that after having their needs met "slowly our people start seeing what socialism is all about."[67] And yet, this linkage strategy was eventually dropped for the sake of organizing in Puerto Rico to advance the Puerto Rican struggle for national liberation.[68]

On the electoral front, dim prospects did not deter the author of *A Puerto Rican in New York*, Jesús Colón, from running for controller under the Communist Party label in 1969. Colón had first run for a seat on the city council in 1953 as an American Labor Party candidate. In 1969, he shared his Marxist-Leninist credentials and his position on issues, such as day care, discrimination, housing, and education, with the Women's Rights Committee of the New Democratic Coalition. "The time will come in these United States," he told the group, "when the dictatorship of the proletariat or some step toward it in the form of a national front of the exploited of all races and creeds will come to power as one of the highest expressions of this now misused and ill-used word: democracy." For Colón, democracy meant universal day care, education, jobs, and housing for everyone. He supported the availability of contraceptive devices, sex education, and a woman's right to an abortion. Above all, he was for "all power to the people." Three words summarized his program: abundance, justice, peace.[69] According to a Communist Party post-election report, Colón was not prepared for his candidacy. Party members had not been consulted on the decision to run candidates in general and many party cells refused to work on behalf of candidates. Interestingly, some members were not enthusiastic about candidates who were from the working class. In Colón's case, only thirty-five people worked on his campaign compared with 300 in a previous race. The party spent only around $9000 on his race compared with about $40,000 for a different (unnamed) candidate.[70]

On November 19, 1969, the MPI issued a public statement deploring the conflict between Puerto Ricans and blacks over anti-poverty funds. Speaking on behalf of the MPI, Benjamín Ortíz and Arlene Bayó declared:

> In Washington, white millionaires have invented a modern and more effective way to quell the fighting spirit of the repressed. It is called the War on Poverty and it is led by the Office of Economic Opportunity. This is a new capitalist investment, carried out by the state with taxpayers' money, for a concrete purpose: to squash the rebellion of the poor; to buy the conscience of a few political leaders (who were supposed to represent us) with a new kind of soporific: the money they distribute. This is like giving us cake to pacify us and to prevent us from recovering the power they have taken away from us.[71]

In their statement, Ortíz and Bayó wondered if Puerto Ricans in New York had been contaminated by the racism of American society to the point that they could not see their own race. They were black! Instead of fighting blacks for anti-poverty funds, Ortíz and Bayó said, Puerto Ricans should be working in unity with blacks against opportunistic politicians and professionals such as Herman Badillo. To make their case for solidarity, they reminded their readers that the War on Poverty was the result of the struggle of blacks against oppression. If Puerto Ricans bene-fited from anti-poverty programs, they claimed, it was because of their collaboration with blacks as much as it was the result of their own efforts. They did not bother to explain how it was possible for the War on Poverty to be both a working-class accomplishment and a capitalist scheme to oppress the working class. Instead, Ortíz and Bayó urged Puerto Ricans to reject politicians who encouraged division and conflict between them and blacks. "That rotten leadership," they wrote, "deserves only our repudiation."[72]

The capstone to radical Puerto Rican politics during the 1960s was the convention held in December 1969 of students from colleges in New York City and Newark that spawned the Puerto Rican Student Union. "We clearly understand," reads their founding manifesto, "from years and years of being hit over the head with it, that the only way that our people will become free from disease, poverty, ignorance, oppression, exploitation, and cultural and physical genocide is through the use of force." Their sense of urgency was keenly exaggerated in claiming that "unless we act now, we may be the last Puerto Ricans on this planet." Their statement of principles added:

> We want you to dig yourself. Understand what you are, what you have become. Work very hard to see where you have come from. Fight to find out who are our ancestors, so that you may know what to say to our children. And then go out, get together with brothers and sisters like yourselves and act like the warriors that we are. Begin to serve our community, fight for it to control every institution in it, and defend it by any and every means necessary.[73]

At the end of the decade, the reaction of participants to the presence of radical groups in the 1969 Puerto Rican Day Parade best describes com-munity sentiments toward radicals compared with feelings toward those whom radicals decried as a "rotten leadership." On June 8, more than 100,000 participants marched along Fifth Avenue, while an estimated 250,000 watched from the sidelines. Radicals were the least appreciated of all who paraded. As the delegations from the Communist and Puerto Rican Nationalist parties approached the main platform, they were booed by the crowd. Once Communists and Nationalists began chanting "Yankee Go Home!" the spectators responded with cries of "Traitors!" Manuel Mariotta, from *El Diario-La Prensa*, wrote: "The extremists tried to tarnish the Parade but were not able to. Thousands of flag-waving parti-cipants showed their support for democracy and freedom for all peoples throughout the world."[74] Badillo and the president of Puerto Rico's

Senate, Rafael Hernández Colón, two mainstream politicians, received the highest acclaim from the crowd.

The politics of inclusion: structural ideation, contingency, and power

Puerto Rican political participation in New York City during the 1960s had consequences for voting rights and electoral enfranchisement (elimination of literacy test and voter registration campaigns), for civil rights (creation of a police review board), for minority representation (appointments during the Lindsay administration, election to city council, borough presidency, and state assembly), and public policy (access to War on Poverty resources, education battles, and school decentralization). Puerto Ricans were victims of covert repression and police brutality but they also were agents of democratic participation within civil and political society. Their activities had significant effects in enhancing the level of political inclusion in New York during this period.

Radicals spent a significant amount of time, energy, and resources spinning their wheels. Their focus of attention limited their ability to work on issues of importance to the community. The YLO was an exception but their practical impact was small. The political commitment of radicals was strong and intense but their strategic vision was ideological and ungrounded. As a key participant in the community control struggle of 1968 put it, they

> failed to see the importance of what was going on there. ... Parents were looking for ways of improving not only schools but police, sanitation concerns, and unemployment. Political groups [of the left] gave lip service but did very little to turn things around.[75]

If the most significant contribution of radical Puerto Rican politics in New York was that it "successfully deterred ... [the] annexation" of Puerto Rico to the United States, then the movement was truly Quixotic; annexation was the movement's windmills.[76] Based on the primary sources examined for this chapter, it is safe to say that annexation of Puerto Rico was not something the US government wanted to accomplish. Secondary sources also support this conclusion.[77] The impact of radical politics was thus largely unintended. The services the YLO provided were meant to radicalize their recipients but for the most part they forestalled the development of a radical consciousness by ameliorating the problems they addressed. The pressures exerted by radical organizations were meant to end colonialism in Puerto Rico but their legacy was a string of mainstream community institutions, such as the Center for Puerto Rican Studies at Hunter College, Hostos Community College, El Museo del Barrio, and the Caribbean Cultural Center. At best, radical politics was training grounds for participation in those community institutions and, later on, in mainstream politics for activists like Felipe Luciano, Juan González, and Pablo Guzmán, among many others.[78] Some call this co-optation; others call it selling out. I choose to call it roundabout inclusion, a form of delayed political gratification.

Regarding power, the variegated nature of Puerto Rican political expression makes it difficult for any one single theory to explain the Puerto Rican experience in New York. In power elite theory the political game is uniformly rigged in favor of the socioeconomically powerful. The pluralist model suggests fair play among interests. Even in instances in which inequality is pronounced—inequality of access to decision-making hubs, of interest in the political process, and of available resources—the effects are not considered cumulative. According to the pluralists, at any given moment anyone can break through and successfully vie for power. Structuralist explanations reduce political to economic or social power. Neostructuralist theories qualify the relationship between politics and economics in a way that makes them a pluralism without *naïveté*; neostructuralists of the "dominant political coalition" variety are pluralists who have been mugged by reality.

So where does the case of Puerto Ricans fit? As far as a theory of power is concerned, it belongs everywhere and nowhere in particular. Each approach is useful to understanding their experience. Elsewhere I have claimed that whether a set of political agents is able to access power or not at a given point in time depends on the degree to which they are able to reconcile what they are capable of doing with what the systemic setting allows.[79] This is not a theory of compromise. It is a theory of inclusion that revolves around the notion of contingency. Political agents operate in contexts not of their own making. The result is what I call structural ideation, meaning that because agents don't control the past they assume that the present does not belong to them. Is this any different from path dependency? Only in the sense that path dependency claims to have explanatory power and structural ideation produces beliefs that obfuscate the explanation of power. When structural ideation occurs, the circumstances set before political agents are conceived as impervious forces, pre-existing, fixed, difficult, if not impossible to change. Within that framework it is easy to either feel impotent about the possibility of shaping the future or to conceive of change only in terms of systemic transformation; you can't do anything or you must destroy everything if you want to create something new. Structural ideation is a cognitive handicap. It prevents political agents from seeing their opportunities and taking them. Contingency is about doing the opposite. You compromise if that is what it takes to succeed and you agree that unless you succeed there is no virtue in compromise. The point is that reconciling capability with feasibility may mean compromise but it is not about compromise. It is about avoiding structural ideation. It is about accomplishing goals with whatever resources may be at hand, attacking the *status quo* from all possible angles even if the attacks are sporadic and disconnected.

Puerto Rican politics during the 1960s was the opposite of structural ideation. It was a set of programs and activities variously informed by theories, ideologies, value systems, and attitudes without much coherence or coordination, determined to achieve socioeconomic and political equality for the community. From their respective vantage points, intentionally and by chance, mainstream political leaders and radicals, insiders and outsiders, enhanced the level of political representation of the community, raised awareness about its plight, educated many and inspired others to take up the Puerto Rican cause. In that process, the community was empowered—that is, its position in the city's opportunity structure improved over time—even if traditional loci of power excluded many of its members. At the end of the 1960s, Puerto Ricans were a fixture of the city. They were political players who also experienced under-representation and relative disadvantage.

Were under-representation and relative disadvantage examples of what Rodolfo Rosales calls the illusion of inclusion?[80] Power can be quite elusive when the capacity for social production of any given group is limited. During the 1960s, Puerto Ricans won some and lost many. Was this because the game was rigged against them? Did they actually lose everything because they did not win it all? That is the kind of conclusion that the idea of illusory inclusion suggests. This idea is another expression of structural ideation. Only the system is real and stable, and any efforts to change the balance of power that fail to produce systemic change must be unreal, illusory. Puerto Ricans during the 1960s did not transform their condition *in toto* but the changes they effected were real and some quite substantial. There's nothing illusory about the process of institutional development that produced community organizations such as the Puerto Rican Forum, the Puerto Rican Family Institute, the Legion of Voters, or the YLO. The Puerto Rican Amendment to the Voting Rights Act leveled the electoral playing field for those who were eager to participate but unable to do so because of their language.

Fernando Guerra and Luis Ricardo Fraga have suggested that in order to be effective in the political process actors must distinguish between contextual and strategic conditions.[81] Contextual conditions are factors that actors cannot control, such as whether elections are competitive or not, and strategic conditions include controllable factors, such as the level of voter registration in a particular electoral race. Did Puerto Ricans continue to experience under-representation and relative disadvantage because their actions took place when contextual conditions overwhelmed strategic factors? The Guerra and Fraga distinction is analytically useful but it is also another instance of potentially demobilizing or counterproductive structural ideation. If contextual factors are negative and immovable, why bother to intervene? How do you objectively determine that objective conditions are not ripe for political intervention? Was Badillo crazy when he challenged Perricone? He had no money and there was not much of a Puerto Rican vote that he could count on. *Objectively* speaking, he should have retreated to his study. But he didn't.

The distinction between contextual and strategic conditions replicates the Machiavellian conceptualization of political action as driven by a mixture of *Fortuna* and *Virtù*—chance and determination—in which *Fortuna* and *Virtù* are distinct categories. But the Puerto Rican experience in New York suggests something different. Chance is never one hundred percent chance and determination is never one hundred percent determination. Even when the context does not appear to be favorable, it is possible to intervene and to effect desired political outcomes or alter the contextual framework. Badillo did this when he went out to register voters that the political machine did not want. Not only did he increase the pool of voters but he also took advantage of the tools offered by the legal system to change its rules. To do this it helped that he was a lawyer. His status as a lawyer was not enough, though. The fact that he could pass for Italian put him in a position where he was able to use strategic information that was useful to his quest.[82] In this case, there was determination within chance and chance within determination. Structural ideation makes understanding this possibility difficult.

For Puerto Ricans in New York inclusion during the 1960s was about access to power. Their ability to exercise power in the political arena was limited and fleeting. The variegated nature of their efforts testifies to the essentially contingent character of political action. By the end of the 1960s, they had been seriously courted by a major presidential candidate and a Puerto Rican had been appointed head of his local campaign, thousands had met in Central Park in preparation for their participation in the Poor People's Movement Campaign led by Martin Luther King, Jr., and Badillo had run for mayor.[83] By then, they had also taken advantage of numerous opportunities provided by the War on Poverty to promote better schools, improved housing, more hospital services, increased employment opportunities, and greater political participation.[84] In 1968 alone, fifteen Puerto Ricans ran for office and four were elected: Robert García (district 29), Armando Montano (district 77), and Manuel Ramos (district 79) made it to the state assembly, and Manuel A. Gómez joined Emilio Núñez, originally from Spain, on the state Supreme Court.[85] In 1969, they had the opportunity to demonstrate their solidarity with workers across ethnicity and race when none other than A. Philip Randolph asked Joseph Monserrat to join him in support of striking GE workers. Monserrat agreed instantly.[86]

In 1969, it was evident that no single political leader spoke for the Puerto Rican community. Once Badillo's mayoral aspirations were derailed, the political leadership of the community split its support between incumbent Lindsay and his challenger, the so-called "subway liberal" Mario Procaccino. Speaking on behalf of the Puerto Rican–Hispanic Committee for Procaccino, Irma Vidal Santaella blasted the Lindsay administration and her former ally Badillo.

> We reject Lindsay because he has divided the city, pitting Puerto Ricans against blacks and blacks against Jews through the distribution of anti-poverty funds. His government is a threat to the unity of the Puerto Rican community. I don't understand how Badillo can support him after attacking him during the primaries. Now he says Lindsay is a great mayor. When is he telling the truth and when is he lying?[87]

Lindsay won in part because of a surge in black and Puerto Rican support, from 35 percent in 1965 to 70 percent in 1969. At the same time, none of the five Puerto Rican candidates running won. The community was anything but unified.

Puerto Rican politics in New York City during the 1960s was an odd mix: pluralist, elitist, structurally limited, contingent, uncoordinated, and infused with determination to achieve inclusion. This case shows that leadership matters, context is important, numbers make a difference, alliances are critical, disruption is sometimes essential. The challenge is knowing when and how to do what, when the match between capability and feasibility is effective, and when and how to articulate interests in such a manner that it produces optimal political effects. Structural ideation forecloses such calculations and contingency makes it difficult, although not impossible, to carry them out. Political inclusion as experienced and fashioned by Puerto Ricans in New York City during the 1960s provides a good antidote to the sense that lack of control of the past disables agents from controlling the present and from shaping the future.

Notes

1 See Carlos E. Santiago, *Labor in the Puerto Rican Economy: Postwar Development and Stagnation* (New York: Praeger, 1992).
2 See José Hernández-Alvarez, *Return Migration to Puerto Rico* (Berkeley: University of California Press, 1967).
3 Based on a three-year estimate, the American Community Survey of the US Census Bureau suggests a further decline in the Puerto Rican population to 9.4 percent of the city total (784,065 people). See 2006–8 American Community Survey, US Census Bureau; http://factfinder.census.gov (S0201: Selected Population Profile in the United States. Puerto Rican. American Community Survey).
4 See "City Finds Gains By Puerto Ricans," *New York Times*, February 16, 1964, 63.
5 These options were favored, respectively, by Oscar Lewis, *La Vida, A Puerto Rican Family in the Culture of Poverty—San Juan and New York* (New York: Random House, 1965); Patricia Cayo Sexton, *Spanish Harlem, An Anatomy of Poverty* (New York: Harper & Row, 1965); and Jesús Colón, *A Puerto Rican in New York and Other Sketches* (New York: International Publishers, 1982).

6 See Michael Lapp, "Managing Migration: The Migration Division of Puerto Rico and Puerto Ricans in New York City, 1948–68," Ph.D. Diss., Johns Hopkins University, 1990, 307.

7 Josephine Nieves interview, May 24, 1988, by Amílcar Tirado and Carlos Sanabria, Archives of the Center for Puerto Rican Studies, Hunter College, City University of New York. Hereafter referred to as Centro Archives.

8 See Albert O. Hirschman, *Exit, Voice, and Loyalty: Responses to Decline in Firms, Organizations, and States* (Cambridge, MA: Harvard University Press, 1970).

9 Herman Badillo interview, August 10, 2006, by José E. Cruz.

10 See "Congresistas Electos," *El Diario de Nueva York*, November 9, 1960, 2; "Se Calcula Que 300 Mil Hispanos Votaron En New York Durante Las Elecciones Del Martes," *El Diario de Nueva York*, November 10, 1960, 10. The November 9 story names the Puerto Rican challenger both as "Luis F." and "F. Luis" while the November 10 story names him as "F. Luis." His actual name was Faustino Luis.

11 Badillo interview.

12 See "Citizens of Convenience," editorial, *El Diario-La Prensa*, June 13, 1963, 21.

13 See "'Prueba de Literacia [*sic*]' Debe Cesar Afirman Líderes de la Comunidad," *El Diario-La Prensa*, June 13, 1964, 1.

14 See Juan Cartagena, "Latinos and Section 5 of the Voting Rights Act: Beyond Black and White," *National Black Law Journal* 18, no. 2 (2005): 201–23.

15 See "Puerto Rican Groups Here in Vote Registration Drive," *The Worker*, October 6, 1963, 1.

16 See Estado Libre Asociado de Puerto Rico, Departamento del Trabajo, División de Migración, *Informe Anual, Año Fiscal 1964–65*, 103–04, 106. Migration Division Collection, Annual Reports, Box 2, Centro Archives.

17 See *Informe Anual, Año Fiscal 1964–65*, 114–16, 119.

18 See *Informe Anual, Año Fiscal 1964–65*, 112, 113.

19 See Mike Davidow, T.R. Bassett, and Fred Gilman, "464,000 Join Boycott, Demand End of Jim Crow School Pattern Now," *The Worker*, February 4, 1964, 1.

20 See Fred Gilman, "Public Refuses to Take Cops' Alibi on Killing," *The Worker*, February 25, 1964. Jesús Colón Papers, Newspaper Clippings, Box 2, Folder 2, Centro Archives.

21 See Mike Davidow, "6,000 Cross Brooklyn Bridge in Unity Anti-Bias March," *The Worker*, March 3, 1964. Colón Papers, Newspaper Clippings, Box 2, Folder 2.

22 See Mike Davidow, "City Hall March Sunday Will Protest Slaying," *The Worker*, March 1, 1964. Colón Papers, Newspaper Clippings, Box 2, Folder 2. See also Fred Gilman, "City Sued for $1,000,000 for Cop's Slaying of Youth," *The Worker*, March 3, 1964, 8; Fred Gilman, "Committee Fights Police Brutality," *The Worker*, March 8, 1964. Colón Papers, Newspaper Clippings, Box 2, Folder 2; Fred Gilman, "Harlem Rally Denounces 'Frisk' and 'No Knock' Laws," *The Worker*, March 10, 1964, 8.

23 See Luisa A. Quintero, "Marginalia," *El Diario-La Prensa*, June 30, 1964, 16.

24 See "Mobilization of the Legion of Voters," editorial, *El Diario-La Prensa*, November 9, 1964, 15.

25 See Doug Archer, "1,500 at East Side Rally Hit Anti-Youth Witchhunt," September 6, 1964. Colón Papers, Newspaper Clippings, Box 2, Folder 2.

26 See Jack Barnes, "La Politica en Nueva York," *El Tiempo*, October 10, 1964, 9.

27 Badillo interview.

28 Badillo interview.

29 Badillo interview.

30 See Mike Davidow, "Badillo Victory Sets New Stage for Puerto Rican Representation," *The Worker*, October 5, 1965, 8. Colón Papers, Newspaper Clippings, Box 2, Folder 6.

31 See "Gerena Valentín Backed for Council," Colón Papers, Newspaper Clippings, Box 2, Folder 6. No paper or date indicated on this clipping.

32 See "Vote Will Also Decide Makeup of Legislature, City Council," reprinted from *The Worker*, October 31, 1965. Colón Papers, Newspaper Clippings, Box 2, Folder 6.

33 See "Endorses Badillo," *New York Times*, October 26, 1965. Colón Papers, Newspaper Clippings, Box 2, Folder 6.

34 See Commonwealth of Puerto Rico, Department of Labor, Migration Division, *Monthly Activities Report of the Migration Division, November 1965*, 7. Migration Division Collection, Monthly Reports, Box 3.

35 See Estado Libre Asociado de Puerto Rico, Departamento del Trabajo, División de Migración, *Informe Anual, Año Fiscal 1966–67*, 126, 129, 133. Migration Division Collection, Annual Reports, Box 2.

36 See Commonwealth of Puerto Rico, Department of Labor, Migration Division, *Monthly Activities Report of the Migration Division, August 1966; September 1966*, 6, 7, respectively. Migration Division Collection, Monthly Reports, Box 4.

37 See "Roberto Lebrón Anuncia su Candidatura a Congresista," *El Diario-La Prensa*, March 23, 1966. Colón Papers, Newspaper Clippings, Box 2, Folder 7; "Let's Unite," editorial, *El Diario-La Prensa*, April 26, 1966. Colón Papers, Newspaper Clippings, Box 2, Folder 7.

38 See Luisa A. Quintero, "Marginalia–Gran Jurado," *El Diario-La Prensa*, October 6, 1966, 22. Colón Papers, Newspaper Clippings, Box 2, Folder 7.

39 See "91% Quiere Votar en Plebiscito de P. Rico," *El Diario-La Prensa*, December 16, 1966, 5. Colón Papers, Newspaper Clippings, Box 2, Folder 7.

40 See Commonwealth of Puerto Rico, Department of Labor, Migration Division, *Monthly Activities Report of the Migration Division, November 1966*, 7. Migration Division Collection, Monthly Reports, Box 4.

41 See Bernard Weinraub, "New Police Board has two Negroes and Puerto Rican," *New York Times*, July 12, 1966, 1.

42 See Memo of Jason R. Nathan to John V. Lindsay, August 4, 1967; Memo of Walter Washington to Jason R. Nathan, August 4, 1967; Memo of Samuel Ganz to John V. Lindsay, August n.d, 1967; Memo of Timothy W. Costello to John V. Lindsay, August 4, 1967; Report to the Mayor of Follow Up Activities in the Department of Social Services to the Puerto Rican Community Conference, August 4, 1967; Memorandum to Mayor Lindsay from August Heckscher, August 4, 1967; Memo of Deputy Commissioner in Charge of Community Relations to Police Commissioner, August 4, 1967. John V. Lindsay Papers, Subject Files 1966–73, Box 94, Folder 1712, Municipal Archives, New York City.

43 See News Release, Office of the Mayor, John V. Lindsay, April 21, 1967. Lindsay Papers, Subject Files 1966–73, Box 94, Folder 1714.

44 See More E. Side Violence: 4 Arrested, 3 Cops Hurt, July 25, 1968. Lindsay Papers, Subject Files 1966–73, Box 97, Folder 1787; Memo of Deputy Commissioner in Charge of Community Relations to Police Commissioner, August 4, 1967. Lindsay Papers, Subject Files 1966–73, Box 94, Folder 1712.

45 See Memo from John V. Lindsay to Conference Committee Members, August 3, 1967. Lindsay Papers, Subject Files 1966–73, Box 94, Folder 1712.

46 See "Llaman 'Falsa' Una Campaña En Apoyo Nueva Constitución," *El Diario-La Prensa*, November 1, 1967, 4; "Se Oponen a Constitución 16 Organizaciones de N.Y.," *El Diario-La Prensa*, November 1, 1967, 14; "Si Aprueban Nueva Constitución, le Subirán Alquiler," *El Diario-La Prensa*, November 6, 1967, 4; Kirtland I. King, "Lucha Constitución Dejará Cicatrices," *El Diario-La Prensa*, November 8, 1967, 2.

47 See "A Decisive 'No,'" editorial, *El Diario-La Prensa*, November 9, 1967, 25.

48 See "Piden se Espere Descentralización de las Escuelas," *El Diario-La Prensa*, November 1, 1968, 10.

49 See Richard Reeves, "Analysis of Recent Voting Patterns Illustrate Reasons for Changes in Lindsay's Re-election Strategy," *New York Times*, October 6, 1969, 38; Alfonso A. Narvaez, "Puerto Rican Prospect: 10% of Population, 0% of Political Power," *New York Times*, October 15, 1969, 30.

50 See Letter of Edward H. Levi to Peter Rodino, May n.d., 1975. Rafael Anglada López Papers, Series VIII, Subject Files, Box 20, Folder 5. Centro Archives.

51 See Memo from SAC, San Juan to Director, FBI, June 12, 1961. López Papers, Series VIII, Subject Files, Box 20, Folder 4.

52 See Memo from SAC, New York to Director, FBI, November 29, 1961. López Papers, Series VIII, Subject Files, Box 20, Folder 4.

53 See Memo from SAC, New York to Director, FBI, February 27, 1962. López Papers, Series VIII, Subject Files, Box 20, Folder 4.

54 See Memo from SAC, New York to Director, FBI, January 30, 1964. López Papers, Series VIII, Subject Files, Box 20, Folder 4.

55 See Memo from SAC, New York to Director, FBI, October 9, 1964. López Papers, Series VIII, Subject Files, Box 20, Folder 4.

56 See Commonwealth of Puerto Rico, Department of Labor, Migration Division, *Monthly Activities Report of the Migration Division, July 1966*, 7. Migration Division Collection, Monthly Reports, Box 4.

57 See Movimiento Pro Independencia, Puerto Rico, Compatriotas de Brooklyn, n.d. Colón Papers, New York Organizations, Box 1, Folder 4. Translated from the Spanish by José E. Cruz.

58 See Secretaría de Organizacion del MPI, "Companero," April 11, 1967. Colón Papers, New York Organizations, Box 1, Folder 4.

59 See "Women to Demonstrate Friday at Army Induction Center," *The Worker*, May 23, 1967. Colón Papers, Newspaper Clippings, Box 2, Folder 10.

60 See Circular letter of Luis González to Movimiento Pro Independencia members, June 27, 1967. Colón Papers, Correspondence, Box 4, Folder 4.

61 See Circular letter of Luis González to Movimiento Pro Independencia members, June 11, 1968. Colón Papers, Correspondence, Box 4, Folder 4.

62 Richie Pérez interview, June 28, 1988, by Carlos Rodriguez Fraticelli. Centro Archives; *Palante, Siempre Palante*, video documentary, produced and directed by Iris Morales, Latino Education Network Service, 1996.

63 See Felipe Luciano and Hiram Maristany, "The Young Lords Party, 1969–75," *Caribe* 7, no. 4 (1983), 7; Miguel "Mickey" Meléndez, *We Took the Streets, Fighting for Latino Rights with the Young Lords* (New York: St Martin's Press, 2003), 87. According to Juan González, the YLO did not exist before September 1969. See Luisa A. Quintero, "No Somos Comunistas," *El Diario-La Prensa*, February 17, 1970, 16.

64 Pérez interview.

65 Pérez interview.

66 Pérez interview.

67 See *El Pueblo Se Levanta* VHS. Third World Newsreel, 1970.

68 See Johanna L. del C. Fernandez, "Radicals in the Late 1960s: A History of the Young Lords Party in New York City, 1968–74," Ph.D. Diss., Columbia University, 2004.

69 See Letter of Jesús Colón to Women's Rights Committee, October 10, 1969. Colón Papers, Correspondence, Box 6, Folder 7.

70 See "Report on the Elections of November 4, 1969." Colón Papers, Series IV, Box 1, Folder 3; Narvaez, "Puerto Rican Prospect." According to Narvaez, Colón ran for council president. A November *New York Times* report has him running for "Controller." See "List of Candidates in Tomorrow's Races," *New York Times*, November 3, 1969, 53.

71 See Movimiento Pro Independencia, Misión Vito Marcantonio, Declaración de Prensa, November 19, 1969. Colón Papers, New York Organizations, Box 1, Folder 4. Translated from the Spanish by José E. Cruz.

72 See Declaración de Prensa.

73 See Puerto Rican Student Union, "Somos Puertorriquenos y Estamos Despertando," n.d. Diana Caballero Papers, Series VI, Organizations, Box 24, Folder 14, Centro Archives.

74 See Manuel Mariotta, "Más de 350 Mil en el Desfile," *El Diario-La Prensa*, June 9, 1969, 3.

75 See James Jennings and Francisco Chapman, "Puerto Ricans and the Community Control Movement: An Interview with Luis Fuentes," in *The Puerto Rican Movement: Voices from the Diaspora*, eds. Andrés Torres and José E. Velázquez (Philadelphia: Temple University Press, 1998), 291.

76 See Andrés Torres, "Introduction, Political Radicalism in the Diaspora–The Puerto Rican Experience," in *Puerto Rican Movement*, 17.

77 According to Edgardo Meléndez, the foremost expert on the issue of Puerto Rican annexation, the agenda of the US government for Puerto Rico between 1959 and 1965 focused on reforming the commonwealth. If there ever was a plan to make Puerto Rico a state of the union during the 1960s, it was mostly spearheaded by pro-statehood forces in Puerto Rico. The federal government did not reciprocate their efforts. See Edgardo Meléndez, *Puerto Rico's Statehood Movement* (New York: Greenwood Press, 1988), 83–114; Ronald Fernandez, *The Disenchanted Island: Puerto Rico and the United States in the Twentieth Century* (New York: Praeger, 1992), 195–222; Ronald Fernandez, *Cruising the Caribbean* (Monroe, ME: Common Courage Press, 1994), 328, 429–30.

78 See Torres, "Introduction," 18.

79 See José E. Cruz, *Identity and Power, Puerto Rican Politics and the Challenge of Ethnicity* (Philadelphia: Temple University Press, 1998), 18.

80 See Rodolfo Rosales, *The Illusion of Inclusion, the Untold Political Story of San Antonio* (Austin: University of Texas Press, 2000).

81 See Fernando Guerra and Luis Ricardo Fraga, "Theory, Reality, and Perpetual Potential: Latinos in the 1992 California Elections," in *Ethnic Ironies, Latino Politics in the 1992 Elections*, eds. Rodolfo O. de la Garza and Louis DeSipio (Boulder, CO: Westview Press, 1996), 131–45.

82 Badillo interview.

83 See Commonwealth of Puerto Rico, Department of Labor, Migration Division, *Monthly Activities Report of the Migration Division, February 1968*, 15. Migration Division Collection, Monthly Reports, Box 5; John Carro interview, June 7, 1988, by Carlos Sanabria. Centro Archives; "Puerto Rican Poor Organize March," May 28, 1968. Colón Papers, Newspaper Clippings, Box 3, Folder 2; "En Peligro Residentes, Edificios Abandonados, Surgen Comités Pro-Badillo Para Alcalde," *El Tiempo*, March 14, 1969, 19. Colón Papers, Newspaper Clippings, Box 3, Folder 5; Alberto Alonso, "Herman Badillo, Alcalde de N.Y.!, Es Consigna de Activistas Hispanos," *El Diario-La Prensa*, March 13, 1969, 31.

84 See "Comité Pro Bien Comunal," Photograph, *El Diario-La Prensa*, October 10, 1968, 5; Letter of Herman Badillo to Nelson A. Rockefeller, October 16, 1968; Letter of Nelson A. Rockefeller to Herman Badillo, October 22, 1968; Letter of Herman Badillo to John V. Lindsay, October 30, 1968; Letter of John V. Lindsay to Herman Badillo, November 6, 1968. Lindsay Papers, Subject Files 1966–73, Box 12, Folder 160.

85 See Jeronimo Berenguer, "Triunfan Boricuas en Elecciones N.Y.," *El Tiempo*, November 7, 1968. Colón Papers, Newspaper Clippings, Box 3, Folder 1.

86 See Letter of A. Philip Randolph to Joseph Monserrat, December 8, 1969, Joseph Monserrat Papers, Series V, Organizations, Box 10, Folder 17. Centro Archives.

87 See "Procaccino Se Convertirá en un Cruzado contra las Drogas," *El Tiempo*, August 20, 1969, 11. Colón Papers, Newspaper Clippings, Box 3, Folder 5.

6   Inclusion, Exclusion, and Citizenship

Kathleen Sullivan and Patricia Strach

In 1992, gay rights activists "were begging Bill Clinton about—literally—about whether he was going to say the word 'gay' in his convention speech. Even say it." They had "to threaten a walkout to get it in."[1] By the time Barack Obama ran for office in 2008, he promised broader rights for gays and lesbians and signed legislation making violence against persons based on sexuality a hate crime. But the "Don't Ask, Don't Tell" policy that keeps gays from military recognition, along with a host of benefits that come with legally recognized marriage, were still sticking points. Much had changed in the years that passed between the two administrations. Thinking about citizenship in terms of inclusion and exclusion, we might say that gays and lesbians are better included (have greater input) in the political process but are still excluded from equal rights and recognition in institutions such as the military and marriage. In this case, citizenship is about who gets what, where citizens are measured by their ability to influence the political process and their eligibility for various government programs and aid.

Another way to understand inclusion and exclusion, however, is to re-think the place of individuals and groups in the policy process. Rather than assume citizens stand on either side of the process—on the left, where they make their voice heard like the activists who urged Clinton to say "gay," or on the right, where they are (in)eligible for various government programs and aid like openly serving in the military—we suggest locating citizens *within* the process. Americans find themselves within governing when they are called on to carry out various government policies. The state or federal government might call upon citizens to temporarily assume public roles, as when citizens are called upon to serve in the military or as jurors, prosecution witnesses, or even rescue personnel. The government also calls upon citizens in their personal lives, such as parents who research schools, apply for admission, and provide transportation when they use education vouchers to send their child to school, or homeowners who navigate complex federal, state, and local policies that provide incentives to buy property in a particular location or at a particular time. In addition, Americans are within governing when the government relies on their status to accomplish particular goals, such as companies defined as "employers" that provide subsidized healthcare to individuals defined as "employees." A lens of governance examines the non-governmental actors that the state enlists to accomplish its objectives, illuminating an additional relationship between state and citizens. Through this lens, we can see how doing the work of government shapes the civic membership of citizens.

From the thinnest theoretical account of citizenship to its fuller forms, citizens are most often measured by their ability to provide input into the political process and by their eligibility for its outputs as beneficiaries of government programs. For example, liberal citizenship includes the positive rights of political participation and the negative freedoms from unnecessary state intervention, but little else.[2] The broader accounts of multicultural citizenship, republican (participatory) citizenship, difference citizenship, and gender-inclusive citizenship, all expand the definitions and expectations for participation or else for the demands and requirements of equality in government policies.[3] T.H. Marshall's three forms of citizenship—civil, political, and social—are similarly defined by participation and eligibility.[4]

Like the theoretical literature, empirical work in political science also emphasizes citizens' input through voting, interest group and party pressure, and public opinion.[5] It also addresses the outcomes, in particular how inequalities persist and may even be fostered by state institutions.[6] Recent scholarship has even tied the outputs to inputs, demonstrating how the interactions of citizens with government feed back into the process by shaping their political participation.[7] The picture we get is rich and varied, but it shares in common a notion of citizenship that seems to rest on either side of the state rather than squarely within it.

Yet we know society's persistent inequalities are not divorced from what happens within that black box. Ascriptive characteristics, such as race and gender, are fundamental to how governing works. Policies affect citizens "differently depending on their age group, employment status, and income."[8] White supremacy has served as a form of statebuilding, sex serves as a basis for social ordering, and heteronormative standards of marriage establish marriage as a foundation for national identity.[9] How policymakers think about particular groups of people—the social construction of target populations—plays a role in how policies are designed.[10] Though we know that the categories of race, gender, sexuality, and class have been deployed in governing, we know less about how other seemingly personal characteristics and particular social relationships, such as parent–child, employer–employee, and town–resident, have also been utilized to accomplish the work of government. In this chapter we ask, "How does the state utilize citizens' day-to-day identities as part of governing?" In thinking about the everyday means that the state uses in governing, we are also led to ask, "What are the obligations and burdens as well as the benefits and privileges that befall citizens?" We elaborate the concept of governance as a starting point to do just that.

Governance

Scholars are increasingly employing the term "new governance" to describe a government that is providing fewer direct services and more in conjunction with quasi-public, non-profit, and private organizations.[11] Lester Salamon explains,

> instead of the centralized hierarchical agencies delivering standardized services that is caricatured in much of the current reform literature and most of our political rhetoric, what exists in most spheres of policy is a dense mosaic of policy tools, many of them placing public agencies in complex, interdependent relationships with a host of third-party providers.[12]

Laurence Lynn, Carolyn Heinrich, and Carolyn Hill define governance broadly as "regimes of laws, administrative rules, judicial rulings, and practices that constrain, prescribe, and enable government activity, where such activity is broadly defined as the production and delivery of publicly supported goods and services."[13] American government has always relied on nongovernmental actors to administer its goals. Federal and state governments in the early republic established mixed enterprises, blending public and private features in quasi-public corporations, markets, and transportation systems in order to foster economic development.[14] From the quartering of soldiers in the homes of ordinary citizens during the Civil War to the processing of Medicare paperwork in more recent times, American government has continued such public–private partnerships.[15]

Though it is clear that American government relies on established third-party actors (from nonprofits to private companies) and enlists a set of tools (from grants to loans to contracts) to do so, established organizations are not the *only* group of actors that carry out governmental objectives, and concrete tools are not the *only* set of instruments that can be used to promote, encourage, or coerce compliance. Indeed, when we look more closely we can see that the state repeatedly calls on citizens in their day-to-day identities to act on its behalf. From parents with school vouchers to homeowners who decipher incentives in the tax code to employers who subsidize healthcare costs, the state relies on citizens in their private roles and relationships to each other. It creates, utilizes, or fosters social relationships in order to identify suitable administrators and provide a means to sustain obligations and privileges.[16] Social relationships matter because they define the lines that connect citizens to one another, to the state, and to a host of other institutions. They also define statuses through which citizens assume certain roles to one another, to institutions, or to both.

Thinking about parents as the administrators of school voucher programs lets us see that American government relies on a series of relationships, between parents and children, between children and schools, between government and all three, to define the statuses of "parent," "eligible school-age child," and "eligible school." Governance allows a conceptual turn from looking at the actors and institutions of the state as separate entities to examining the relationships the state fosters to achieve its objectives and the consequent effects on citizenship. Visually, it is a shift from looking at the "dots" (official state agencies and programs) to the "lines" that connect those dots to citizens (personal, civic, and social relationships).

Recognizing this relation between citizens, between citizens and institutions, and between citizens, institutions, and government, invites us to rethink some of the normative presumptions of studies of citizenship, particularly the impulse to provide universal rights and benefits. An individual's multiple relationships provide multiple and sometimes conflicting status categories. One individual might act as a parent responsible for fulfilling obligations to his/her child, an employee eligible for particular benefits, or a head of household responsible for the accounting and receipt of tax obligations. Membership is an important part of citizenship not only in determining who may participate in the political process or who may receive social benefits, but also in defining legitimate relationships *within* the state, ranging from members of a community eligible for disaster aid to members of a family legally responsible for one another's debt. Although universal language is usually invoked to talk about the rights of citizenship, the state routinely differentiates individuals by their relationships with other institutions and citizens. Classes, distinctions, and statuses, however, tend to signal inequality in the citizenship literature. For Marshall, writing after World War II, when the state was in the process of extending rights to various groups that had previously been denied those rights, citizenship was about belonging in equal terms. He defined citizenship as "a status bestowed on those who are full members of a community."[17] To be denied full membership was to be denied a right of citizenship. Social class stood out as an indicator of inequality. More recently, governments have used ascriptive statuses as a marker for differential, and unequal, treatment of citizens.[18] But status is also a marker of a relationship between some individuals and others. When viewed through the lens of governance, status can provide information about the work that government is doing, and the means it is relying upon to do it. The differentiation of citizens by age, race, gender, and employment status, among other things, relies on social relationships and points to those places where government sustains or generates differences in the pursuit of other objectives. If we view these distinctions as markers of the roles and relationships that government has cultivated to serve as resources for administration, then it leads us to ask, "What work is the government attempting to accomplish in sustaining, even generating, these distinctions?"

Recognizing differential status does not mean we give up on the project of equal citizenship; indeed, it invites us to think even more seriously about the operations of power and hierarchy. When government relies on the status of citizens, whether it is coercing or cajoling or providing incentives, it exercises power to get citizens to do its work.[19] In the absence of a contract that connects government with the third-party organization carrying out public goals, we must look for power in the social relations it defines and maintains. Such exercises of power may not be readily apparent, or they may appear to be benevolent or benign, as in the postindustrial workplace where a professional environment masks mechanisms of control.[20] In such situations, workers are situated as both a subject of needs and an object of surveillance, unaware of the ways in which power is acting upon them, operations of power that Foucault identifies in his concept of governmentality.[21] The mechanisms of discipline seep through social relationships so that government objectives can be accomplished without an explicit demonstration of government power or a feeling of coercion on the part of the citizen.[22] Governmentality also occurs in state agencies and organizations as well as in a host of other relationships, such as in the family and at the workplace. Feminist theorists have long maintained that gendered roles in the family affect citizenship.[23] Our own work has examined in depth the role of the family in American governance.[24]

Though disciplinary mechanisms may pervade a social relationship, the relationship itself provides opportunities for resistance. Freedom can be found by renegotiating the terms of the relationship and disrupting institutional rules and surveillance. Disability, for example, is a status created and imposed by the state, but it can also be renegotiated from the bottom up as a site of resistance. The disabled subject is a member of a class that citizens may move in and out of. The disabled subject can also bring his/her knowledge of the nonstandard to make a claim to negotiate and even unseat standard practices.[25] Workers of various disabilities can forge bonds based on their corporal needs, such as supporting women who need facilities in a lunchroom for pumping breastmilk.[26] Noncitizens can also claim rights as workers, invoking federal regulations, universal human rights, and dignity of person claims to challenge and resist ill treatment by floor supervisors.[27] Such renegotiations of status can be extended to gendered citizenship, where gendered subjects can appropriate the category of citizenship and make a claim to embodied citizenship, thus introducing more experience into the category.[28]

Like disability, the family is not a fixed status. It has to be constructed, and it is capable of further classification in order to distinguish different kinds of families. Through the policing of families, the state has historically acted through the family. When the state relies on families, it draws upon them in their social classes, thus reproducing class distinctions in this instrumentalism. Upper-class families were restructured for the purposes of protecting children. With domestic servants seen as a source of pathology among wealthy children, mothers could reclaim their role by following the advice of doctors. The resulting practice was one in which "the doctor prescribes, the mother executes."[29] Through such practices, the upper-class family sets itself apart as autonomous, while the mother could claim her own authority within the family, thus skirting its patriarchal authority.[30] Working-class families, meanwhile, were cast as perpetually in struggle against the vices of the streets. Members were pitted against one another, to exercise surveillance upon one another. Those who were castaways of the family were classed as vagabonds. The police were available to exercise authority upon these "family's rebels."[31] The family is a universal category, but social differentiation led to differential civic production of the citizens who were members of the families of different social classes. The state's treatment of class issues can be reframed around models of family, and the state can then discipline individuals through their conformity or lack of conformity to expected behavior within the family. Foucault positions the family as an instrument for management in modern states. Information that needs to be gained about citizens by government or provided to citizens from government can be transmitted through the family. The family can inculcate appropriate sexual behaviors, implement demographic shifts, maintain consumption patterns, and fulfill many other governmental goals.[32]

Rather than attempt to universalize citizenship and its privileges, it would be productive to find ways to address citizens at the point at which their privileges and obligations are affected. Legal scholars have led the way by addressing threats to accountability and democratic norms when governments contract out public work to private companies. Democratic norms can be sacrificed if there is a lack of oversight and accountability.[33] The contract, statutory, and regulatory powers, as well as the common law, are all resources that preserve public norms when the state transfers policy administration to private institutions. The contract can incorporate accountability mechanisms, which might include training requirements, performance benchmarks, accreditation, and self-evaluation.[34] All of these mechanisms turn to the relationship between governments and contractors to establish terms of behavior and accountability. Although the governance we describe in this chapter lacks a formal contract, the contract can be seen as an analogous line connecting the government with the relevant institution or individual, a resource that either party may infuse with public norms to equalize or ameliorate status differentials.

Insights from governance

Social relationships, and the statuses that result from them, invite us to consider not just different characterizations of persons but also how government accomplishes its objectives, the power it exercises upon citizens in doing so, and the effect on individual lives when particular relationships become important for policy aims. In the following sections of this chapter, we look at four policy areas to demonstrate the insights that a governance perspective offers. Together, our four cases illustrate the role third parties play in governing across several policy areas and constituencies. Combining the insights of governance with attention to citizenship—the benefits, opportunities, and shaping of civic identity—allows us to capture how citizenship is located within governance.

Doing one's job may be doing the work of government

Over the course of American history, fears over drink, drugs, tobacco, and sex have invited public intervention into what could be considered private concerns. Nongovernmental actors have been critical to the politicization of a seemingly private issue into one that warrants government intervention into private behaviors. As Rogan Kersh and James Morone recount, the process starts with professional and civil associations that generate social disapproval, medical experts who issue reports, and self-help movements that provide encouragement and enthusiasm. Citizenship categories are constructed as these groups go on to label "the demon user" and "the demon industry." Finally, interest groups ramp up the pressure until government intervenes and these nongovernmental activities become absorbed into a formal public policy.[35]

Governance recognizes that private actors are intrinsically involved in the development of a policy issue, and its attention to third-party actors helps to highlight the processes of citizen construction that accompany that development. There is evidence that the entry of different groups— health, medical, consumer, environmental, family—into the public concern over obesity has already generated the categorization of citizens and the rise of experts. The very groups that are *agents* in advancing federal obesity policy are simultaneously *objects* of citizen construction. The health expert emerges as the authoritative figure. The mother at home dispensing snacks stands in relation to this doctor/expert, ceding her authority to become a medium for the doctor's prescriptions. If federal regulatory policy does take place, it will only target those who did not comply in the transitioning social relations at this current stage. They will then become objects of formal regulation should a federal obesity policy develop. The wholesome bread-making mothers will, meanwhile, appear to be autonomous; their own position in a relation of social regulation going unnoticed.

Once the government takes on a policy, we can expect to see the public sphere acting upon the private, with the government controlling the conditions of sale, raising prices through sin taxes, litigating against producers, regulating marketing and advertising, and conducting education campaigns.[36] Thinking in terms of governance posits an alternative set of relationships between citizens, citizens and institutions, and citizens, institutions, and government that can be utilized in the generation and implementation of policy. Federal subsidies will become critical to encouraging some industries that contribute to obesity patterns, such as the manufacturers of high-fructose corn syrup, to offer lower-priced alternatives. Medical associations can work through pediatricians to advise parents about family nutrition practices. Schools can be enlisted to run programs akin to "Just say no," replete with looming authority figures. In these alternative sites, the federal government cedes bureaucratic control to other institutions, such as professional associations, schools, and families, which have developed networks to affect public-health policy.

Once the federal government enacts a formal policy, the act of categorization will take place along the lines of good/bad mother, reliable/ unreliable childcare center, and healthy/unhealthy schools. These lines have already been forming as policy networks have mobilized around the issue. Governance shows that federal regulation rests not on the failure of parents but on the inability of social modes of regulation in the development phase to capture all parents. The holdouts are the "casualties" of the regulatory system.[37] In contrast, the good mother/care provider/school official triumvirate will emerge to join the ranks of the yeoman farmer, freedman, industrial worker, and victim as the most recent reiteration of the "idealized citizen."[38]

Power and agency in the construction of civic identity

The construction of identity is a two-way street, with government shaping the civic identity of citizens, while citizens simultaneously contribute to the construction of their own identities as well as a broader national identity. Native Americans occupy a distinct legal status within American law that challenges the dualistic distinction of being included or excluded in the polity. Rather than situate themselves within one category, indigenous people have capitalized on their ambivalent status, occupying "the third space of sovereignty."[39] By refusing to occupy a fixed position in imperialistic binaries, indigenous people have combined their tribal identities with contemporary conditions. They are both outside the boundaries in terms of their tribal status and inside the boundary in terms of their position as minority groups. As such, they transcend and challenge spatial and temporal boundaries. The result is a "haunting" of American dreams. Current discursive engagements between the United States and Native Americans present an image that challenges the understood fixtures of the relation between the two parties, thereby unsettling national identity.[40]

Governance reminds us that this negotiation of civic identity requires institutions and that those institutions, too, can be sites of further citizen formation. In 1871 President Grant announced a policy to foster civilization among Native Americans.[41] The federal government, through either the military or other federal agencies, was not well suited for achieving this goal in its new relation with Native Americans. Instead, the government relied on public sentiment to promulgate it.[42] As government officials well understood, state actors and institutions could not carry out the day-to-day work of advancing civilization among Native Americans; it would take "Christian missionaries, teachers and farmers among the Indians."[43] The federal government had already established networks of governance in relying on Christian missionaries in the earlier phases of federal Indian policy. In the early part of the "Allotment and Citizenship" era, the federal government had appointed religious leaders as Indian agents and as members of the Board of Indian Commissioners, as well as promising ongoing support of Indian missions.[44] Religious norms facilitated policies that trained Native Americans to live among whites, dress like whites, and take up agriculture, a form of "gentle genocide."[45] Similarly, philanthropists were appointed to the Board of Indian Commissioners, an institution designed to serve as a watchdog of the Bureau of Indian Affairs. On the East Coast, voluntary associations also sprung up in the name of Indian reform. The Indian Citizenship Committee in Boston, the Women's National Indian Association, the Indian Rights Association in Philadelphia, and the Lake Mohonk Conference of Friends of the Indian all expressed a commitment to civil and political rights for Native Americans and disseminated this idea in the broader political culture.[46]

On the one hand, these groups pressured federal policymakers to change policy toward Native Americans, and in this sense they were activists providing input into the policy process. But, on the other hand, they were also third-party actors situated within the web of governance. The government relied on such groups to conduct work that state actors were not suited to do. Transitioning from a military-based policy to a social-formation policy required cultural tools. The government relied on reform groups to shape public sentiment for the new policy as well as to formulate the process of social formation, thus altering the education, labor, and living patterns of Native Americans. Humanitarians stressed the need for agricultural labor as a means of encouraging civilized ways of life. These sentiments would underlie the need for individual allotments of land.[47] While these volunteers had Native American citizenship as their object, they themselves were transforming their civic identity by doing the work of government. Women found a space for political activity. Volunteers constructed a notion of civilization that defined their own citizenship as well as providing a model to which Native Americans were to conform.

By 1887 the policymakers in Washington were ready to take over. Congress passed the Dawes Act, allotting land and encouraging individual ownership as a means to destroy tribal arrangements and foster individual habits of property ownership. The federal government was ready to call on bureaucrats to implement these new policies. The Bureau of Indian Affairs grew dramatically in the 1880s, increasing the number of its police and educational employees.[48] With Native Americans recognized as persons rather than as nations, the federal government could now assume criminal jurisdiction over their individual behavior. Social formation could then occur by criminalizing undesired activity, including sun dances, polygamy, practices of medicine men, thefts, destruction of property, and intoxication.[49] The federal government also offered aid to churches that maintained schools on reservations.[50] Finally, it could extend marital relations to indigenous people to confer the privilege of head of household upon married men and norms of modesty and domesticity upon married women.[51] The governance of Native American affairs continued as a hybrid of public and private administration, which had been critical to both the development of public policy and the shaping of citizenship.

Identifying the origins of status categories

As social relationships and statuses are important for understanding civic identity, the creation and maintenance of status categories are worth unearthing. Federal policymakers may draw these categories from preexisting sources, giving official weight to the actions of groups, agencies, and other levels of government. The education provisions of the GI Bill provide an illustration. Though the GI Bill was fashioned to give veterans a chance to enroll in universities, the bill did not create the status of veteran or student. Instead, it drew extensively upon the practices of existing organizations, notably the VA (Veterans Affairs/Veterans Administration), American Legion, and the education network consisting of colleges, universities, education boards, and state governments across the nation, to define those statuses.

At the end of World War II, there were competing definitions of "veteran." A key difference between President Franklin D. Roosevelt's backed bill and the American Legion bill, which would eventually become the "GI Bill," was whether or not to include merchant seamen. For both the VA and the Legion, a veteran was defined by his or her formal relationship to the armed services. Even though the *tasks* of the merchant marines— "[carrying] troops ammunition, and supplies to ... theaters of war"—were similar to the *tasks* of many Army and Navy personnel, the *formal relationship* was quite different.[52] Merchant marines served under either the War Shipping Administration or the United States Army Transport Service and the VA was adamant about "a clear distinction being drawn as between members of the armed forces in active service and those engaged in civilian occupations for the Government or for the several welfare agencies such as the American Red Cross and similar organizations."[53] Veterans were those individuals who served in the Army, Navy, Marine Corps, and Coast Guard, not the women at home who went to work in the factories, not the farmers whose "food won the war," and not the civilians who fought at sea.

Just as the status of "veteran" was taken from existing sources, Congress and the VA relied on existing statuses of "student," giving colleges and their state overseers wide leeway. The GI Bill left the veterans' choice of schools (once they met certain minimum standards) and schools' choice of veterans to their own criteria.

> Each eligible veteran was privileged to elect his own course of instruction and to enroll in any approved education ... establishment of his choice which would accept him, and (subject to his period of eligibility) could continue such course to completion provided his conduct and progress remained satisfactory *according to the prescribed requirements of the educational ... institution attended* [emphasis added].[54]

FDR reinforced the roles of states and colleges upon signing the GI Bill into law, saying that "certification of trainees and students should reside in the States and localities."[55] Ultimately, to receive GI benefits, soldiers had to be admitted to a college or university by that institution's criteria and standards.

Student status, therefore, was based on rules already in place, defined in large part by a host of individual educational institutions. However, that status did not remain fixed; veterans transformed it considerably. GIs changed their own life-prospects when soldiers of working-class families had opportunities to go to college (and beyond) they never thought possible.[56] These soldiers became members of the middle class, giving their own children and the children of lower-income families across America the ability to also extend their education. The GI Bill essentially democratized higher education. Leading college presidents and deans not only praised the work ethic and maturity of veterans, but also, based on their experience with the GI Bill, began to question what accessibility of universities for an even broader population might mean. The Reverend Edward J. O'Donnell, president of Marquette University, noted, "if the economic barriers were removed, many students who would not otherwise be able to attend college could do so with profit."[57] The GI Bill broke down the barriers to college for working- and middle-class Americans as well as "ethnic, racial, and religious groups that had previously had little hope of such opportunities."[58]

The government, for its part, relied on the GI Bill to take care of returning soldiers. For all intents and purposes, the GI Bill's education provisions were enacted to ease the transition to peacetime. Yet, the bill had lasting effects. It forever connected military service and higher education. Even today, the Army enlists new recruits with the promise of a college education. In addition to the direct relationships it fostered between the state and its citizens, the GI Bill also relied on statuses of "veteran" and "student" that were taken from existing models and modified in the process. In this regard, one's status as a US citizen mattered less than one's status as a "veteran" and "student." Far from being given, these statuses were defined and re-defined by the VA, American Legion, Congress, and scores of colleges and universities across the nation.

Transforming status categories and relations

Many scholars have looked at how policies and programs put in place by the federal government differ. They have found that there are two tiers of welfare. Programs for advantaged categories are designed to give beneficiaries more autonomy and are generally seen as "earned," while programs for disadvantaged categories are paternalistic and seen as "handouts." There are also differences between those programs that are governmental and those that are provided through more indirect means, such as employer-provided health and retirement benefits. Although we could study the origins and development of these programs, we need to think more specifically about how they shape our very notion of citizenship. Governance highlights how social relationships undergird social-welfare provision in the United States and how the use of those relationships for governmental purposes transforms them.

When employers are encouraged to provide benefits to their workers, it has an effect on who gets health insurance as well as on the willingness of Americans to support the public provision of such benefits.[59] But it also transforms the employer–employee relationship. Once employer-provided benefits were in place, employment itself was re-created. Citizens were inextricably linked to the state through a host of social relationships rather than a universal notion of citizenship. Social-welfare provision in the United States has not been defined by citizenship—where citizens receive guaranteed healthcare—but by one's status as a worker. Furthermore, prior to employer-provided healthcare, *other* institutions, individuals, and relationships were called on to do this work.

Prior to employer-provided healthcare, fraternal organizations provided such assistance as life insurance, "cash payments to compensate for income from working days lost and the care of a doctor. Some societies ... founded tuberculosis sanitariums, specialist clinics, and hospitals."[60] The level of service, however, varied considerably and individual organizations were often segregated on the basis of race, sex, and class. For most Americans, membership in a fraternal organization was the defining relationship for receiving healthcare benefits. Because blacks were prohibited from white organizations, and women from men's organizations, the organizations— whether white or black or men's or women's—themselves became predicated on race and sex, reinforcing those differences through different roles and rituals, and, in the process, often providing aid for people excluded from the public sphere.[61] Though the members of fraternal organizations were overwhelmingly workers, employer-provided health insurance nonetheless displaced "membership" in a voluntary organization for "employment" in a corporation or business as the criterion for receiving such benefits.

Employer-provided healthcare has altered the relationship between employers and employees, ratcheting up the responsibilities for both parties. Though government policies encourage healthcare (for example, through favorable tax incentives), private companies must determine which employees will be covered, what they will provide employees, and with which health insurance organization they will contract. Employer-provided healthcare places a burden on companies and their human resource management for funding and administering such programs. It also places a burden on employees in two ways. First, like their employers, employees are feeling the rising costs of healthcare. The Department of Health and Human Services estimates that nationwide healthcare expenditures have grown from $27.6 billion in 1960 to $2.2 trillion in 2007—in constant dollars a 508 per cent increase—overwhelming private business, governments, and families who shoulder the costs.[62] But even though everyone is feeling the pinch of increasing healthcare premiums, employees are picking up a growing share of the tab. Over the past twenty years, the ratio of employer to employee contributions to private healthcare costs (where equal contributions would be "1") has steadily decreased from 1.92 in 1987 to 1.67 in 2007.[63] Second, in addition to the costs involved, employer-provided healthcare has turned employees into a type of secondary provider for their families. Private health insurance in the United States covers not only a particular employee, but also his/her spouse and dependents as well. Just as private companies must administer and fund health benefits for their employees, employees are responsible for administering and paying for the health benefits of their families. To give a sense of the extensiveness of this type of secondary provision, 54 per cent of all children under six years old are covered through "private insurance obtained in the workplace."[64] Clearly, youth are ineligible for workplace benefits *except* through their parents or guardians. The development of employer-provided healthcare, as opposed to universal government care or expanded fraternal organization coverage, has essentially indentured employees, especially those with families, to their employer for continued healthcare benefits.

Employer-provided healthcare has also altered government healthcare. The federal government has relied on the status of worker to limit government provision strictly to "non-workers" and to identify and provide for "non-working" populations. The healthcare reform bill passed in 2010 promises to further expand the role of employers in healthcare provision. In its healthcare policy and through its tax code, the federal government defines a classificatory framework for "employees" (the recipients of private, non-taxable healthcare benefits), "elderly" (recipients of Medicare), "poor" (recipients of Medicaid), "disabled" (recipients of Social Security Disability Insurance), "children" (State Children's Health Insurance Program), and a host of family relations ("spouse," "child," and "dependent"). Tying health benefits to employment has enforced particular jobs and occupations as "work" and marginalized others. While assembly line employees at General Motors and supervisors at General Electric receive wage compensation and health benefits, scores of agricultural workers and domestic aids receive none in return for their labor. In providing health benefits on two tiers, the government both reinforces particular forms of employment as "work" and defines one's citizenship through a host of *other* relationships, from income level to family status.

Governance requires thinking about the organization through which one receives social-welfare provision, even if that organization is non-governmental. Healthcare provision in the United States relied initially on "membership" in fraternal organizations and later on "employment" in particular kinds of companies. Governance also entails following the "lines" or the relationships and statuses that make such provision possible. In regard to healthcare, the federal government has used employee status to subsidize healthcare provision through the tax code and other types of incentives, and to define public provision for non-workers, especially the "elderly," "needy," and "disabled." These various forms of provision make healthcare available to a broad segment of the population but they also transform the relationships on which they are built.

Conclusion

When we think about how citizens are included or excluded in the polity, we often measure whether their voices are heard in the public-policy process and whether they are eligible for particular programs and types of assistance. This way of thinking about citizenship is important for identifying inequality and working to change it. But if we want to know more about how governing works and the consequences for citizenship when governing relies on our "personal" relationships, we must also think about how citizens are called on to carry out the work of government.

When we do, we can identify the institutions that are important in making government operate, and not only those defined as governmental, such as the federal agencies important in formulating obesity policy, but also those that are explicitly non-federal or nongovernmental, such as medical associations, schools, and parents. We can then understand the range of institutions that are employed to create citizens, such as the philanthropic societies and religious organizations that the federal government used to make Native Americans citizens. Furthermore, we can see how citizenship relies on status categories policymakers "borrow" from other institutions. In the case of the GI Bill, the American Legion defined "veterans" and schools and universities defined "students." Finally, we can identify how status categories in federal policy transform our "personal" relationships, as when the provision of healthcare gives new weight to the employer–employee relationship.

Because government relies on these status categories to enlist citizens to do its work, studies of citizenship should make sense of differentiated citizenship. The lens of governance helps us to see why it is not so important to get rid of those categories as to be attentive to what happens when someone is denied access to a differentiated status, such as when the state denies the right of marriage to homosexual couples. A person who is not able to be recognized as a wife or father or as a head of household because of the denial of same-sex marriage is not only losing rights and recognition; that individual will also not be enlisted by government when it decides to make use of that status category. Hence, the citizen is missing out on both the privileges and obligations of citizenship as an administrator of government policy, in addition to whatever material losses his/her dependents may incur. On the other hand, the experiences of the disabled worker or Native American point to the possibilities of resisting and reshaping existing categories. The politics of citizenship is happening when citizens are singled out in a particular status and are doing the work of government. A project of equality should ensure that everyone is entitled to do that work.

Notes

1 See Adam Nagourney, "Political Shifts on Gay Rights are Lagging Behind Culture," *New York Times*, June 28, 2009.
2 See John Locke, *Two Treatises of Government*, ed. Peter Laslett (Cambridge, UK: Cambridge University Press, 1988).
3 For these other conceptions of citizenship, see Jean Bethke Elshtain, "Antigone's Daughters: Reflections on Female Identity and the State," *Democracy* 2 (1982): 45–59; James Fishkin, *Democracy and Deliberation: New Directions for Democratic Reform* (New Haven, CT: Yale University Press, 1991); Kathleen B. Jones, "Citizenship in a Woman-Friendly Polity," *Signs* 15, no. 4 (1990): 781–812; Will Kymlicka, *Multicultural Citizenship: A Liberal Theory of Minority Rights* (Oxford, UK: Oxford University Press, 1995); Jane Mansbridge, *Beyond Adversary Democracy* (Chicago: University of Chicago Press, 1983); Iris Marion Young, *Justice and the Politics of Difference* (Princeton: Princeton University Press, 1990).
4 See T. H. Marshall, *Citizenship and Social Class* (Cambridge, UK: Cambridge University Press, 1950).
5 For this empirical work, see Scott Althaus, *Collective Preferences in Democratic Politics: Opinion Surveys and the Will of the People* (New York: Cambridge University Press, 2003); R. Douglas Arnold, *The Logic of Congressional Action* (New Haven, CT: Yale University Press, 1990); Walter Dean Burnham, *Critical Elections and the Mainsprings of American Politics* (New York: Norton, 1970); Martin Gilens, "Political Ignorance and Collective Policy Preferences," *American Political Science Review* 95, no. 2 (2001): 379–96; Kenneth M. Goldstein, *Interest Groups, Lobbying, and Participation in America* (Cambridge, UK: Cambridge University Press, 1999); Gary Jacobson, *Politics of Congressional Elections* (New York: Longman, 2003); Earl Latham, "The Group Basis of Politics: Notes for a Theory," *American Political Science Review* 46, no. 2 (1952): 376–97; David R. Mayhew, *Congress: The Electoral Connection* (New Haven, CT: Yale University Press, 1974); Mancur Olson, *The Logic of Collective Action: Public Goods and the Theory of Groups* (Cambridge, MA: Harvard University Press, 1965); Benjamin Page and Ian Shapiro,

The Rational Public: Fifty Years of Trends in Americans' Policy Preferences (Chicago: University of Chicago Press, 1992); E. E. Schattschneider, *Party Government* (New York: Farrar & Rinehart, 1942); John R. Zaller, *The Nature and Origins of Mass Opinion* (New York: Cambridge University Press, 1992).

6 See Robert C. Lieberman, "Race, Institutions, and the Administration of Social Policy," *Social Science History* 19 (1995): 511–42; Suzanne Mettler, *Dividing Citizens: Gender and Federalism in New Deal Public Policy* (Ithaca, NY: Cornell University Press, 1998); Rogers Smith, *Civic Ideals: Conflicting Visions of Citizenship in U.S. History* (New Haven, CT: Yale University Press, 1997).

7 See Andrea Louise Campbell, *How Policies Make Citizens: Senior Political Activism and the American Welfare State* (Princeton, NJ: Princeton University Press, 2003); Suzanne Mettler, *Soldiers to Citizens: The GI Bill and the Making of the Greatest Generation* (New York: Oxford University Press, 2005); Joe Soss, "Lessons of Welfare: Policy Design, Political Learning, and Political Action," *American Political Science Review* 93, no. 2 (1999): 363–80.

8 See Suzanne Mettler and Andrew Milstein, "American Political Development from Citizens' Perspective: Tracking Federal Government's Presence in Individual Lives over Time," *Studies in American Political Development* 21 (2007): 125.

9 See Julie Novkov, *Racial Union: Law, Intimacy, and the White State in Alabama, 1865–1954* (Ann Arbor: University of Michigan Press, 2008), 6; Gretchen Ritter, *The Constitution as Social Design: Gender and Civic Membership in the American Constitutional Order* (Stanford, CA: Stanford University Press, 2006); Priscilla Yamin, "The Search for Marital Order: Civic Membership and the Politics of Marriage in the Progressive Era," *Polity* 41, no. 1 (2009): 86–112.

10 See Anne Schneider and Helen Ingram, "Social Construction of Target Populations: Implications for Politics and Policy," *American Political Science Review* 87, no. 2 (1993): 334–47.

11 See Gerald Garvey, *Facing the Bureaucracy: Living and Dying in a Public Agency* (San Francisco: Jossey-Bass, 1993); Donald F. Kettl, *Sharing Power: Public Governance and Private Markets* (Washington: Brookings Institution, 1993); Laurence E. Lynn, Carolyn J. Heinrich, and Carolyn J. Hill, *Improving Governance: A New Logic for Empirical Research* (Washington: Georgetown University Press, 2001); James G. March and Johan P. Olsen, *Democratic Governance* (New York: Free Press, 1995); Lester M. Salamon, "The New Governance and the Tools of Public Action: An Introduction," in *The Tools of Government: A Guide to New Governance*, ed. Lester M Salamon (New York: Oxford University Press, 2002), 1–47; Lester M. Salamon, "Rethinking Public Management: Third-Party Government and the Changing Forms of Government Action," *Public Policy* 29, no. 3 (1981): 255–75.

12 See Salamon, "New Governance," 3.

13 See Laurence E. Lynn, Carolyn J. Heinrich, and Carolyn J. Hill, "Studying Governance and Public Management: Challenges and Prospects," *Journal of Public Administration Research and Theory* 10, no. 2 (2000): 235.

14 See Brian Balogh, *A Government out of Sight: The Mystery of National Authority in Nineteenth-Century America* (New York: Cambridge University Press, 2009).

15 See Donald F. Kettl, "The Transformation of Governance: Globalization, Devolution, and the Role of Government," *Public Administration Review* 60, no. 6 (2000): 488–97. Unlike much of the "new governance" literature, we believe that the federal government has always relied on nongovernmental actors to achieve its objectives. We borrow from public administration the lens that allows us to see the resources government marshals through time by different organizational structures. We break with public administration scholars in that our analysis: 1) does not make normative claims about the desirability of such provisions; 2) includes a much broader range of institutions; and 3) illuminates rather than hides questions of power.

16 See Patricia Strach and Kathleen Sullivan, "The State's Relations: What the Institution of Family Tells Us about Governance," *Political Research Quarterly* (forthcoming).

17 See Marshall, *Citizenship and Social Class*, 18.

18 See Smith, *Civic Ideals*.

19 See Anne Schneider and Helen Ingram, "Behavioral Assumptions of Policy Tools," *Journal of Politics* 52, no. 2 (1990): 510–29.

20 See Ruth O'Brien, *Bodies in Revolt: Gender, Disability, and a Workplace Ethic of Care* (New York: Routledge, 2005), 93–102.

21 See Michel Foucault, "Governmentality," in *The Foucault Effect: Studies in Governmentality*, eds Graham Burchell, Colin Gordon, and Peter Miller (Chicago: University of Chicago Press, 1991), 100.

22 See Michel Foucault, *Discipline and Punish: The Birth of the Prison* (New York: Vintage, 1995).

23 See Carole Pateman, *The Sexual Contract* (Stanford, CA: Stanford University Press, 1988).

24 See Patricia Strach, *All in the Family: The Private Roots of American Public Policy* (Palo Alto, CA: Stanford University Press, 2007); Kathleen Sullivan, *Constitutional Context: Women and Rights Discourse in Nineteenth-Century America* (Baltimore: Johns Hopkins University Press, 2007).

25 See Ruth O'Brien, *Crippled Justice: The History of Modern Disability Policy in the Workplace* (Chicago: University of Chicago Press, 2001), 112. The Roth chapter in this volume also explores this theme.

26 See O'Brien, *Crippled Justice*, 114.

27 See Paul Apostilidis, "Hegemony and Hamburger: Migration Narratives and Democratic Unionism among Mexican Meatpackers in the US West," *Political Research Quarterly* 58, no. 4 (2005): 647–58.

28 See Ritter, *The Constitution as Social Design*, 310–12.

29 See Jacques Donzelot, *The Policing of Families* (Baltimore: Johns Hopkins University Press, 1977), 18.

30 See Donzelot, *Policing of Families*, 45.

31 See Donzelot, *Policing of Families*, 24.

32 See Foucault, "Governmentality," 92.

33 See Martha Minow, "Outsourcing Power: Privatizing Military Efforts and the Risks to Accountability, Professionalism, and Democracy," in *Government by Contract: Outsourcing and American Democracy*, eds Jody Freeman and Martha Minow (Cambridge, MA: Harvard University Press, 2009), 110–27; Paul R. Verkuil, "Outsourcing and the Duty to Govern," in *Government by Contract*, 310–34; Laura A. Dickinson, "Public Values/ Private Contract," in *Government by Contract*, 336; Gillian Metzger, "Private Delegations, Due Process, and the Duty to Supervise," in *Government by Contract*, 335–62.

34 See Dickinson, "Public Values/Private Contract," 336.

35 See Rogan Kersh and James Morone, "How the Personal Becomes Political: Prohibitions, Public Health, and Obesity," *Studies in American Political Development* 16, no. 2 (October 2002): 162–75; Rogan Kersh and James Morone, "The Politics of Obesity: Seven Steps to Government Action," *Health Affairs* 21, no. 6 (November/December 2002): 142–53.

36 See Kersh and Morone, "How the Personal Becomes Political," 172.

37 See Donzelot, *Policing of Families*, 24.

38 See Jonathan Simon, *Governing through Crime: How the War on Crime Transformed American Democracy and Created a Culture of Fear* (New York: Oxford, 2007), 77.

39 See Kevin Bruyneel, *The Third Space of Sovereignty* (Minneapolis: University of Minnesota Press, 2007).

40 See Bruyneel, *Third Space of Sovereignty*, 20.

41 See Brian Dippie, *The Vanishing American: White Attitudes and U.S. Indian Policy* (Lawrence: University Press of Kansas, 1982), 144.

42 See Francis Paul Prucha, *The Great Father: The United States Government and American Indians* (Lincoln: University of Nebraska Press, 1984), 609.

43 See Merrill E. Gates, "Land and Law as Agents in Educating the Indians," in *Americanizing the American Indian, Writings by the "Friends of the Indian," 1800–1900*, ed. Francis Paul Prucha (Cambridge, MA: Harvard University Press, 1973), 56; quoted in Robert B. Porter, "The Demise of the Ongwehoweh and the Rise of the Native Americans: Redressing the Genocidal Act of Forcing American Citizenship upon Indigenous Peoples," *Harvard Blackletter Journal* 15 (1999): 117.

44 See Robert Keller, *American Protestantism and the United States Indian Policy, 1869–82* (Lincoln: University of Nebraska Press, 1983), 18.

45 See Keller, *American Protestantism*, 154.

46 See Carol Nackenoff, "Constitutionalizing Terms of Inclusion: Friends of the Indian and Citizenship for Native Americans, 1880s–1930s," in *The Supreme Court and American Political Development*, eds Ronald Kahn and Ken I. Kersch (Lawrence: University Press of Kansas, 2006), 366–413.

47 See Prucha, *Great Father*, 619.

48 See Prucha, *Great Father*, 242.

49 See Prucha, *Great Father*, 218. For contemporary uses of criminal law by the state to construct categories of criminals, victims, and administrators, see Simon, *Governing through Crime*.

50 See Prucha, *Great Father*, 693.

51 See Nancy F. Cott, *Public Vows: A History of Marriage and the Nation* (Cambridge, MA: Harvard University Press, 2000), 121.

52 See E. S. Land, "War Shipping Administration Views on Certain Benefits to Seamen," (Washington, 1944), 1045–48.

53 General Frank T. Hines, director of Veterans Affairs, summed up the agency's long-running opposition to aiding "civilians" in a letter to Elmer Thomas (D-OK), chairman of the Senate Committee on Education and Labor. Hines wrote: "Inclusion of any particular group of civilian employees under laws specifically conferring benefits upon persons who served in the active military or naval service of the United States and honorably discharged there from, would constitute a material departure from the long-established policy followed by the Congress of limiting veterans' benefits to those persons who performed active military or naval service." See Frank T. Hines, "Letter to Elmer Thomas, Chairman of the Senate Committee on Education and Labor, November 6, 1943," *Congressional Digest* 23, no. 3 (1944): 90. In testimony before the Senate Committee on Education and Labor, Lieutenant L. J. Calhoun explained that military officials did not oppose funding programs for merchant marines. Rather they opposed providing them benefits as part of the GI Bill. See L. J. Calhoun, "Testimony before the Senate Committee on Education and Labor, December 14, 2003," *Congressional Digest* 23, no. 3 (1944): 96.

54 See "General Accounting Office Report of Survey—Veterans' Education and Training Program" (Washington: General Accounting Office, 1951), 37.

55 See "The Osborn Committee Reports on Post-War Education for Service Men," *Congressional Digest* 23, no. 3 (1944): 70, Franklin D. Roosevelt, "President Roosevelt Urges Aid for Veterans' Education," *Congressional Digest* 23, no. 3 (1944): 69.

56 See Suzanne Mettler, "The Creation of the GI Bill of Rights of 1944: Melding Social and Participatory Citizenship Ideals," *Journal of Policy History* 17, no. 4 (2005): 345–74.

57 See Benjamin Fine, "Educators Praise Their GI Students," *New York Times*, October 11 1949.

58 See Mettler, *Soldiers to Citizens*, 57.

59 See Jacob S. Hacker, *The Divided Welfare State: The Battle over Public and Private Social Benefits in the United States* (Cambridge, UK: Cambridge University Press, 2002).

60 See David T. Beito, *From Mutual Aid to the Welfare State: Fraternal Societies and Social Services, 1890–1967* (Chapel Hill: University of North Carolina Press, 2000).

61 See Theda Skocpol and Jennifer Lynn Oser, "Organization despite Adversity: The Origins and Development of African American Fraternal Associations," *Social Science History*

28 (Fall 2004): 367–437; Bayliss Camp and Orit Kent, "'What a Mighty Power We Can Be': Individual and Collective Identity in African American and White Fraternal Initiation Bonds," *Social Science History* 28 (Fall 2004): 439–83.

62 Authors' analysis of data from: "Health, United States, 2009" (Washington: US Department of Health and Human Services, 2009), Table 123.

63 Authors' analysis of data from "Health, United States, 2009," Table 134.

64 See "Health, United States, 2009," Table 137.

Part II
Politics of exclusion

7 The Micro-politics of Immigration

Local Government Policies of Inclusion and Exclusion

Nadia Rubaii-Barrett

Immigration is widely perceived to be a national or international phenomenon and thus immigration policies are assumed to be the responsibility of national or international actors. Among the many policy realms assigned to local governments, immigration is not generally included. Yet the effects of immigrants, both positive and negative and real and perceived, are on the minds of many local government leaders. And the experience of immigrants, whether they are excluded from or included as part of communities, is largely a function of local policies. Some who study immigration have gone so far as to assert that, contrary to popular perceptions and formal legal responsibilities, "ultimate political control over unwanted migration lies at the municipal, not the national, level."[1]

Elected and appointed officials from cities, counties, towns, and villages across the United States have responded to the challenges and opportunities of immigration with a wide variety of policies. Michael Wishnie refers to this time as a "surge in immigration policy at the local level."[2] A handful of policies—those with vocal supporters or opponents, those interpreted as being extreme in their support of or opposition to immigrants, and those that have generated legal challenges—have received some media coverage. On the whole, however, local government responses have not been the subject of much systematic attention or scholarly research.

An examination of past and present local government responses to immigrants using both a chronological perspective and a cross-sectional snapshot suggests considerable variety across time and place. In the absence of a framework for categorizing and analyzing local government responses to immigration, it is difficult to assess whether there is consistency or significant change over time in the extent to which immigrants are included or excluded by local governments. This chapter provides a brief overview of changing patterns of immigration in the United States and of the long-standing, but often overlooked, history of local government policies regarding immigrants. Existing models are then used as a starting point for developing a three-dimensional model of the micro-politics of immigration. Once presented, the model is applied to a variety of local government policies to illustrate the complexity of examining the concepts of inclusion and exclusion as they relate to immigrants.

Changing patterns of immigration

The United States has a long and contentious history regarding immigration.[3] Although we often speak of waves or phases of immigration, and characterize the earlier waves as less troubling and more easily assimilated, "each phase of immigration has been 'the new immigration' at its time; each has been viewed with alarm; each has been described as certain to deteriorate the physical quality of our people and destroy the standards of living and of citizenship."[4] While most immigrant groups begin their experience fighting against exclusionary pressures in their efforts to be included in American society, once they are included those same groups resist the inclusion of different immigrant populations later on. Each new immigrant group has become the scapegoat for whatever problems society is facing at that time—the problems of industrialization and urbanization in the 1830s and 1840s, the Depression in the 1930s, stagflation in the 1970s, or terrorism since 2001—even if the relationship is spurious.

Immigrant assimilation is a matter of enduring contention, as "some Americans found promise of new vigor and growth in a country composed of diverse ethnic populations, [while] others saw threats to the very core of that nation's heritage in the presence of these strange people."[5] The ongoing internal struggle is captured in a line from President Theodore Roosevelt's 1903 State of the Union address: "We cannot have too much immigration of the right kind, and we should have none at all of the wrong kind." The "wrong kind" of immigration has, at different times in our history, referred to the Chinese, Italians, Hebrews, Poles, Slovaks, Irish, and, more recently, Mexicans and Arabs.[6]

While all immigrants have encountered problems of citizenship, language, lack of experience with democratic politics, and the immediate priority of economic survival, the older waves of immigrants had the slight advantage of more similar languages, religious beliefs, and appearances, as well as a cultural kinship to the nation's Anglo-Saxon Protestant founders, with the exception of Irish Catholics, who were treated as "different" on that basis.[7] The original "old" immigrant groups, those who arrived before 1910, came largely from northwestern parts of Europe. The "new" immigrant groups who arrived between 1910 and the 1930s came from southern, central, and eastern parts of Europe, and were, at the time, considered less desirable and harder to assimilate. They were even more visibly different from the "native stock" and generated a more xenophobic response. Differences in "coloring, physique, customs, and languages aroused new fears that these strangers would be unable to assimilate."[8] This sentiment from the early twentieth century could just as easily be applied to the current wave of immigrants.

We speak about waves of immigration at a national level, but this masks the local variations at the local level. Even in the 1870s, there were noticeable differences in the immigrant populations among cities. Irish immigrants dominated the immigrant populations in cities such as Boston (65 percent) and Philadelphia (54 percent), whereas German immigrants comprised a larger share of the immigrant population in Cincinnati (62 percent), Columbus (52 percent), and St Louis (52 percent). Other cities lacked a single nationality among their immigrant populations; for example, the immigrants in Syracuse, New York, consisted of 38 percent Irish, 36 percent German, and 10 percent from England and Wales.[9]

The United States has experienced sizeable increases in the overall numbers of immigrants. Between 1880 and 1930, 28 million foreign-born people arrived in the country, increasing the total foreign-born population from 6.7 million (9.7 percent) to 14 million (14.7 percent).[10] Legal restrictions on immigration adopted in 1924, the Great Depression, and World War II combined to dramatically cut the number of new foreign arrivals and eventually resulted in noticeable declines in the share of the population comprising foreign-born individuals. More recently, demand for unskilled labor in northern and western cities created a need for additional immigrants. As of 2000, an unprecedented number of immigrants, both legal and illegal, were in the United States. They totaled 34 million people, comprising 12 percent of the nation's population. The number of illegal or undocumented immigrants is of particular concern to some.[11] The United States experienced slight decreases in the influx of new immigrants beginning in 2009 in response to the economic recession, but there was no significant outflow of immigrants. Issues related to the number of immigrants in the country thus remain relevant.

In addition to increases in the sheer numbers of immigrants, the composition of recent immigrant populations also differs from earlier generations. At the start of the twenty-first century, immigrants were arriving in the United States from a broader range of countries, many of whom represent nationalities that differ more visibly from native populations. Recent immigrants also speak a greater number of languages that are more distinct from English.[12] Among the first-wave immigrants to the United States (those arriving before 1880), the continent-of-origin diversity was low. Fully 88 percent of the immigrant population was from Europe, and most were from northwestern European countries. By the year 2000, the European share of immigrants to the United States had dropped to 69 percent, and these were from a larger number of more widely dispersed countries on the continent. A small but growing percentage of immigrants are from Asia, but the most dramatic increases are among immigrants from the Americas.[13]

Immigration scholar Alejandro Portes noted that "[t]he surge of immigration into the United States during the past 30 years has brought a proliferation of languages, and with it fears that the English language might lose its predominance and cultural unity may be undermined."[14] Historically, notions of race were largely based on language, and language barriers continue to present challenges for communities, particularly given that the number of different non-English native languages spoken by immigrants has expanded dramatically.[15] In a study of state government responsiveness to language diversity, the authors found that some states recognized the need to make information available in languages extending well beyond English and Spanish, including, for example, Armenian, Cambodian, French, German, Chinese, Vietnamese, Swedish, Japanese, Arabic, Hindi, Hmong, Tagalog, and Urdu.[16] In a 2006 resolution expressing support for comprehensive immigration reform, the city of Boston, Massachusetts, referred to "more than 140 foreign languages spoken by residents, and more than 33% of the population speaking more than one language at home."[17]

The typical pattern of language usage among immigrants is a rapid shift from monolingual non-English speakers in the first generation to bilingualism in the second generation and monolingual English by the third generation.[18] Contrary to popular perceptions, more recent immigrants are learning English quicker than earlier waves of immigrants. Fewer than one-half (45 percent) of old immigrants spoke English within their first five years in the United States, another 30 percent learned English within the next five years, and more than 90 percent spoke English after 20 years or more in the country. In contrast, almost 80 percent of new immigrants (including Latino immigrants) speak English within their first five years. New immigrants have higher English proficiency after five years than the older immigrants had after ten years.[19] Even immigrants living in the ethnic Cuban, Nicaraguan, and Haitian enclaves of south Florida demonstrate rapid English acquisition.[20] Yet, the perception persists that non-English-speaking immigrants pose a threat to the English language and American culture.[21] While efforts to enact a national law or amend the United States Constitution to declare English the official language have repeatedly failed, several states have adopted such policies and, more recently, local language restrictions have been enacted as well.

A final challenge facing local governments stems from the fact that the increasing numbers of diverse non-English-speaking immigrants coming to the United States are dispersed throughout large- and small-sized communities across the country.[22] Immigrants no longer limit themselves to major metropolitan areas that have served as traditional gateways and instead increasingly settle in southeastern and interior states.[23] Although the largest numbers of immigrants still congregate in large urban centers, with "more than a third of the national total ... located in the Los Angeles and New York metropolitan areas alone, [and] another fifth in Miami, Houston, Chicago, San Francisco, and Boston," a growing number of smaller, more rural communities are also experiencing increased immigration.[24] A major factor in this new pattern of immigrant settlement is the availability of jobs.[25] For these communities even a small increase in immigrants is notable as many are simultaneously experiencing declines in their native populations.

Local governments and immigration

There is an extensive body of literature concerning immigration issues, ranging from studies of global migration patterns to personal narratives. At the international and national levels of analyses, these studies examine the supply and demand or push–pull factors affecting migration patterns, and provide comparative studies of national immigration and border control policies.[26] Within the United States, research has examined the changes in values about immigration and naturalization, and corresponding changes in national immigration policies over time.[27]

The sub-national level of study is more limited and generally takes the form of descriptive case studies of the experiences of a particular immigrant group in a single city or state, or engages in very limited comparisons.[28] At the state level, James Gimpel provided a cross-state comparison of immigration patterns in seven states between 1970 and 1990.[29] Even while categorizing states as high or low in terms of their immigration and internal migration rates, Gimpel acknowledged (and illustrated with maps) the extensive variation in experiences within each state when looking at the county level of analysis.[30]

Except for an occasional reference to specific local communities within the context of ethnic studies or case studies of a particular community, most of the literature neglects local governments. It is well documented, however, that local communities experience immigration differently— economically, socially, and politically—than states or the country as a whole.[31] Repeated studies indicate that immigrants generally pay their way at the national level; that is, they contribute more in taxes and to the economy than they receive in benefits. At the state level, their contribution varies from net gain to net loss depending on the state. Most, but not all, of the studies that have looked at the economic impact of immigrants on local governments have concluded that they require more in expenditures than they provide in revenues.[32]

In sum, "[m]ost of the discussions about immigration theory and policy occur on the national and international level, but immigration's effect actually manifests itself at the local level where residents live and receive services."[33] National governments may control policies regarding the admission and legal status of immigrants, but it is at the local level that policy decisions directly influence the degree of inclusion or exclusion experienced by immigrants. How then have local governments responded to immigrants in their midst? What kinds of policies have they adopted and where do those policies fall along the continuum from inclusion to exclusion? Answering these questions requires both a historical and a cross-sectional examination of local policies.

Local immigration policy

Despite widely held perceptions that immigration is and always has been a national government responsibility, local governments have a long history of establishing and implementing policies regarding immigration. The United States Constitution clearly assigns to the national government the powers to define the terms of naturalization and paths to citizenship. Over the years, Congress has enacted a number of statutes articulating immigration policies and procedures and established agencies to enforce those policies. In recent years, the perception of immigration as a national policy issue has been reinforced by high-profile discussions of immigration reform as part of presidential campaigns and as the repeated subject of proposed legislation in the Congress. Yet, the perception that immigration is primarily a national government function does not accurately reflect the ubiquity and importance of local immigration policies.[34]

The national government was largely absent from the immigration policy arena in the early years of the republic. It did not get involved in regulating immigration until 1875, when Congress targeted criminals and prostitutes for exclusion. Then, in 1882, Congress enacted the first in a series of Chinese exclusion bills. Prior to that time, there was significant activity on the local and state levels. State and local policies date back to a 1658 order from New Plymouth regulating immigration and include a multitude of policies adopted by New York and other port cities over the next two centuries.[35] When the national government did get involved, whether in the form of restrictions on certain populations, literacy tests, quota systems, elaborate systems of preferences, or employer sanctions, it used a "police power" model that drew largely upon the experiences and policies of local and state governments.[36] Despite the passage of major immigration laws in 1986, 1990, and 1996, there has been "no substantial policy changes concerning immigrant volume, composition and incorporation" at the national level, and talk of reform continues.[37]

National immigration and naturalization laws serve a basic gatekeeping function. They determine who shall or shall not be allowed legal entry into the United States and who shall or shall not be allowed to become a citizen. But, without examining local policies, we can not have a full understanding of the reception of immigrants and their incentives or abilities to assimilate.[38] As local communities experience different rates of ethnic change, they will respond differently in what they expect the national government to do regarding immigration.[39] As they have in the past, they will also fill any perceived void in national immigration policies.

Over time, some localities have steadfastly resisted the influx of immigrants, others have been passive receivers of immigrant populations, and still others have competed to appeal to potential settlers. The number of local governments that have recently adopted policies directed at immigrants has increased as has the variety of strategies they have employed. The pro-immigrant organization, Fair Immigration Reform Movement (FAIR), maintains a list of recent local ordinances, labeling them as either pro-immigrant or anti-immigrant and indicating whether they focus on housing, employment, language, government services, police enforcement, or some combination of the above.[40] As of 2010, more than 100 local jurisdictions appear on the list, with more than three-quarters identified as having passed or considering an anti-immigrant ordinance of some sort, usually with a particular focus (language or employment, for example). The pro-immigrant ordinances, while fewer in number, are generally more comprehensive in scope. The local policies range from fines, fees, literacy tests, or language requirements imposed on immigrants, stringent enforcement of criminal justice, employment, housing, zoning, solicitation, and other policies to either protect immigrants from the unscrupulous or to target them as troublemakers, and, finally, the provision of services and benefits to make immigrants feel more welcome and to ease the process of assimilation. This array of local policies clearly reflects the fact that political inclusion and exclusion exist along a continuum.

Given the range of local responses, it is unclear whether any consistent factors are at play over time and across jurisdictions. A 2010 study purports to explain local opposition to immigrants using a "politicized places" model that attributes opposition to sudden demographic changes occurring at the same time as a rise in national anti-immigrant rhetoric.[41] This model is intuitively compelling but limited in applicability because it neglects to include the localities that adopted pro-immigrant policies under the same conditions. The "politicized places" model then does not provide a model for understanding *different* local responses to immigration.

A framework for the micro-politics of immigration

A framework for understanding different local responses to immigration would not only help us understand past and current policies but also anticipate future ones. Two existing models offer starting points for the development of this more comprehensive model.

There is widespread agreement that the characteristics of settler societies are important for integration.[42] The speed of immigrant absorption depends on many factors, including language, religion, and race, and the contexts of reception are important as well. According to Portes and Borocz, host societies may respond in one of three ways.[43] The first option effectively *handicaps* immigrants or excludes them from the community. Government officials take a dim view of immigrants and attempt to reduce or suppress their influx. As a result, patterns of settlement are precarious and economic mobility is blocked. A second option is a more *neutral* response in which immigration is permitted or tolerated but not actively encouraged. In this case, government officials hold no strong stereotypes of immigrants and allow them to freely compete with the native-born. The third option is to *advantage* and include immigrants through active legal as well as material assistance from the host government. While some local government responses to immigration fit neatly into the Portes and Borocz model, others are difficult to categorize. For example, is stringent enforcement of limits on occupancy of rental units intended to handicap immigrants, treat them neutrally, or protect (read, advantage) them? The Portes and Borocz model provides a useful starting point for discussion, but it is limited by its one-dimensional approach.

Although not developed explicitly in reference to immigration, Thomas Sinclair's model provides some additional factors to consider.[44] Focusing on the challenges that face local communities and governments when new residents ("strangers") arrive, Sinclair arrayed community responses along a single dimension consisting of three options, defense, retreat, or integration. The *defense* approach attempts to keep strangers from moving in or staying, or forces them to conform to existing values and beliefs. *Retreat* redefines boundaries to exclude areas where newcomers congregate or live, changing the physical dimensions of the community to keep it separate from the newcomers. *Integration* redefines social relationships to include strangers as members of the community. Taken alone, these options roughly correspond to the ones Portes and Borocz presented more than a decade earlier. Sinclair's real contribution lay in the typology of communities he developed based on a consideration of two dimensions, degree of institutional attachment to community and degree of institutional attachment to government. He labeled cities with high attachment for both "symbiotic," with high attachment to community and low attachment to government "enclave," with high attachment to government and low attachment to community "pluralistic," and with low attachment to both "transient." He posited that the response to strangers both affects and is affected by the type of community. The reaction of a community to strangers, in the form of defense, retreat, or integration, is driven by whether the community is symbiotic, enclave, pluralistic, or transient but the influx of strangers may also lead to changes in the type of community. Transient communities may have an easier time adjusting to the influx of strangers precisely because they lack strong attachments with the government or community. In contrast, symbiotic communities may have a defensive or retreating response in an effort to protect their existing relationships.

Sinclair reinforces the value of examining local government responses. He asserts that governments have the responsibility to respond to the needs of all their citizens, whereas other community institutions have some choice about whether to help assimilate strangers into the community.

Governments cannot change beliefs, but they can structure policies to provide incentives and inducements to change behavior. When governments target strangers, they send a message that the strangers must conform; when they legitimize the position of strangers, they send a message that the community needs to adjust. Sinclair's model adds to our understanding of local government responses to immigration in that it helps explain why some communities may react differently to seemingly similar immigration experiences as well as why policies may change over time. The model falls short, however, in that it ultimately resorts back to a single dimension of response categories.

In the context of local government responses to immigration, the notion of three options arrayed along a single dimension does not adequately address the factors that have been or might be used by local governments in determining what action, if any, to take. The existing dimensions also limit our ability to assess the full level of inclusion or exclusion applied to immigrant populations by local governments in the United States. A more comprehensive model would include three separate, but interrelated, dimensions: 1) attitudes about immigrants; 2) theories of assimilation; and 3) perceived congruence between local and national interests.

The first dimension of this model addresses the local community's attitudes about immigrants. This dimension is similar to the ones described above, but differs in that it extends beyond a simple three-point negative–neutral–positive range to encompass six, more nuanced, points. It also focuses on underlying attitudes as contributing factors toward community actions rather than synonymous with those actions. The most extreme negative view of immigrants is one that characterizes them as a threat to the community's way of life. Included in this view are perceptions of immigrants as dangerous criminals who threaten public safety, people whose different culture threatens community values, and people whose different languages threaten the primacy of the English language. A slightly less hostile view of immigrants, although still largely negative, portrays them as a drain on public resources. They are not necessarily evil, but they do impose an economic cost on the community. The third option is neutrality, in which the community articulates no clear opinion of immigrants. A fourth option is to characterize immigrants as actual or potential victims in need of protection from harm and abuse. This view is neither a strictly negative nor positive perception but it is also not neutral. A somewhat more positive view of immigrants looks at them as useful in serving a larger community interest. They may be perceived as an abundant and cheap source of needed labor or as potential voters or supporters. This view is not entirely positive because it holds the potential for the exploitation of immigrants for the benefit of others. The final and most positive position on this first dimension represents the idea that immigrants are important, deserving, and contributing members of the community whose diversity will strengthen it.

The complex views people have about immigrants are not fully captured by a simple attitudinal dimension, even if it is expanded beyond the earlier positive–neutral–negative options. Language policies are particularly difficult to categorize using a single dimension. In addition to representing a generally positive or negative view of immigrants, local government responses also reflect underlying views regarding the extent to which and the manner in which immigrant populations can and should assimilate into the local community. The second dimension thus considers different theories of assimilation. Regardless of whether a local community holds a positive or negative view of immigrants, local government responses reflect underlying (or sometimes explicit) assumptions about the process by which assimilation can or should occur. I have identified four potential positions along this dimension. At the extreme negative position are those communities that reject outright the notion that assimilation is possible or desirable for the current group of immigrants. A second possibility is to assume a "tough love" position; that is, assimilation can only occur when immigrants are forced to adopt the customs and language of the locality. A third option is to expect assimilation to occur naturally over time, requiring no explicit action other than patience. Finally, it is possible that assimilation could occur through mutual accommodation in which immigrants are integrated into the community and both new immigrants and longer-term residents adjust their behaviors to each other.

Obviously, local governments in the United States do not operate in a vacuum. They are part of a federal system with evolving patterns of intergovernmental relations. Taking a cue from Sinclair, I contend that local government responses must also be evaluated in terms of the actions of another actor, in this case the national government. Early local government policies regarding immigration were made in the absence of national law; more recent actions have occurred within the context of extensive national law on immigration. Local governments can not help but respond to the actions or inactions of the national government. The third and final dimension of this model represents the degree to which local officials perceive that their local interests coincide with the interests of the national government and are adequately addressed by national policy. On this dimension, I suggest four options: 1) the interests of the local and national government clearly coincide but the local government sees the need for more extensive or effective implementation and enforcement; 2) the interests of the local and national governments coincide and the local government is willing to merely assist the national government; 3) the local government does not indicate whether its interests coincide with those of the national government or not; or 4) the local government perceives distinct and conflicting interests. The first option would be characterized by local government policies that are similar to national policies but which extend beyond the scope of those policies and provide for extensive local enforcement. Under the second option, we would expect the local government to

Table 7.1 Three dimensions of local government response to immigrants

Dimension 1: attitudes about immigrants	*Dimension 2: theory of assimilation*	*Dimension 3: congruence of local and national interests*
Threat to community	Not possible or desired	Local interests extend beyond national interests
Drain on public resources	Requires tough love	Local and national interests coincide
Neutral	Occurs naturally with the passage of time	No indication/unclear
In need of protection	Requires mutual accommodation	Local and national interests conflict
Useful		
Contributors to community		

facilitate and actively assist in the enforcement of national policies. The third option would be associated with a passive local government on the issue of immigration or one that focuses primarily on the use of traditional local powers. The fourth option would warrant distinct local policy action to circumvent or counter national policy. How the position of a local government on this congruence dimension translates into policy depends on the nature of the national policies in place at a particular point in time. It should be noted that it is also possible for communities to experience inconsistencies between local and state policies. In 2010, for example, the state of Arizona took steps to override immigrant-friendly local policies. Unlike the ubiquity of national immigration policy, state policies are, however, more of the exception than the rule and thus are not included in the model.

Collectively, the three dimensions of attitudes about immigrants, theories of assimilation, and congruence of local and national interests provide a contextual framework for understanding the micro-politics of immigration. Table 7.1 summarizes this framework.

Clearly, where a local government falls on any of the three dimensions is a function of unique situational factors. The model does not address those unique factors, but instead provides a means by which local policies can be understood in relation to one another. In the following section, I apply the model to the real world.

Applying the model

To appreciate the utility of this three-dimensional model, I categorize a variety of past and current local government responses to immigration. I also explain how the model contributes to our ability to categorize and better understand those responses. In this way, we can assess whether local governments have significantly changed the manner in which they respond to immigrants, or if responses that appear to be different are, in fact, different manifestations of the same underlying factors.

Taxes, fees, and intergovernmental reimbursements

As already stated, the earliest immigration policies were adopted by cities and states receiving immigrants through their ports. Cities developed laws to protect their communities from the potential burdens of foreigners who might become a drain on public resources. Early limitations were based primarily on individual characteristics rather than group characteristics. Governments attempted to bar entry to those few "lunatics, idiots, the lame or infirm, paupers or indigents" who were likely to become a burden on society.[45] Poor laws, head taxes, and bonding were among the most common techniques. These policies initially applied to only those deemed likely to become public charges but were later expanded to apply to all immigrants as a means of generating revenue.[46] They reflected a view of immigrants as a potential drain on public resources who were likely to assimilate only through the passage of time. They also reflected perceptions on the part of local government officials that local and national interests were distinct, given that the federal government had not yet recognized a need to regulate immigration. The intergovernmental aspects of immigration were apparent at these early times as well, as localities, most notably New York, sought state support for the foreign poor. The formation of a coalition of counties along the United States–Mexico border to lobby collectively for federal reimbursement of their immigration expenses is a more recent manifestation of this view of immigrants. These counties differ significantly in their receptivity to immigrants, particularly undocumented or illegal immigrants, but are in agreement that the federal government should reimburse them for the costs associated with serving a population that is supposedly a federal government responsibility.[47]

Competition for immigrants

When local governments began to perceive immigrants less as a drain on resources and more as useful workers in their local economies, policies shifted accordingly and competition for immigrants increased. In earlier periods, New Jersey was able to entice vessels to drop foreigners at their ports to avoid the taxes imposed in nearby New York City.[48] More recently, an aggressive recruitment strategy has been utilized by the city of Schenectady, New York. The mayor is actively recruiting Guyanese immigrants to move from New York City to Schenectady as part of an economic revitalization strategy. More than 2000 Guyanese people have responded and moved to this city of 61,000, buying up run-down properties, working in blue-collar jobs, and developing new restaurants and shops.[49] In this case, the local government recognizes the value of immigrant workers in supporting the local economy, especially in the context of slowing rates of native population growth.

Neutrality

Whether they take explicit action or not, local governments across the country are feeling the effects of immigration. More than 3000 Somali immigrants have settled in Lewiston, Maine, attracted by good schools, low crime rates, and inexpensive housing.[50] This development has generated some conflict within the community, with rallies and counter-demonstrations organized by both opponents and supporters. In this case, the local government has taken a position of neutrality, allowing immigrants to assimilate over time, and not directly challenging or supporting national policy.

Political bosses and party machines

Local responses to earlier waves of immigrants were also characterized by inclusion in the community through local "political bosses" and "party machines."[51] The political boss and party machine approaches to immigration reflected a shift to a more utilitarian view of immigrants, while maintaining separate local and national interests, and the expectation that assimilation would occur over time with the assistance of such non-governmental institutions as churches, community groups, civic associations, mutual-aid societies, and settlement houses.

Day labor centers

A controversial local strategy that has received considerable media attention is the construction, funding, and operation of day labor centers or hiring halls. Across the United States, roughly 120,000 laborers gather at more than 400 locations "seeking work as construction workers, landscapers, painters, roofers, and drywall installers."[52] Day labor centers provide a central location for workers, often undocumented, to link with employers (often contractors or homeowners) for short-term employment. Los Angeles opened the first such center in 1989 and other cities have followed suit.[53] The actions of the town of Herndon and Fairfax County, Virginia, to fund such a center have been challenged in court.[54] Some proponents of day labor centers portray the policy in terms of the value of immigrant workers to the local economy; others suggest it is to minimize the potential for exploitation by employers and the risk of unsafe working conditions. This approach clearly challenges national policy and implies that immigrants can assimilate on their own time.

Local identification cards

Only slightly less controversial is the decision by some local governments to provide immigrants, both legal and illegal, with local identification cards. The ID cards are intended to help immigrants assimilate by easing the process of opening bank accounts, renting or purchasing property, using public libraries, and otherwise participating as members of the community. The decision of government officials in New Haven, Connecticut, to provide ID cards may reflect a utilitarian, protective, or positive attitude toward immigrants, assumes they are able to assimilate, and challenges national policy. It is also possible that an ID card policy could be used by a local government with a less positive view of immigrants with the intent of using the IDs as a means of more closely monitoring their activities.

Sanctuary and no questions asked

Local sanctuary policies emerged in the 1980s to provide places of refuge for individuals fleeing persecution in war-torn Central America.[55] In their original form, sanctuary policies represented a view of immigrants as victims in need of local government protection. They also reflected distinct local versus national interests as well as a belief that assimilation will occur naturally over time. Sanctuary policies take several forms, but the basic premise is that a local government asserts that federal employees, not city employees, are responsible for the implementation of immigration policy and that the cities will not do the work of the national government in identifying, reporting, or detaining immigrants. Beginning in 1985, Berkeley, San Francisco, and St Paul adopted such resolutions. These laws are interesting because they provide a very different way of looking at the doctrine of preemption.[56] The doctrine of preemption protects federal interests in maintaining exclusive domain over particular policy areas. Historically, it has been used to prohibit state and local governments from restricting the rights of immigrants. However, in the current context, the federal government is actively seeking state and local assistance, and some local leaders are refusing to cooperate. Most legal scholars conclude that federal law does not preempt local ordinances that bar cooperation with the Immigration and Naturalization Service (INS).[57]

The National Immigration Law Center maintains a list of laws, resolutions, and policies instituted across the United States limiting enforcement of immigration laws by local authorities.[58] The list includes fifty-five local governments representing twenty-one states. Police department officials often support such policies, recognizing that the enforcement of national immigration policies alienates potential crime victims, witnesses, or informants who also happen to be illegal immigrants.[59] An executive order issued by the mayor of New York in 2003 protects immigrant access to city services by restricting the inquiry, collection, use, and disclosure of "confidential information," including immigration status.[60] In 2007, Cook County, Illinois, adopted a "Fair and Equal County for Immigrants" resolution to the effect that conditioning county benefits, opportunities, and services, including law enforcement, health services, and translation services, on citizenship or immigrant status "directly contravenes the County's commitment to ensuring fair and equal access for all of its residents."[61]

The motivation for sanctuary or other "don't ask, don't tell" ordinances regarding immigration status is generally to improve community relations and the effective provision of local services. Highstown, New Jersey, provides a case in point. In 2005, Highstown was the scene of a massive federal raid on an apartment complex that resulted in high levels of fear and distrust among immigrants, both legal and illegal, of all public officials and agencies. City officials considered that counterproductive, and recognized the value to the community of the more than 1300 Latin Americans who had settled in the city in recent years. The mayor credited the immigrants for the economic revitalization of the city through their shops, restaurants, and businesses. As a result, the city enacted a no-questions-asked policy on immigration status. Now the city experiences more open lines of communication with the immigrant community, more trust, and more willingness to report and work with police.[62] In contrast to the original sanctuary policies, these more recent policies view immigrants less as victims in need of protection and more as useful members of the community.

Comprehensive immigration reform resolutions

"No questions asked" and other similar policies are often accompanied by local resolutions calling on the national government to enact comprehensive immigration reform that would make it easier for undocumented immigrants to gain permanent status and ultimately citizenship. Like non-cooperation policies, these resolutions tend to view immigrants either as victims or as useful members of the community. They also assume a direct conflict between local priorities and national policies, as well as that assimilation will occur over time.

Department of Homeland Security training and enforcement

In the post 9/11 environment, the national government increased its efforts to obtain local and state assistance in immigration enforcement.[63] In sharp contrast to sanctuary and no-questions-asked ordinances, some local governments are actively cooperating with the federal government on immigration policies. These communities have signed memorandums of understandings (MOUs) with the Department of Homeland Security to receive immigration-related training and to enforce immigration law. They readily inquire about immigration status, report undocumented persons to the federal government, and participate or assist in raids of housing complexes and places of employment where undocumented persons are believed to reside or work. It is apparent that these communities view immigrants as a threat, that they see their local interests as consistent with national policies, and that they do not consider assimilation to be either possible or desirable.

Local crackdowns

Other communities have taken an even more aggressive approach to immigration restriction and not limited themselves to assisting in the implementation of federal policy. In the Dallas suburb of Farmers Branch, the voters adopted a local policy to crack down on illegal immigrants by requiring apartment managers to verify citizenship or legal status or face a fine.[64] Zero tolerance policies in places like Hazelton, Pennsylvania, impose fines on landlords who rent to illegal immigrants, deny licenses to businesses that employ them, and require that city documents be printed only in English.[65] Both Farmers Branch and Hazelton are facing lawsuits, as are other cities that have adopted similar anti-immigration ordinances, such as Valley Park, Missouri, Riverside, New Jersey, and Escondido, California.[66] These cities perceive immigrants as a threat and assimilation as impossible or undesirable. They also recognize similarities in tone between local and national policies but believe the latter are insufficiently or inadequately enforced.

Language policies

Among the local government responses to immigrants, some communities address the issue of language diversity explicitly. Language policies provide a clear illustration of the limits of a single attitudinal dimension, and the importance of the second dimension regarding theories of assimilation. Reminiscent of earlier uses of literacy tests, some local governments have adopted English Only ordinances to force immigrants to learn and use English quickly. Cities pursue this policy primarily by limiting local government publications, meetings, and communications to English. These ordinances represent a clear disconnect between local and national policies, and a "tough love" theory of immigration. They are harder to interpret in terms of the underlying perception of immigrants. In some cases, they are intended to encourage immigrants to assimilate more quickly and thoroughly, thereby increasing their opportunities for success.[67] In other communities, they are intended to keep or drive out non-English speakers. In still other locales, the motivation appears to be purely economic, as a way to minimize the expense of printing information and providing services in multiple languages.[68]

An alternative local response to the issue of language diversity is to assert the language rights of non-English speakers, to encourage the use of multiple languages by both immigrants and natives, and to provide guarantees that services will not be denied on the basis of language skills.[69] Woodburn, Oregon, has developed incentives to attract and reward employees who are bilingual and culturally competent to serve its increasingly diverse population.[70] The Predominant Language Ordinance of El Cenizo, Texas, represents an effort to facilitate greater and more meaningful participation in local government by Spanish speakers. Similarly, the Equal Access Service Ordinance of Oakland, California, states that "it is of paramount importance that all residents regardless of their proficiency in English have access to City programs and services." The population of Stockton, California, is 23 percent Asian and the city has responded with a refugee job placement center for southeast Asian refugees through which residents of Cambodian and Hmong descent have been trained to work as liaisons in the various city departments that serve their communities.[71] Language rights policies and efforts to encourage bilingualism and multilingualism among immigrants and native populations generally assume that everyone in the community will benefit from such policies. People in these communities view immigrants who do not speak English as potential contributors to the community or as potential victims in the absence of such policies. They do not explicitly support or oppose federal policy, but they do suggest that assimilation will occur through a process of mutual accommodation.

Local regulatory authority

Some communities have attempted to address the influx of immigrants through an enforcement crackdown utilizing ordinances already on the books. Local governments have a long-standing and well-recognized role in community safety, and some problems associated with immigration can be addressed through a strict enforcement of criminal laws.[72] Existing land use ordinances, housing and building codes, and policies regarding driver's licenses, taxi licenses, healthcare, vagrancy, solicitation, minimum wage, and employment conditions may not have been designed to regulate immigration but they can be used that way. This approach can be interpreted in several ways. It may reflect a neutral attitude about immigrants, may be designed to indirectly drive out a potential threat, or may be intended to protect immigrants from potential abuse by unscrupulous landlords, employers, or service providers. More stringent police enforcement can be used to target immigrant populations, as in the case of Hazelton, or to protect them from crime, as in the case of Stockton.[73] Similarly, this approach may be premised on the notion that immigrants will assimilate over time or that they require "tough love" to force them to accept local community norms. This approach does not directly support or challenge federal policy so it is unclear whether these communities perceive congruence or conflict between their interests and national interests.

Inclusion

After unsuccessfully trying a strict enforcement policy, Santa Ana shifted to a much more inclusive strategy. City officials adopted a policy requiring all new hires "including police, fire, library, parks, receptionists, and so on" to be bilingual.[74] By this action, the city government sent a powerful message to the community-at-large that the nature of the city had changed, that immigrants were a valuable part of the community, and that mutual accommodation was an expected aspect of assimilation. City officials publicly recognized that "[i]mmigrants feed the local economy by spending money in the multitude of businesses that support the immigrant community. They also buy homes, use public transportation, make cultural and social contributions, and bring people, energy, and economic growth to depressed areas."[75] As a result, the city was able to tackle a wider range of issues without the usual public pushback, realizing lower crime rates, cleaner neighborhoods, and greater community pride.

Table 7.2 summarizes the information presented in this section. It lists the various local responses and their corresponding status on each of the three dimensions. The cells list a key word and the numerical score for each dimension corresponding to the information presented in Table 7.1. Where a local government response can be a result of one of several possible positions on a dimension, all are listed within the cell.

As illustrated in Table 7.2 the attitudinal dimension, which was the only dimension used in earlier models, is the least discriminating of the three dimensions. More than half of the illustrative responses referenced cannot be neatly placed on that dimension. In many instances, local governments can use the same policy to pursue different attitudinal objectives. Policies about inclusion or exclusion are not simple reflections of community attitudes. They represent a much more complex set of factors, requiring multiple dimensions to explain them. The interplay of the attitudinal dimension and the assimilation dimension seems particularly important to explaining local policy variation.

The three-dimensional model also illustrates that local government policies regularly reflect disagreement with national policies. Immigration policy may be perceived as the responsibility of the national government, but local governments have used and continue to use their own policy initiatives to expand on, respond to, counteract, or directly contradict federal mandates. This incongruence suggests that the national government does not always dominate the intergovernmental policy dynamic on immigration. The diversity of local government responses may also help

Table 7.2 A model of the micro-politics of immigration: three dimensions of local government policies

Policy	Dimension 1: attitudes about immigrants	Dimension 2: theory of assimilation	Dimension 3: congruence of local and national interests
Head taxes	Burden (2)	Time (3)	Separate (4)
Political bosses	Useful (5)	Time (3)	Separate (4)
Literacy tests	Burden (2) Neutral (3)	Tough love (2)	No Indication (3)
Sanctuary policies	Victims (4)	Time (3)	Separate (4)
"No questions asked" or "don't ask, don't tell" policies	Victims (4), Useful (5), or Contributors (6)	Time (3)	Separate (4)
Resolutions calling for Comprehensive Immigration Reform & Paths to Citizenship	Victims (4) Useful (5), or Contributors (6)	Time (3)	Separate (4)
Recruitment of Immigrants	Useful (5)	Time (3)	Separate (4)
Day Labor Centers	Victims (4) or Useful (5)	Time (3)	Separate (4)
Local ID Cards	Threat (1), Neutral (3), Victims (4), Useful (5)	Time (3)	Separate (4)
Strict Enforcement of Existing Regulations	Threat (1), Neutral (3) or Victims (4)	Tough Love (2) Time (3)	No Indication (3)
English-Only Policies	Threat (1), Burden (2), Neutral (3)	Tough Love (2)	Separate (4)
Language Rights	Victims (4), Useful (5), or Contributors (6)	Time (3) and Mutual Accommodation (4)	No Indication (3)
Homeland Security Training for Local Officials	Threat (1)	Not Possible (1)	Coincide (2)
Fines for Landlords or Businesses	Threat (1)	Not Possible (1)	More Extensive (1)
Bilingual Employees	Contributors (6)	Mutual Accommodation (4)	Separate (4)
Federal Reimbursement	Burden (2)	Not Possible (1) or Time (3)	Separate (4)
More Inclusive Decision Making	Contributors (6)	Mutual Accommodation (4)	No Indication (3)

explain why Congress has so much difficulty forging a national consensus on this issue and enacting a comprehensive immigration reform bill. In the absence of a national consensus, local governments have acted to fill the void, yet the diversity of local government responses makes a national consensus even more difficult to attain.

Conclusion

Immigration has always presented both challenges and opportunities for local governments. They have responded over time with a range of policies. Increased immigration, wider dispersion of immigrants, and greater language diversity among immigrants brings these types of challenges to a larger number of communities throughout the United States and thus presents an abundant laboratory for research. There has been little systematic study of local immigration policies and prior models were limited by virtue of their reliance on a single dimension. The model presented in this chapter helps provide a framework for examining concepts of inclusion and exclusion as they are reflected in local government responses to immigrant diversity.

At the macro-level, immigration policies address issues of who is granted admission to the country and with what legal status. At the local level, policies determine whether immigrants are effectively excluded from or included in local communities. The micro-politics of immigration reflects a complex set of political, social, and economic factors. The three dimensions of the model—attitudes about immigrants, theories of assimilation, and congruence between local and national interests—combine to create a framework for explaining varying levels of inclusion of immigrants in local communities. Alone, none of the dimensions contributes much to our understanding of the diversity of local government responses to immigration. But when considered together, they provide such a framework. Because of the critical role of local governments in establishing and implementing immigration policy, immigrants cannot be neatly categorized as a group that has been included in or excluded from American society. There has been too much variation across time and space.

Notes

1 See Ivan Light, *Deflecting Immigration: Networks, Markets, and Regulation in Los Angeles* (New York: Russell Sage Foundation, 2006), 13.
2 See Anthony Faiola, "Looking the Other Way on Immigrants," *Washington Post*, April 10, 2007, A1.
3 See Michael LeMay and Elliott R. Barkan, eds, *U.S. Immigration and Naturalization Laws and Issues: A Documentary History* (Westport: Greenwood Press, 1999).
4 See John P. Gavit, *Americans by Choice* (New York: Harper & Brothers, 1992), 197.
5 See Stanley Lieberson, *Ethnic Patterns in American Cities* (New York: The Free Press of Glencoe, 1963), 1.
6 See Claude S. Fischer and Michael Hout, *Century of Difference: How America Changed in the Last One Hundred Years* (New York: Russell Sage Foundation, 2006).
7 See LeMay and Barkan, *Immigration and Naturalization Laws*.
8 See Lieberson, *Ethnic Patterns*, 7; LeMay and Barkan, *Immigration and Naturalization Laws*, xxxii.
9 See Lieberson, *Ethnic Patterns*, 82.

10 See George Gerstle and John H. Mollenkopf, eds, *E Pluribus Unum? Contemporary and Historical Perspectives on Immigrant Political Incorporation* (New York: Russell Sage Foundation, 2001).

11 See Jerry Seper, "Immigration Enforcement Grows Weaker," *Washington Times*, November 24, 2004, A1.

12 See Michael Fix and Jeffrey S. Passel, *Immigration and Immigrants: Setting the Record Straight* (Washington: The Urban Institute, 1994).

13 The Lien chapter in this volume documents both these increases.

14 See Fischer and Hout, *Century of Difference*, 42.

15 See Leigh Culver, "The Impact of New Immigration Patterns on the Provision of Police Services in Midwestern Communities," *Journal of Criminal Justice* 32 (2004): 329–44; Fix and Passel, *Immigration and Immigrants*; Nancy Foner, Ruben G. Rumbaut, and Steven Gold, eds, *Immigration Research for a New Century: Multidisciplinary Perspectives* (New York: Russell Sage Foundation, 2000).

16 See Nadia Rubaii-Barrett and Lois R. Wise, "Language Minorities and the Digital Divide: A Study of State e-Government Accessibility," *Journal of Public Management and Social Policy* 12 (2006): 5–27.

17 See "New Bostonians 2005" (Boston: Boston Redevelopment Authority, 2005), 14; www.cityofboston.gov/newbostonians/pdfs/demo_report_2005.pdf.

18 See Jack Citrin, Beth Reingold, and Evelyn Walters, "The 'Official English' Movement and the Symbolic Politics of Language in the United States," *Western Political Quarterly* 43 (1990): 535–59.

19 See Fischer and Hout, *Century of Difference*.

20 See Alejandro Portes and Richard Schauffler, "Language and the Second Generation: Bilingualism Yesterday and Today," *International Migration Review* 28 (1994): 640–61.

21 See Citrin, Reingold and Walters, "The 'Official English' Movement."

22 See Fix and Passel, *Immigration and Immigrants*.

23 See Paul Vitello, "As Illegal Workers Hit Suburbs, Politicians Scramble to Respond," *New York Times*, October 6, 2005, A1; William H. Frey, *Diversity Spreads Out: Metropolitan Shifts in Hispanic, Asian and Black Populations since 2000* (Washington: Brookings Institution, 2006).

24 See Gerstle and Mollenkopf, *E Pluribus Unum*, 5.

25 See Frey, *Diversity Spreads Out*.

26 See Peter Andreas and Timothy Snyder, eds, *The Wall around the West: State Borders and Immigration Controls in North America and Europe* (Lanham, MD: Rowman & Littlefield, 2000); Wayne A. Cornelius and Marc R. Rosenblum, "Immigration and Politics," working paper 105, University of California, San Diego, 2004; Fischer and Hout, *Century of Difference*; Nancy Foner, *In a New Land: A Comparative View of Immigration* (New York: New York University Press, 2005); Alejandro Portes and Jozsef Borocz, "Contemporary Immigration: Theoretical Perspectives on Its Determinants and Modes of Incorporation," *International Migration Review* 23 (1989): 606–30; Darren M. Scott, Paul A. Coomes, and Alexei I. Izyumov, "The Location Choice of Employment-Based Immigrants among U.S. Metro Areas," *Journal of Regional Science* 45 (2005): 113–45.

27 See Robert Barde and Gustavo J. Bobonis, "Detention at Angel Island: First Empirical Evidence," *Social Science History* 30 (2006): 103–36; A.W. Carlson, "One Century of Foreign Immigration to the United States—1880–1979," *International Migration* 23 (1985): 309–34; Roger Daniels, "Immigration Policy in a Time of War: The United States, 1939–45," *Journal of American Ethnic History* 25 (2006): 107–16; Peter Duignan and Lewis H. Gann, eds, *The Debate in the United States over Immigration* (Stanford, CA: Hoover Institution Press, 1998); Nancy Foner, "The Challenge and Promise of Past–Present Comparisons," *Journal of American Ethnic History* 25 (2006): 143–52; Donna R. Gabaccia and Vicki L. Ruiz, eds, *American Dreaming, Global Realities: Rethinking U.S. Immigration History* (Urbana: University of Illinois Press, 2006); Edward P. Hutchinson, *Legislative History of American Immigration Policy, 1798–1965* (Philadelphia: University

of Pennsylvania Press, 1981); Charles Jaret, "Troubled by Newcomers: Anti-immigrant Attitudes and Action during Two Eras of Mass Immigration to the United States," *Journal of American Ethnic History* 18 (1999): 9–39; Karen J. Leong, "Foreign Policy, National Identity, and Citizenship: The Roosevelt White House and the Expediency of Repeal," *Journal of American Ethnic History* 22 (2003): 3–30; Erika Lee, "Enforcing the Borders: Chinese Exclusion along the US Borders with Canada and Mexico, 1882–1924," *Journal of American History* 89 (2002): 54–86; Edith Lowenstein, *The Alien and Immigration Law: A Study of 1446 Cases Arising under the Immigration and Naturalization Laws of the United States* (Westport, CT: Greenwood Press, 1972); Mae M. Ngai, *Impossible Subjects: Illegal Aliens and the Making of Modern America* (Princeton, NJ: Princeton University Press, 2004); Dorothee Schneider, "Naturalization and United States Citizenship in Two Periods of Mass Migration: 1894–1930, 1965–2000," *Journal of American Ethnic History* 21 (2001): 50–82; Peter H. Schuck, *Citizens, Strangers, and In-Betweens: Essays on Immigration and Citizenship* (Boulder: Westview Press, 1998); Suzanne Shanahan and Susan Olzak, "The Effects of Immigrant Diversity and Ethnic Competition on Collective Conflict in Urban America: An Assessment of Two Moments of Mass Migration, 1869–1924 and 1965–93," *Journal of American Ethnic History* 18 (1999): 40–64.

28 See John Bodnar, "Immigration and Modernization: The Case of Slavic Peasants in Industrial America," *Journal of Social History* 10 (1976): 44–68; Ellen Eisenberg, "Transplanted to the Rose City: The Creation of East European Jewish Community in Portland, Oregon," *Journal of American Ethnic History* 19 (2000): 82–97; John J. Grabowski, "Prospects and Challenges: The Study of Early Turkish Immigration to the United States," *Journal of American Ethnic History* 25 (2005): 85–100; Anita O. Gustafson, "North Park: Building a Swedish Community in Chicago," *Journal of American Ethnic History* Winter (2003): 31–49; Stacy Harwood and Dowell Myers, "The Dynamics of Immigration and Local Governance in Santa Ana: Neighborhood Activism, Overcrowding, and Land-Use Policy," *Policy Studies Journal* 30 (2002): 70–91; Mark Kanazawa, "Immigration, Exclusion, and Taxation: Anti-Chinese Legislation in Gold Rush California," *Journal of Economic History* 65 (2005): 779–805; Philip Kasinitz, John Mollenkopf, and Mary C. Waters, "Becoming Americans/Becoming New Yorkers: Immigrant Incorporation in a Majority Minority City," *International Migration Review* 36 (2002): 1020–37; Gloria R. Lothrop, "Italians of Los Angeles: An Historical Overview," *Southern California Quarterly* 85 (2003): 249–300; Ruben Martínez, *The New Americans* (New York: New Press, 2004); K. Bruce Newbold and John Spindler, "Immigrant Settlement Patterns in Metropolitan Chicago," *Urban Studies* 38 (2001): 1903–19; Barbara J. Rozek, *Come to Texas: Attracting Immigrants, 1865–1915* (College Station: Texas A&M University Press, 2003); Joan L. Saverino, "'Domani Ci Zappa': Italian Immigration and Ethnicity in Pennsylvania," *Pennsylvania Folklife* 45 (1995): 2–22; Roger Waldinger, "From Ellis Island to LAX: Immigrant Prospects in the American City," *International Migration Review* 30 (1996): 1078–86.

29 See James G. Gimpel, *Separate Destinations: Migration, Immigration, and the Politics of Place* (Ann Arbor: The University of Michigan Press, 1999).

30 See James G. Gimpel, *Separate Destinations*.

31 See Mark Ellis, "Unsettling Immigration Geographies: US Immigration and the Politics of Scale," *Tijdschrift voor economische en sociale geografie* 97 (2006): 49–58; Fix and Passel, *Immigration and Immigrants*; Eric S. Rothman and Thomas J. Espenshade, "Fiscal Impacts of Immigration in the United States," *Population Index* 58 (1992): 381–415.

32 See *Impact of Undocumented Persons and Other Immigrants on Costs, Revenues, and Services in Los Angeles County* (Los Angeles County, Internal Services Division, 1992); John Isbister, *The Immigration Debate: Remaking America* (West Hartford, CT: Kumarian Press, 1996).

33 See Stacy Harwood and Dowell Myers, "The Dynamics of Immigration and Local Governance in Santa Ana: Neighborhood Activism, Overcrowding, and Land-Use Policy," *Policy Studies Journal* 30 (2002): 70.

34 See Peter Skerry, "Many Borders to Cross: Is Immigration the Exclusive Responsibility of the Federal Government?" *Publius* 25 (1995): 71–85.
35 See Benjamin J. Klebaner, "State and Local Immigration Regulation in the United States before 1882," *International Review of Social History* 3 (1958): 269–81.
36 See LeMay and Barkan, *Immigration and Naturalization Laws.*
37 See Ellis, "Unsettling Immigration Geographies," 52.
38 See LeMay and Barkan, *Immigration and Naturalization Laws.*
39 See Ellis, "Unsettling Immigration Geographies," 49–58.
40 See www.fairimmigration.org.
41 See Daniel J. Hopkins, "Politicized Places: Explaining Where and When Immigrants Provoke Local Opposition," *American Political Science Review* 104 (2010): 40–60.
42 See Jeffrey G. Reitz, ed., *Host Societies and the Reception of Immigrants* (San Diego: University of California, San Diego, 2003).
43 See Portes and Borocz, "Contemporary Immigration."
44 See Thomas A.P. Sinclair, "From Community-Building to Governing Strangers: Reconceptualizing Institutional Relationships among Governments, Community Organizations, and Individuals," *American Review of Public Administration* 32 (2002): 312–25.
45 See LeMay and Barkan, *Immigration and Naturalization Laws.*
46 See Klebaner, "State and Local Immigration Regulation."
47 See Tanis Salant, Christine Brenner, Nadia Rubaii-Barrett, and John Weeks, *Illegal Immigrants in U.S./Mexico Border Counties: The Costs of Law Enforcement, Criminal Justice and Emergency Medical Services* (United States/Mexico Border Counties Coalition, 2001); www.bordercounties.org.
48 See Klebaner, "State and Local Immigration Regulation."
49 See Sarah Kershaw, "For Schenectady, a Guyanese Strategy: Mayor Goes All Out to Encourage a Wave of Hardworking Immigrants," *New York Times*, July 26, 2002, B1.
50 See William Finnegan, "New in Town," *New Yorker*, December 11, 2006, 46.
51 See Evelyn S. Sterne, "Beyond the Boss: Immigration and American Political Culture from 1880 to 1940," in *E Pluribus Unum*, 33–66.
52 See David Downey, "All in a Day's Work," *Planning* (April 2006): 7.
53 See Downey, "All in a Day's Work," 6–11.
54 See Margaret Hobbins, "The Day Laborer Debate: Small Town, U.S.A. Takes on Federal Immigration Law Regarding Undocumented Workers," *Connecticut Public Interest Law Journal* 6 (2006): 111–41.
55 See Miriam J. Wells, "The Grassroots Reconfiguration of U.S. Immigration Policy," *International Migration Review* 38 (2004): 1308–47.
56 See Ignatius Bau, "Cities of Refuge: No Federal Preemption of Ordinances Restricting Local Government Cooperation with the INS," *La Raza Law Journal* 7 (1994): 50–71.
57 See Rebecca Chiao, "Two Sides to Preemption: Comments on Bau," *La Raza Law Journal* 7 (1994): 72–80.
58 See www.nilc.org.
59 See Laurel R. Boatright, "Clear Eye for the State Guy: Clarifying Authority and Trusting Federalism to Increase Nonfederal Assistance with Immigration Enforcement," *Texas Law Review* 84 (2006): 1633–74.
60 See New York City Executive Order No. 41, "City-wide Privacy Policy and Amendment of Executive Order No. 34 Relating to City Policy Concerning Immigrant Access to City Services," September 17, 2003.
61 See Cook County Resolution 07-R-240, "Resolution Declaring Cook County a 'Fair and Equal County for Immigrants,'" approved and adopted on June 5, 2007. The full text of the resolution is available at the following web address: www.cookcountyclerk.com/countyboard/boardmeetings/Pages/default.aspx {search under June 5, 2007 board meeting}.
62 See Faiola, "Looking the Other Way."

63 See Boatright, "Clear Eye for the State Guy."
64 See Anabelle Garay, "Local Immigration Laws Bring High Costs," *Cox Newspapers Washington Bureau*, May 5, 2007.
65 See Faiola, "Looking the Other Way."
66 See Garay, "Local Immigration Laws."
67 See Frank Van Tubergen, *Immigration Integration: A Cross-National Study* (New York: LFB Scholarly Publishing, 2006).
68 See Eunice Moscoso, "Cities and Towns Pass English Language Laws," *Cox Newspapers Washington Bureau*, December 7, 2006.
69 See Kenya Hart, "Defending against a 'Death by English': English-Only, Spanish-Only and a Gringa's Suggestions for Community Support of Language Rights," *La Raza Law Journal* 14 (2003): 177–224.
70 See Julie C.T. Hernandez, John C. Brown, and Christine C. Tien, "Serving Diverse Communities—Best Practices," *PM: ICMA Public Management Magazine* 89 (2007): 12–17.
71 See Hernandez, Brown, and Tien, "Serving Diverse Communities."
72 See *The Role of Local Government in Community Safety* (US Department of Justice, Office of Justice Programs, Bureau of Justice Assistance, April 2001; NCJ 184218).
73 See Hernandez, Brown and Tien, "Serving Diverse Communities."
74 See Harwood and Myers, "Dynamics of Immigration," 84.
75 See Harwood and Myers, "Dynamics of Immigration," 88.

8 Outside the Binary

Transgendered Politics on a Global Stage

Jenna Basiliere

In 1996, after a long and tenuous debate around the issue, the European Court of Justice ruled that discrimination based on sex-reassignment was ostensibly discrimination based on sex, and therefore in violation of European Union (EU) law. This moment illustrates one strategy in the struggle to incorporate issues of gender diversity into international policy. The EU ruled that sex-reassignment surgery was protected based on the procedure's adherence to normal standards of sexual identification. What this provision does not address are the rights of gender-variant individuals who do not undergo sex-reassignment surgery and are thus less visible within the established system of sex-based recognition. Organizations such as the International Lesbian, Gay, Bisexual, Trans and Intersex Association (ILGA) are actively working to get gender-variant populations represented by international human rights legislation. The ILGA focuses much of its effort on the United Nations and the Universal Declaration for Human Rights, arguing that: "[h]uman rights principles, as we now know them, began in the years after World War II with provisions in the UN Charter (1945) and the Universal Declaration of Human Rights (1948). There was simple binary thinking in those days. There are men and women. They enter into marriage. They have kids. Families are to be protected."[1] This critique of binary thinking brings to light a number of larger questions, including: What is the role of legislation concerning gender equality in the movement for international human rights? Can these same provisions for treatment of gender be extended to protect the rights of gender-variant individuals? Is the human rights framework the appropriate model for protecting those with gender-variant identities?

To address these questions, it is first necessary to understand the relationship between gender expression and provisions for human rights. The effort to integrate a gender analysis into development work has become significantly more forceful since the Convention on the Elimination of All Forms of Discrimination Against Women (CEDAW), which the United Nations general assembly adopted in 1979, and the Fourth World Conference on Women, which was held in 1995 in Beijing.[2] However, the vast majority of this dialogue still focuses on gender roles assigned for men and women, and the need for women to gain further rights within the domestic sphere.[3] Even the most progressive aspects of the gender and development discourse tend to discuss the roles of women and men in terms of a gender binary.

Clearly, international development initiatives need to address issues of gender diversity. These initiatives are often challenged by the difficulties in quantifying the exact size of the transgender population worldwide. Since gender diversity is not formally regulated or measured in most places of the world, the available data covers only those individuals who seek psychological attention or undergo sex-reassignment surgery. There is little data available on those who do not seek out medical interventions and, according to Femke Olyslager and Lynn Conway, even this data set is skewed. The generally accepted media reports claim that transsexualism is found in approximately 1:30,000 males and 1:100,000 females. However, Olyslager and Conway found that "more recent data and alternative methods for estimating the prevalence of transsexualism … indicate that the lower bound on the prevalence of transsexualism is at least 1:500, and possibly higher."[4] This discrepancy in the estimated size of the trans-sexual population highlights one of the primary challenges in doing international justice work around gender diversity, that is, the frequently indefinable and culturally contingent nature of gender-diverse populations. To that end, this chapter looks to theorize ways that gender diversity activism in the United States can help the gender and development dialogue expand to include those types of bodies and identities that transgress traditional gender norms. Given the cultural sensitivity of gender expressions, gender norms, and gender roles as well as the danger of colonial thinking when talking about gender roles transnationally, we need a flexible framework that allows for variations in cultural norms and ideologies.

To begin, this chapter examines the theoretical frameworks of gender and development, gender mainstreaming, and theories of the gender binary in an attempt to illustrate the general principles of the current dialogue around transnational gender equality. Then, I discuss the struggle for the acceptance of gender diversity in the United States and existing attempts to insert protections around gender identity into the human rights dialogue. Finally, using the World Bank as a specific case study, I consider the practical applications of the gender and development framework and illustrate the ways that its policies not only rely on but also perpetuate notions of "man" and "woman" as exclusive gender categories. I propose my own revisions to World Bank documents that draw on the strengths of the gender and development model while incorporating the theoretical influences of the US-based struggle for transgender rights. Ultimately, I illustrate the radical possibilities of an activism that allows these two theoretical spaces to congregate.

A brief history of gender and development

Any examination of the theories and practices of gender and development first must look into the historical conditions that led to the incorporation of women into international development. Prior to 1970, development policies concerning women were interested only in the welfare of wives and mothers, primarily in the contexts of protecting the health of male children and lowering fertility rates in overpopulated countries. These assumptions were first challenged by the Danish economist Ester Boserup, who made the (then) groundbreaking claim that women did not always benefit when male heads of household gained increased income and social status.[5]

This welfare-based approach eventually gave way to the Women in Development (WID) approach, which was introduced at the 1975 World Conference of the International Women's Year in Mexico City and the United Nations Decade for Women (1976–85). These public events illustrated the major preoccupations with women's issues in the 1970s and 1980s.[6] The WID framework focused primarily on ways to incorporate women into the already existing development framework, assuming that the same economic relief strategies that worked for men could be unilaterally applied to women with only minor changes to allow for gendered differences in need.

After the WID approach, there were a number of slightly nuanced strategies for dealing with gendered issues in development that focused on the construction of gender roles and the sociological necessity of investigating gender roles independently before attempting to address gendered issues of development. Ultimately, all of these approaches settled down into the framework that we now identify as Gender and Development (GAD).[7]

The exact tenets of the GAD approach vary from practitioner to practitioner, making a specific definition difficult to pin down. In the interest of clarity, I will employ Janet Momsen's definition:

> Based on the concept of gender (the socially acquired ideas of masculinity and femininity) and gender relations (the socially constructed pattern of relations between men and women) they analysed how development reshapes these power relations. Drawing on feminist political activism, gender analysts explicitly see women as agents of change. They also criticize the WID approach for treating women as a homogeneous category and they emphasize the important influence of differences of class, age, marital status, religion and ethnicity or race on development outcomes.[8]

As we can see from Momsen's explanation, the GAD approach is a calculated reaction to the weaknesses of the WID ideology. Drawing heavily from standpoint feminist theory, the GAD approach prioritizes differences among women and recognizes the importance of acknowledging differences in specific intrinsic needs.[9] Another facet that separates GAD from WID is that the GAD framework is not solely concerned with women's issues but is more concerned with the gendered nuances of oppression. Additionally, the GAD framework allows for the contributions of men who share concerns of justice and equality, a sharp divergence from the female-only solidarity valued by early feminists working in the development field.[10] The primary change the GAD approach brought to dialogues around social justice was the desire to re-conceive the development framework in a way that takes into account gendered differences.

Gender mainstreaming, or, the naturalization of patriarchal control

GAD work operates primarily through a strategy called gender mainstreaming. This concept was first introduced at the 1985 Third World Conference on Women in Nairobi and was then formally incorporated at the 1995 Fourth World Conference on Women in Beijing. Ultimately, the goal of gender mainstreaming is to revisit and assess all development policies in specific relation to their impacts on men and women. The United Nations has defined this approach as:

> Mainstreaming a gender perspective is the process of assessing the implications for women and men of any planned action, including legislation, policies or programmes, in all areas and at all levels. It is a strategy for making women's as well as men's concerns and experiences an integral dimension of the design, implementation, monitoring and evaluation of policies and programmes in all political, economic, and societal spheres so that women and men benefit equally and inequality is not perpetuated. The ultimate goal is to achieve gender equality.[11]

In the past ten years, the great majority of national governments, NGOs, and international development institutions have adopted the concepts of gender mainstreaming and recognized the importance of gender equality. Almost all of their definitions and understandings come from the above United Nations definition.[12] From this definition, we can see that gender mainstreaming fits within the GAD field because of the focus on integrating the concerns of women as well as men into a broader set of development programs.

GAD and gender mainstreaming have encountered heavy critiques.[13] However, the primary critiques of gender mainstreaming have focused on the fact that the GAD framework is not all that far removed from the previous WID framework. Men have always been present and consulted in the development dialogue, therefore shifting the gendered discussion from solely focusing on women to focusing on both women and men does not actually change much.[14] What this critique lacks is an understanding of the fact that the dualistic categories of "men" and "women" are actually the most problematic. While the GAD framework professes to be anti-dualistic and attempts to shift away from essentializing categories that ignore nuances of race, class, ethnicity, and religion, it ignores the dualism inherent in categorizing human beings into only two gendered categories.[15]

Arguments against gender binaries

Systems of gendered interactions are culturally specific, yet they share with each other imbedded systems of inequality. As Ridgeway and Smith-Lovin note:

> Gender is a system of social practices within society that constitutes people as different in socially significant ways and organizes relations of inequality on the basis of the difference. The continued, everyday acceptance of the gender system requires that both people's experiences and widely shared cultural beliefs confirm for them that men and women are sufficiently different in ways that justify men's greater power and privilege. ... Gender is distinctive, however, in that its constitutive cultural beliefs and confirmatory experiences must be sustained in the context of constant interaction, often on familiar terms, between those advantaged and disadvantaged by the system.[16]

As I use the term "gender binary," it refers to the fact that many cultures give children two options when learning sex roles, the masculine role traditionally associated with men and the feminine role traditionally associated with women. From a psychological perspective, one traditional way of describing this phenomenon is through the use of gender schema theory. Gender schema theory proposes that children learn gender roles through a readiness to encode and organize social information according to the traditional cultural roles assigned to men and women.[17] What I would like to draw from gender schema theory is the notion that there is a space to resist the imposition of culturally imposed roles. Given this understanding, it is important to create space within the development discourse to allow for those individuals who choose to resist enforced gender and sex role stereotyping.

The existing prevalence of gender–binary thinking in development work is apparent in the language of the report titled "Gender and Development: Concepts and Definitions."[18] This report was published by BRIDGE, an organization devoted to identifying and synthesizing key issues and debates within the GAD movement. It is a heavily cited document and is representative of broader understandings of gender within the development field. The Bridge Report begins by providing brief definitions of some of the important concepts in gender and development, and then goes on to define each of these concepts in greater depth. The concepts outlined in this report are culture, gender analysis, gender discrimination, gender division of labor, gender equality and equity, gender mainstreaming, gender needs, gender planning, gender relations, gender training, gender violence, intra-household resource distribution, national machineries for women, patriarchy, sex and gender, social justice, WID/ GAD, women's empowerment, and women's human rights.

Of particular concern within The Bridge Report is its working definition of the distinction between sex and gender. The report emphasizes the importance of making this distinction but its working definition of gender still leaves much to be desired:

> how a person's biology is culturally valued and interpreted into locally accepted ideas of what it is to be a woman or man. "Gender" and the hierarchical power relations between women and men based on this are socially constructed, and not derived directly from biology. Gender identities and associated expectations of roles and responsibilities are therefore changeable between and within culture. Gendered power relations permeate social institutions so that gender is never absent.[19]

This definition allows little space for individual identities that do not fit within a culturally mandated binary. By limiting gender to simply the definitions of "man" and "woman," there is a wide range of identities that are excluded from the equation. Acknowledging the differences between sex and gender as well as the culturally constructed nature of gender are certainly two steps in the right direction, but we need to push the paradigm further to become more inclusive.

The limitations of thinking in terms of a gender binary are also apparent in The Bridge Report's definition of gender violence. It defines gender violence as "any act or threat by men or male-dominated institutions that inflicts physical, sexual, or psychological harm on a woman or girl because of their gender."[20] Certainly, violence against women is a serious problem that must be addressed in an aggressive manner. But to make this framework more inclusive, the discussion should be opened up to include other types of violence. To begin with, the analysis makes no mention of the gendered nature of the violence that women commit against men. Men are typically in greater positions of social privilege and therefore much more likely to commit violence against women, but it is important to acknowledge that the phenomenon of women committing violence against men also exists. Additionally, violence against individuals who are non-normatively gendered, whether they are transgendered, gay, lesbian, or bisexual, is an international problem. We need to enter these individuals and groups into the international discourse in order to afford them the protections already sliding into place for women around the world. As indicated by such international events as Transgender Day of Remembrance, this issue has gained increased visibility and international documents should reflect that fact.

The language deployed in The Bridge Report is just one illustration of the limitations of thinking within a gender binary when doing transnational justice work. As we move away from thinking in terms of two (and only two) gendered options, we will be able to provide more people more protection than in existing human rights paradigms.

The marriage of gender theory and gender activism

Often, there is a discursive divide between those who theorize gender diversity and those who work on the activist front. However, it is only through the interaction of these two seemingly divergent worlds that we can achieve effective social change. To demonstrate that all hope is not lost, I would like to look at the work of an intellectual who has successfully bridged this gap, Kate Bornstein. Through her work, I hope to show the radical potential that gender theory holds in providing a model for a larger social transformation. Bornstein's work is particularly notable because she openly rejects the gate-keeping language that marks much academic work. While still maintaining a theoretical base, her writing presents itself in a way that is accessible to the general (literate) population. Furthermore, her performance pieces give theoretical access to groups of people who might otherwise be denied access through their inability to read and write. In this way, she illustrates the radical potential for theory, and specifically theories of gender diversity, to impact a larger social audience. The first step in bridging the gap between activists and academics is clearly through the facilitation of open communication. Bornstein's work provides a way to begin thinking about how to do that.

Aside from its accessibility, Bornstein's theories about gender offer an excellent model for thinking about how to discuss gender and international development policies. Bornstein proposes a four-part model for examining gender: gender assignment, gender identity, gender roles, and gender attribution. These four processes do not stand alone, but rather intersect to form the way we understand gender. Gender assignment refers to the gender assigned at birth, based on biological sex. Gender identity is determined by an individual, and answers the question "Who am I?" Gender roles are the societal expectations for gendered behavior. Finally, gender attribution refers to the assumptions society makes about an individual's gender identity.[21]

In looking at Bornstein's analysis, it becomes clear that not all aspects of a gendered existence are autonomous. An infant holds no control over the gender assigned at birth, just as a social actor has little control over culturally prescribed gender roles. Gender attribution is a little trickier, because it relies on cues (physical, behavioral, textual); however, it also relies on the perceptions of society at large, those doing the attributing. Gender identity is the only real space in this model where social agency is available. What Bornstein's model demonstrates is the amount of social force exerted over gendered experiences requiring them to conform to a master narrative. In light of all of that force, Bornstein calls for academics and activists alike to embrace and fight for the rights of those whose gender identities do not prescribe to a social norm.

Integrating Gender into the World Bank's Work: A Strategy for Action

In 2002, the World Bank released a policy paper designed to incorporate gender into its daily operations. This paper, "Integrating Gender into the World Bank's Work: A Strategy for Action," encountered heavy resistance from feminist scholars.[22]

The World Bank paper begins by making a business case for gender mainstreaming, outlining the relationships between gender equality, poverty, growth, and development effectiveness. The bank's basic strategy has three steps. First, a Country Gender Assessment (CGA) analysis must be completed for each country that receives support from the bank. This analysis should examine the gendered impact of development activities in the respective country and evaluate areas in which the bank could facilitate improvement. Second, the bank must develop and implement policy and operational interventions in response to the CGA. Third, the bank will monitor the implementation and results of the policy and operational interventions. The paper then goes on to explain the advantages of gender mainstreaming, the challenges to mainstreaming gender within the bank's work, and the comparative advantage that the bank possesses within the GAD framework. The specific policy and implementation shortcomings of this document have been discussed elsewhere, and with a very critical lens, so that is not the purpose of my analysis. Rather, I would like to examine the ways that the discourse of gender is used and manipulated within the bank's policy language. Following that analysis, I will propose revisions to strengthen the inclusiveness of the bank's development strategies.

The definition of gender employed by the World Bank seeks to reinforce binaries of "man" and "woman." Furthermore, the bank's definition of gender relies on the assumption that there are aspects of gendered behavior that are biologically determined. To the potential horror of many members of the feminist community, it seems that this definition of gender is the only definition that the bank analysts have ever encountered. The definition is:

> The term gender refers to culturally based expectations of the roles and behaviors of males and females. The term distinguishes the socially

constructed from the biologically determined aspects of being male and female. Unlike the biology of sex, gender roles and behaviors can change historically, sometimes relatively quickly, even if aspects of these roles originated in the biological differences between the sexes. Because the religious or cultural traditions that define and justify the distinct roles and expected behaviors of males and females are strongly cherished and socially enforced, change in gender systems is often contested.[23]

Within this definition, the authors attempt to make a distinction between biological sex and gender; however, the assertion that gendered behaviors may be based on biological differences between the two sexes serves to counteract this idea. Additionally, the way the authors have structured this definition leaves no space for the idea of an intersex body, or a gender identity that is completely removed from cultural expectations. Within this framework, there are only two types of gender allowed, and they are culturally assigned genders based on biological differentiations.

According to the World Bank, a traditional gender assessment usually includes a profile of the different socioeconomic roles of males and females (which only covers the domestic and private spheres), a review of the country's policies and their relative gender sensitivity, and a review of the bank's policies and their relative gender sensitivity.[24] The CGAs can either be independent documents or they can appear as a section in a larger poverty analysis. Despite the fact that these assessments have gender in their title, they still frame their analysis in terms of males and females. Since male and female are indicators of biological sex and not gender, the bank's policy as it currently stands could be more accurately labeled as a "Country Sex Role Assessment." One serious weakness of the document is that it does not differentiate between culturally imposed roles assigned on the basis of biological sex and autonomously selected expressions of gender identity.

The World Bank provides a list of key issues that gender analysts should examine when performing a CGA. Among this list of key issues are gendered differences in access to transportation, education and literacy, healthcare, employment, leisure time, legal protections, and market participation. With the exception of market participation, which is reserved for last on the list of issues to be addressed, all of the other issues concern women's role within the domestic and private spheres. The sections on gendered differences in employment and education acknowledge that women are bound to be at a disadvantage in the public sphere based on their household duties rather than attempt to deconstruct the notion that women should be the prime caregivers and therefore solely responsible for daily domestic chores.

Possibilities for transformation

While the World Bank's gender strategy is a positive move in the direction of gender equality, the framework could be re-conceived in a manner that would place the bank on an even more progressive course. As Bornstein's work illustrates, a script that relies on notions of "man" and "woman" as unified and definable categories excludes a part of the population from the rights of social protection. The first step in re-conceiving the bank's gender framework is to re-evaluate the premise of the document. The current framework relies on an understanding of the business case for gender mainstreaming. Instead, I propose an argument for gender equality that draws its basis from the Universal Declaration of Human Rights and claims a unilateral right to basic human dignities.[25] The fact that the declaration does not currently directly address issues of gender makes an even stronger case for using this framework in an argument for gender equality. If the number of powerful and influential development organizations that recognize gender equality as a significant human rights issue increases, it will eventually prompt a shift towards an understanding that gender equality is central to the human rights discourse.

The second aspect of the World Bank's framework that should be revised is its working definition of gender. As it currently stands, the bank uses an understanding of gender that directly equates biological sex with one prescribed gender role. This definition of gender should be expanded to allow for identities and expressions that do not prescribe to a direct association with an understanding of biological sex. The opening up of this gender definition does not come without the danger of ethnocentrism. In discussing issues of gender expressions that deviate from social norms, it is important to acknowledge that not all societies and cultures operate with the same cultural understanding that Euro-American societies have of issues of gender identity and transgenderism.[26] There are, however, identities in many cultures that parallel what we know as transgenderism. Judith Butler provides an excellent framework for looking at transgressive gender identities cross-culturally:

> One speaks, and one speaks for another, to another, and yet there is no way to collapse the distinction between the other and myself. When we say 'we' we do nothing more than designate this very problematic. ... They are part of any normative aspiration of a movement that seeks to maximize the protection and the freedoms of sexual and gender minorities, of women, defined with the broadest possible compass.[27]

Using Butler's framework, I propose that the World Bank re-word its definition of gender so that the term is positioned as an autonomous expressive choice. We still need to acknowledge that in many cultures gender roles are conceived in terms of a social relationship based on biological sex; however, we also need to recognize the individuals who do not fit within that framework. I thus propose that an additional statement be added to the end of the bank's definition of gender:

While the above definition certainly holds true in the majority of cases, it is important to note that there are individuals who break away from the prescribed gender roles of their respective cultures. The World Bank needs to open space in their discourse to allow for these individuals as well as those bound by traditional cultural roles.

Along with this new definition of gender, the role of the CGA needs to be re-evaluated to accommodate the new understanding of gender. As it stands right now, the CGA focuses on profiling the different socioeconomic roles of males and females, and deconstructing the way government policies treat men and women differently. All of this work is extremely valuable; however, the role of the CGA needs to be expanded to evaluate the social conditions of a larger group of people. I propose that the CGA include an analysis of the gender dynamics within the country that extends beyond the roles of men and women. Additionally, it should engage in some sort of analysis that attempts to gauge how many individuals living outside of traditional gender roles are present within a given society and the policy and institutional protections that these individuals may or may not be afforded. The gender-responsive policy and operational interventions that the World Bank's gender team proposes also should take into account the needs of individuals who do not simply fall into the categories of "man" and "woman."

The last revision I would propose to the World Bank's gender framework is a reconfiguration of its seven key challenges to gender mainstreaming. These challenges present a framework for the types of challenges that the bank considers in its work, and that is why it is pivotally important that they reflect gender fluidity. The seven challenges that the bank already recognizes should be expanded to include institutionalized violence against individuals based on gender expression and sexuality.

While revising the World Bank's understanding of gender is certainly a positive start, it would be naïve to believe that simply changing the phrasing of a policy document is sufficient. A recent analysis of the bank's gender policy found that the number of "gender experts" has increased significantly over the past couple of years, but the numbers still paled in comparison to experts working on other areas of interest. Furthermore, a spot-check of bank employee awareness found that very few people who were not specifically commissioned to work on gender issues had ever read the policy document, and in many cases they did not even know that it existed.[28] The bank should not only revise its understanding of gender but also require its employees to gain a familiarity with the nature of gender and gendered oppressions.

A proposal for future action

As I have demonstrated in this chapter, there is a significant need for a revision of the definition of "gender" within the current GAD framework.

One possible vehicle for a further course of action is the incorporation of the International Bill of Gender Rights (IBGR) into the framework. The IBGR is one of the most recent attempts to articulate a framework of human rights for transgendered individuals. This bill of rights calls for the right to define gender identity, the right to free expression of gender identity, the right to secure and retain employment, the right of access to gendered space, the right to control and change one's own body, the right to competent medical and professional care, the right to freedom from involuntary psychiatric diagnosis, the right to sexual expressions, the right to form committed loving relationships, and the right to conceive, bear, or adopt children.[29] Just as CEDAW re-conceived the ways that violence against women mattered, the International Bill of Gender Rights can serve to radically alter the way that gendered experiences are approached within the development context.

The GAD approach has many strengths, and the push to make sure that women are included and represented in all aspects of international development is very important. GAD strategies, such as the CEDAW, the Beijing Platform for Action, and the incorporation of gender into the United Nation's Millennium Development Goals, have certainly had a positive impact on the lives of women from many countries. However, the current definitions of gender used within the GAD framework are seriously limiting the scope of its effectiveness. As long as gender is defined in terms of the socially constructed notions of what it means to be a man and what it means to be a woman, there are always going to be individuals who are excluded from the discussion because of their failure to conform to these norms.

Based on Bornstein's scholarship, it is simple to see how expanding the current understandings of gender and its relationship to biological sex will allow for individuals with a more fluid range of identities to fall under the protection of wealthy development organizations. In particular, one finds in her work an urgent need to close the divide between theory and activism; or, in this case, the divide between more legal-based social movements and grassroots social activism. It is not enough to just work on the formal frameworks for dealing with gender. These efforts must be combined with efforts to prevent social discrimination against gender-variant individuals. Significant changes in international development policy could help to address some of those concerns, but they cannot stand alone.

Notes

1 See Douglas Sanders, "Transgender Rights," http://ilga.org/ilga/en/article/mdO32ZR1AY.
2 CEDAW is often credited with bringing issues of women's rights to the forefront of the international development dialogue. In particular, CEDAW makes the assertion that all women have the right to live a life free from discrimination based on their biological sex. Currently, there are only two countries in the world that have not

ratified CEDAW. However, it is important to note that many of the countries who have ratified CEDAW have been unable or unwilling to properly enforce its tenets.

3 See E. M. Rathberger, "WID, WAD, GAD: Trends in Research and Practice," *Journal of Developing Areas* 24, no. 1 (1990): 489–502.

4 See Femke Olyslager and Lynn Conway, "On the Calculation of the Prevalence of Transsexualism," in *WPATH 20th International Symposium* (Chicago: International Journal of Transgenderism, 2007), 2.

5 See Ester Boserup, *Women's Role in Economic Development* (London: Allen & Unwin, 1970).

6 See S. Razavi and C. Miller, "From WID to GAD: Conceptual Shifts in the Women and Development Discourse," United Nations Research Institute for Social Development, Geneva, 1995.

7 See Razavi and Miller, "From WID to GAD."

8 See Janet Henshall Momsen, *Gender and Development* (London: Routledge, 2005), 13.

9 For an excellent definition of feminist standpoint theory, see Nancy Hartsock, "The Feminist Standpoint: Developing the Ground for a Specifically Feminist Historical Materialism," in *Feminism and Methodology*, ed. Sandra Harding (Bloomington: Indiana University Press, 1987), 157–80.

10 See Rathberger, "WID, WAD, GAD."

11 See "Report of the Economic and Social Council for 1997," www.un.org/documents/ga/docs/52/plenary/a52-3.htm.

12 See C. Moser, "Has Gender Mainstreaming Failed? A Comment on International Development Agency Experiences in the South," *International Journal of Feminist Politics* 7, no. 4 (2005): 576–90.

13 For example, see Moser, "Gender Mainstreaming"; S. Chant and M. Gutmann, "Men-Streaming Gender? Questions for Gender and Development Policy in the Twenty-First Century," *Progress in Development Studies* 2, no. 4 (2002): 269–82; Cecile Jackson, "Rescuing Gender from the Poverty Trap," in *Feminist Visions of Development: Gender Analysis and Policy*, eds Cecile Jackson and Ruth Pearson (New York: Routledge, 1998), 39–64.

14 See Chant and Gutmann, "Men-Streaming Gender."

15 For an illustrative example of this problematic dualism, see Martha Nussbaum, *Women and Human Development: The Capabilities Approach* (Cambridge, UK: Cambridge University Press, 2005).

16 See Cecilia Ridgeway and Lynn Smith-Lovin, "The Gender System and Interaction," *Annual Review of Sociology* 25, no. 1 (1999): 192.

17 See Sandra Bem, "Gender Schema Theory: A Cognitive Account of Sex-Typing," *Psychological Review* 88, no. 4 (1981): 354–64; Calvin Mercer and Thomas Durham, "Religious Mysticism and Gender Orientation," *Journal for the Scientific Study of Religion* 38, no. 1 (1999): 175–82.

18 See Hazel Reeves and Sally Baden, "Gender and Development: Concepts and Definitions," BRIDGE Report No. 55, Institute of Development Studies, University of Sussex, 2000. Hereafter referred to as The Bridge Report.

19 The Bridge Report, 30.

20 The Bridge Report, 22.

21 See Kate Bornstein, *Gender Outlaw: On Men, Women, and the Rest of Us* (New York: Vintage, 1994).

22 For examples, see Elaine Zuckerman and Wu Qing, "Reforming the World Bank: Will the New Gender Strategy Make a Difference? A Study with China Case Examples," Heinrich Foundation, Washington, 2005; Phillip Jones, "The World Bank and the Literacy Question: Orthodoxy, Heresy and Ideology," *International Review of Education* 43, no. 4 (1997): 367–75; Stephen Fidler, "Who's Minding the Bank?" *Foreign Policy* 126 (2001): 40–50.

23 See "Integrating Gender into the World Bank's Work: A Strategy for Action," World Bank, Washington, 2002, 2.

24 See "Integrating Gender," 2.

25 See "Universal Declaration on Human Rights," www.un.org/en/documents/udhr/.

26 From a Euro-American cultural perspective, "transgender" is an umbrella term used to describe individuals who have cultivated an understanding of their gender identity that exists outside the traditional definition of "man" and "woman." This label can be used to describe a wide variety of gender expressions, ranging from a male-to-female or female-to-male transsexual to an individual who identifies as genderqueer or androgynous. For further information about transgenderism, see Pat Califia, *Sex Changes: The Politics of Transgenderism* (San Fransisco: Cleis Press, 1997).

27 See Judith Butler, "Global Violence, Sexual Politics," in *Queer Ideas: The David Kessler Lectures in Lesbian and Gay Studies* (New York: The Feminist Press at the City University of New York, 2001), 201.

28 See Zuckerman and Qing, "Reforming the World Bank."

29 See "International Bill of Gender Rights," in *Transgender Rights*, eds Richard M. Juang Paisley Currah, and Shannon Price Minter (Minneapolis: University of Minnesota Press, 1996).

9 Politics and the Disabled Body

Diverse Thoughts about Human Diversity

William Roth

Disability is an instance of diversity that can inform other types of diversity. Jean Paul Sartre's classic essay, *Anti-Semite and Jew*, concerns what its title indicates.[1] But it also transcends its title to be a general indictment of oppression and bigotry. I attempt to engage disability as Sartre engaged the Jew, simultaneously honoring disability and using it as exemplary of diversity in class, gender, race, ethnicity, age, and more. None of these categories is simply biological.[2]

"Disability" is a word that has been jostled by history, appropriated by various social sectors, and defined and refined by public and corporate policy. It is a word that means different things to different people, who, nonetheless, may act as if they are remarkably certain about the word and what it signifies.[3] To modern medicine, disability means chronic illness.[4] To government bureaucracies, it means the inability to work (or work full-time) for physical or health reasons.[5] To K-12 schools, it means some deficiency in need of "special remediation."[6] To a capitalist economy, it is an abstract derivative of abstract human capital. To corporations, it means statistically less productive employees and less significant consumers. One could clearly go into more extensive detail and easily fetch further examples. According to many such definitions, there are approximately fifty million disabled people in the United States.

All the above discourses are important because they indicate how society works. But all convey abstractness, disembodiedness, social appropriation. It would seem that, in some sense at least, they ought to be talking about concrete people with disabilities, about life and death, about the disabled body and experience. That they do not should be troubling to people with disabilities.

Disabled people have begun to question the language that ensnares, to organize in a society that oppresses, and to theorize what it means to be disabled and act with a disability.[7] Such activism has been characteristic of many oppressed people. Indeed, much of the current discourse of disability derives from the discourse of other oppressed people, such as people who are poor, people of color, women, gays and lesbians, religious groups, and the many others who, although commonly referred to as minorities, in obvious fact constitute a majority of the species.

A common move made by people with disabilities is to think ourselves a minority and to recognize the social and cultural constructions of disability that resemble the social and cultural constructions that many other oppressed people have struggled against.[8] Particularly during the last decade, the discourse of disability has been concerned not only with what people with disabilities share with other oppressed people but also with what makes them different, such as the significance of beauty and ugliness or of demeaning charities and telethons.[9] This move is important to the freedom of people with disabilities. As was and is true of the discourses of class, gender, sexual orientation, and race, the discourse of disability promises to contribute to the discourse of freedom by examining, exposing, and critiquing current structures of power, oppression, and domination.

The body as a medical field once dominated the discourse of disability. The discourse of medicine had to be overcome, rejected, and transcended for the freedom of people with disabilities, for an understanding of disability, and for an emancipation of disability from those countless professions, businesses, and charities that are invested in, require, and use it. But in rejecting the medical model that dominated professional discourses about disability, people with disabilities often distanced themselves from their own bodies. An abstract humanism ignored the concreteness of disabled experience, marked an aspiration of assimilation, denied culture, study, and value to disability, and displaced disability from the concrete ground it occupied that could be used to critique other cultural issues as well as itself.

The vibrant discussion of disabled bodies, disabled culture, disability studies, and disability politics beyond independence and toward cooperation, democracy, equality, and freedom promises to change not only the way people in general theorize disability but also the way people with disabilities themselves theorize disability.[10] In this transformation, the body plays a central role.[11]

Power has many euphemisms, not only with words such as "cooperation," "discipline," and "input" but also with the obfuscating misuse of the word "empowerment" in pop psychology and the human services, as if one with power could or would empower one without power. Elites rarely have an interest in others gaining power. Indeed, they usually have an interest in others losing power. Of course, elites have something to gain from fostering the illusion of power in others but that is quite different from actually enhancing their power. Moreover, elites may not even be able to enhance the power of others. The most that they can do is to remove the chains, surveillance, and countless other operations of power so that the person encumbered by them might regain her own freedom. Bureaucracies, for example, often save money by euphemistically empowering other people to fend for themselves and feeling virtuous in the process. People with disabilities are generously endowed with reasons to be suspicious, unappreciative, and weary of euphemisms. In this essay, I will use the word "empower" to refer to the enhancement of the power of bureaucracies and other agencies of domination.

Prior to the 1970s, court decisions had guaranteed disabled children a public education, minus funding, and they had been more or less integrated into systems of public education. The Education for All Handicapped Children's Act of 1975, which in 1990 morphed into an act with the felicitous acronym IDEA (Individuals with Disability Education Act), provided funding, although not enough. While these acts were originally intended to be civil rights acts, an accommodating special education industry perverted them into traditional service acts.[12] Still, a significantly greater proportion of disabled children went to school, graduated from high school, and found a place in higher education or at work. (Of course, there could and should be more of them.) Congress also enacted the Americans with Disabilities Act (ADA) in 1990. This act was a testament to a new politics of disability, which, in the best tradition of American progressive politics, skillfully forged alliances with other oppressed people to secure its passage. But similar to the earlier court decisions and congressional actions, the effect was much less than the promise. The ADA is a perfect example of how progressive legislation can fall prey to the "normal" politics of special interests.

The country has moved substantially to the right. The gap between rich and poor has increased, and disabled people tend to be poor. Public budgets have shrunk, under-funding social programs of all sorts, including programs for disabled people. Corporate power has increased dramatically. What corporations have done with the ADA exemplifies this shift.

Disability is pivotal to appreciating and critiquing many of the domains that surround it. Thought, writing, and action on disability as a social issue flourish but at a level that insufficiently deals with the realities of power. I am concerned with the power that oppresses, subjugates, traumatizes, depresses, dominates, and kills. We can understand none of these abominations without understanding power. My interest in power is, however, more by way of protest than of admiration. What I admire is survival, life, freedom, and heroism, which power could be used to advance, but which, too often, are victimized by it.

In practice, the direction of power often requires the presence of diversity. I will use the words associated with diversity in different ways and from various perspectives. I hope each change of perspective will acquire different reflections, cast new shadows, and reveal new aspects. It is necessary to acknowledge the immediate contributions of feminist thought and practice, the eloquent history and resistance of African Americans, and the actions of the many other groups whose members have been oppressed because of perceived group differences. Of course, this includes disabled people.

Michel Foucault is a man to listen to. I share his appreciation of Jeremy Bentham. Willowbrook was to disability what Bentham's Panopticon was to Foucault's prisons and, by extension, other facets of society.[13] Power, according to Foucault, is much more subtle and endemic than people commonly realize. Power is part of architecture, medicine, corporations, and schools. The clock, time management, and schedule also express power. Power need not have an intentional agent. Foucault claimed that "power is everywhere not because it embraces everything, but because it comes from everywhere."[14]

Disability is a concrete revelation of the actions of power through bureaucracy, medicine, science, institutionalization, education, medication, euphemism, oversight, utilitarianism, psychiatry, markets, and more. Power is not only applied to disability; it also largely creates it. Power can mold disability, disguise it, and enhance it. Power can also do these things with other instances of diversity.

Freedom opposes power. It is not necessary to invoke the delicate and perhaps dangerous concepts of positive freedom, derived from Georg Wilhelm Friedrich Hegel and Karl Marx, although they will sometimes be applicable to my reflections on disability and diversity.[15] I shall instead use freedom as it is understood by most people, with the caution that it is far less common than most people think.

The body politic

Disabled bodies are political in demanding changes to the discourse that constructs disability, political in demanding changes to the structures that, in some measure, create disability and make disability unnecessarily burdensome, and political in representing human embodiment in the face of the machine, bureaucracy, markets, capitalism, globalism, and many other facets of modern "progress" that might not, in fact, be progress at all. The disabled body is political in its concrete and obstinate materiality over and against a world increasingly abstract, digital, virtual, spiritual, and media-manufactured.[16]

For the disabled human body to meaningfully realize its political dimensions, it must organize with other disabled bodies, plunge into the waters of society, and engage the movement of history. Political activism is a proper part of Disability Studies, which, at least to some extent, is, or should be, such activism occurring in academia.

Marx theorized the revolutionary consequences of workers coming together in factories. Disabled people came together in hospitals, institutions, schools, and isolated incarceration. But in concrete historical context, the founding of contemporary Disability Studies occurred in the wake of the African American civil rights movement, the movement against the Vietnam War, the movement to liberate the body in universities where generally well-to-do bodies encountered oppression, and the Women's Movement. Outside such a context, disabled people did not congeal into the Disability Rights Movement, nor could they have.

In the 1960s at Berkeley, when and where many people thought possible what today seems less possible yet is more necessary, Chancellor Edward Strong attempted to close down the CORE (Congress of Racial Equality) table at Sather Gate. This table, among others, had participated in the Black Civil Rights Movement. Indeed, many students at Berkeley arrived by way of the South's Freedom Summer. In lush sexual Berkeley, embodiment, so to speak, embodied, this attempted shutdown led to the student occupation of Sproul Hall and the Free Speech Movement. Students assembled in Sproul Hall, on the steps of Sproul Hall, and in Sproul Plaza next to Sather Gate, with Civil Rights, Student Rights, and the New Left all present.

Meanwhile in Cowell Hospital, Larry Biskamp, Cathy Caulfield, John Hessler, and Ed Roberts, all "severely disabled," as language then had it, were exchanging words after class. Biskamp ended up breaking his curfew by spending the night with "girls," as language then had it, behavior for which students at Berkeley were notorious.

The official sponsorship of this conduct by the California Division of Vocational Rehabilitation (DVR) was too much. Biskamp was kicked out of the university. At this time, the Free Speech Movement was in full swing. If this event had occurred outside the concrete historical context of the Free Speech Movement, itself embedded in the concrete historical context of the Civil Rights Movement, matters might well have turned out differently. For one thing, there would have been no Center for Independent Living in Berkeley. The connection between Civil Rights and Disability Rights was there for the making. It was made in the political activism of the first generation of Disability Rights activists.

Biskamp was soon reinstated, not only because the expulsion was called "double jeopardy" in the thoroughly politicized environment of Berkeley in the 1960s, but also because Michael Fuss of the university's Cowell Residence Program was a friend of Roberts, who was to take something of a leadership position among disabled people in Berkeley. Fuss was critically important, for he was the conduit of the Free Speech Movement to Roberts. In short, the four disabled students absorbed the spirit, if one may use such a word to describe something so concrete, of Berkeley in the 1960s by living there but also through the person of Fuss.

What happened next became our history. As many students at Berkeley knew how, a press conference was called. Coming from the same lexicon as "free speech," "double jeopardy" was used to describe the situation. Both are political, activist, indeed fighting words. DVR didn't know what hit it. Biskamp was reinstated and any future expulsions predicated solely on performance in school. (The Free Speech Movement and Civil Rights Movement knew nothing about the emerging Disability Rights Movement, a situation with many analogues.)

The Disability Rights Movement was born in Berkeley in the 1960s at a university through a political activism connected to academia. Unique and so close was this concatenation that it also produced Women's Studies, African American Studies, and Anti-War Studies, all theorized as part of the academy.

Theory was not put into general practice not because of internal weakness but because of external power; the power of the police, the FBI, and the National Guard, on occasion tear-gas-spraying power, as well as of the government, the 1950s, and the corporation. These forms of power have only increased, becoming even more dominant over both the academy and the external world.

Disabled bodies have the virtues and necessities of rebellion. They are inherently political. The same power that subdued the 1960s subdued the disabled body, sometimes even killing it, by poverty, starvation, lack of healthcare, and pressures toward suicide.

Even if the natural sciences are autonomous, the social sciences and humanities are not.[17] They are theorized, constructed, both the subjects and objects of postmodernism. They are political phenomena, indeed constitutive of the body politic, at least as elites theorize it. Disability Studies is elite because of its location in the academy. A democratic Disability Studies has yet to flourish.

Theorizing and interrogating the disabled body is a necessary project of Disability Studies. It must engage in the relevant emancipatory theorizing, confronting the empowered construction of bodies by corporations, capitalism, and bureaucracy. While the latter demand the virtual interchangeability of bodies, the disabled body embodies the uniqueness of bodies. It exemplifies the recalcitrance, obstinacy, and resistance of the human body to interchangeability.

The democratization of the body politic must also deal with the corporation, theorize it, contextualize it, and engage in discourse about it whose claim to seriousness is that it is against it, finding it abusive of disabled bodies in particular and all bodies in general. Discourse of, by, and for the corporation exists everywhere. Turn on the television, go to school, read the records of any court of law, which far surpass anything encountered by Kafka's Josef K. in a once-upon-a-time modernism.

Corporations, capitalism, and bureaucracy act coercively on bodies in general and on disabled bodies in particular. The example of a workplace housed in a building architecturally inaccessible to a person who rides a wheelchair easily generalizes to other examples of architectural inaccessibility. Broaden architectural accessibility to program accessibility, and yet more disabled people face discrimination. The ADA calls for "reasonable accommodation" without "undue hardship." Undue hardship is pretty much a function of profit.

For this reason, democratic socialism is preferable for people with disabilities. With democratic socialism, firms can decide their own internal workings and come to agreements with other socialist firms. What holds for disabled bodies holds for bodies temporarily disabled, differences in gender, and working conditions for able-bodied people, which are also often frustrating and stressful. Furthermore, the capitalist corporation is not a democracy. Serious democracy includes democracy in the workplace.

The factors of production are standardized and interchangeable, including bodies, disabled and not. The products for sale are also overwhelmingly standardized, affecting not only the disabled body but the able body as the apparatus of the media, advertising, and public relations usually portray them. Young women may think that they look like the size-4, airbrushed, now digitally manipulated ideal used to sell not just clothes but other stuff. The corporation constructs the consumer and what he or she thinks or ought to think. Disabled people are usually yet more different from the imagery, discourse, and construction of corporate practice devoted to marketing, sales, and advertising. This fact is only too obvious. But it is important because the university and Disability Studies exist within this corporate world that, *inter alia*, crushed the possibilities of Berkeley in the 1960s. Disability Studies can be complicit with these vectors of force, although the disabled body finds complicity difficult or impossible. Disability Studies in its manifold forms should not distance itself from the disabled body. That disability and the body are now coupled is an invaluable contribution of contemporary Disability Studies to disabled people who once considered themselves abstractly human, split from their bodies; *individuals, consumers, persons WITH disabilities*.

The corporation that contextualizes modern disability is a powerful counterexample. Corporation (if Latinate) comes from concrete (if dead) bodily roots, *corpus*. Even the Supreme Court has appropriated this language in defining the corporation as an artificial body, hence entitled to the rights of the body under the Fourteenth Amendment.[18]

The "corporate politic" opposes the body politic. We live in a polity more corporate than body. The "corporate politic" is anti-democratic, anti-human, anti-body, and anti-body politic. Its domination of disabled bodies is exemplary of its domination of all bodies.

Empowered bureaucracy

The effects of bureaucracy on diversity and disability are profound. What bureaucracy does about diversity and disability is interesting, empowered, and thorough. Part of what it does is by way of normalization, stratification, and homogenization. For example, the category of mild mental retardation did not exist until bureaucratic compulsory public education required uniform performance by students of a certain age. Students who did not pass muster were held back and not promoted to the next grade; that is, they were literally retarded.[19] Here, bureaucracy caused a disability. Elsewhere, bureaucracy impedes the participation of people with disabilities.

Indeed, people with disabilities possess a biology that does not conform to even the most radical operations of normalization.[20] Nowhere is this truer than in those institutions that we refer to as bureaucracies. Bureaucracies are of concern to people with disabilities not only in the numerous ways they are of concern to everyone but also because bureaucracies may well be in essential conflict with people with disabilities. If so, one obvious reaction would be to say so much the worse for people with disabilities. After all, after a certain point designing environments around them is surely beyond reason. If bureaucracy normalizes people, it does so for efficiency, control, and all of the other good reasons of organizational morality. If organizational morality conflicts with individual morality so much the worse for individuals, who, in any event, can be educated, socialized, and indoctrinated.

Bureaucracies are disturbing for workers in general.[21] For many people with disabilities they are not only disturbing, they are also impossible. Here, as elsewhere, the experience of people with disabilities can critique much of the experience imposed on other people, particularly the vast majority who are oppressed and different. Ultimately, the morality of bureaucracies, like the morality of "cabbages and kings," ought to be inferior to the morality of concrete people, including people who are disabled.[22] That is why the questions of who controls and designs bureaucracies, and why they control and design them, are such important questions.

Sometimes, the coagulations of power, domination, and submission pretend to be something else, as in transforming the power of the army into the discipline of its troops. Institutions are supposed to help; bureaucratic domination can be hidden in a well-run institution. We are told that power is only exercised against enemies or to eradicate sickness and suffering, and that corporations do not dominate submissive workers but rather create wealth and jobs. We often ignore the power so deployed and the enormous power directed inward.

Bureaucracy and domination are reckoned easier than imagination, more efficient than cooperation. Bureaucracy is a clear example of Foucault's power/knowledge. Elites use their knowledge of the social world, in this case the world of elites, to create and control bureaucracies, which, in turn, control other people. In this process, power and knowledge are inseparable.[23]

What bureaucracy does to the bureaucrat is compelling, dominating, and subjugating. The stresses that bureaucracies casually produce for bureaucrats, who obstinately retain some of their humanity, can be overwhelming. People of diversity, such as women, African Americans, and people with disabilities, may especially experience these stresses.

Bureaucracies originate from deep structure rules. These rules are available to any elite. As Napoleon, Lenin, and Mao proved, they are also available to aspiring elites. There is little mystery to bureaucracy then, except for the mystery that many people do not recognize its nature or importance.

Bureaucracies are not natural entities like trees, nor theoretical entities like electrons. Rather, like winks, games, or armies, they are artifacts created by people. Presumably, people create bureaucracies with some purposes in mind and, presumably, bureaucracies express some of those purposes in their effects. One major purpose, as Max Weber so poignantly codified, is domination. It is impossible to comment reasonably on bureaucracy without invoking Weber. Alfred North Whitehead once called Western philosophy a footnote to Plato. To write on bureaucracy is to footnote Weber.

In his "Science as a Vocation," Weber observed that while art does not progress, so that by virtue of his time Pablo Picasso fashioned art somehow more advanced than Michelangelo, science does.[24] Bureaucracy at a later time is generally (though not universally) more advanced, accomplished, powerful, and extensive than bureaucracy at some earlier time. Such progress is possible because bureaucracy and social science apply to the world of people the power that technology and natural science apply to the world of things. Weber foresaw a world increasingly rational and bureaucratic, more today than yesterday, more tomorrow than today.

Similar to the efforts of another social planner, Frederick Winslow Taylor, Weber's codification of bureaucracy achieves its veracity by describing the social world as it should and will be rather than as it is. The story is one of design, engineering, power, and craft. Through their writings, Weber and Taylor provided rule books for an artificial game from which people with disabilities may well be excluded.

The social sciences are notoriously primitive, non-predictive, messy, and over-simplified. Imagine a realm of human action about which it was possible to specify certain laws that would predict future behavior, account for current behavior, and put past behavior into perspective. Suppose such laws were not trivial, but rich, indeed sometimes quite powerful.

Such realms exist and are called games. Consider the game of baseball. We know what constitutes a ball, a hit, and an out. We know the significance of hits and outs for winning or losing the game. We know that to hit a ball out of the field is to score one more point than the number of people already on base. We know that a player who has hit a ball will run to first base and we know that he will take the bases in order. We also have a reasonably good idea that a person who hits a home run will shake the hands of his teammates on his way to the dugout. Within the game of baseball, otherwise strange behavior makes sense. Baseball is an extreme example of Foucault's power/knowledge.

Studying bureaucracy is much like studying baseball. Both have rule books and in both rules largely govern behavior. (In studying bureaucracy, it may be useful to relate it to other social phenomenon. This may also be true of baseball. What are the odds of a consistent home run hitter getting paid more money?)

It is easier to analyze behavior that has been planned, easier to analyze artifact than fact. The analysis is easier when closest to the rules that have established and dominate the artifact, easier still when a rule book exists, and easiest of all when a rule is broken. We are analyzing a system that people have constructed and empowered. The analysis is predicated on its social construction. Knowledge is a result of prior power, the power to insert a certain set of rules, processes, patterns, and blueprints into the world of people, the power to engineer. Engineers often disguise this insertion by setting into motion an apparatus, structure, or system, and then waiting long enough for it to become a "natural" object of investigation.

Weber and Taylor were theorists of bureaucracy. They described how to design a world rather than explain a world already designed. Taylor was a draftsman and an engineer, not the constructor of models of what *is* but an architect drawing blueprints of what *should be*. Taylor extended engineering practices to the engineering of societies. He analyzed those motions of the body necessary to a task and engineered ever more efficient bodily motions. Analysis, dissection, and probing of the human body serve to increase its productivity. But such analysis does not account for the experience of the bodily diversity that is characteristic of disability.

Taylor's analysis was and is a technology that improves the efficiency of what Gary Becker, following Horace Mann, called human capital.[25] Yet, it is not enough to secure the technical efficiency of workers. For a system that allocates rewards unequally, it is also necessary to ensure political submission. As issues became more psychological and political and less medical and economic, engineers called upon social science.

One such instance was the Hawthorne studies. Some rather dubious conclusions were reached.[26] Then prescriptions were derived. Conclusions from prescriptions were less dubious. The implementation of the prescriptions from the Hawthorne studies, however dubious the original studies, engineered a field far more perspicacious than the original. They followed closely the perspicacity of Taylorist engineering, not so different really from the engineering of his (mythical) contemporary Abner Doubleday.

Still, it was not enough, as did Taylor, to engage the body of the worker. In the words of Foucault, in a different context, the soul must be engaged as well.[27] This engagement of the soul marks the move to further schools of management technology, described in some textbooks as having rendered Taylorism obsolete. But Taylorism has not died; it has become a "natural" part of organization. A discussion of social wholes, ultimately one that embraced both individuals and bureaucracies, was, nonetheless, necessary. Enter Weber.

Modern students of bureaucracy often frame their studies as complementing Weber's, as re-pointing cracks in his construction or perhaps adding an electrical system to a building constructed before electricity. Like Taylor, Weber was a social engineer. He achieved his inspired articulation of the rules of bureaucracy, in the first moment, by introspection, an introspection that asked, "If I were to design a bureaucracy, what would it look like?" In answer, Weber had access by his biography to the workings of elites and the methods of domination. In skeleton, his description of bureaucracy was a prescription of how to design a bureaucracy, a rule book for elites. Of course, people with disabilities are much less likely to be elites.

During World War I, Weber himself had a chance to construct a small bureaucracy for his country. Afterward, he took a more ambitious role in helping frame the constitution of the Weimar Republic. The ultimate failure of the second construction doubtless shows the fallibility of human architecture. The enduring quality of bureaucracy shows that human architecture is not always fallible.

Weber introspected, prescribed, and verified prescription against enormous erudition. Fundamentally, however, he was transcribing a rule book for elites who establish bureaucracies. (It is not always the case that a single elite constructs a bureaucracy. In fact, more generally it is a group of elites. Robert Michels sought to show how even exceptions end up as the rule.[28]) How might Weber's rule book have read? It might have read as follows.[29]

1) You should never decide to create a bureaucracy without a reason. Bureaucracies have purposes and means–ends rationalities, and they are tools for domination.

2) You should make your bureaucracy accountable to you. Rumors of bureaucracies accountable to no one except perhaps themselves are ample warning for any sane person. You should create an organization that you can dominate and control. You are aware that control itself is neither good nor bad but that control by you is good. It is sometimes unfashionable to think of bureaucracies as mechanisms of control, but it is more unfashionable for you to design a mechanism that you do not control and that may do you harm.

3) You should establish a hierarchical structure that allows you to achieve control, on the one hand, and purposive rationality, on the other. With hierarchy comes a division of labor.

4) You should give the officials in your bureaucracy fixed areas of jurisdiction so as to avoid conflict with your other projects. Furthermore, you want certain things done and the easiest way to ensure that they get done is to be clear about who does what.

5) You should also give the officials in your bureaucracy official duties. There is a limit to the obligation that they will feel toward you and your colleagues. Prescribing official duties embeds obligation into the very structure of your design. The genius of your bureaucracy will be to embed into its structure a series of mechanisms of efficiency, rationality, control, oppression, and power that will allow you to go about the rest of your business with confidence that your bureaucracy works for you.

6) You should base your bureaucracy on written documents, numbers, and computer systems so that you and your lawyers can keep track of what is going on, so that you and your accountants can inspect ledgers and make appropriate decisions, and so that those under you will have similar records on those under them. Peter Blau's fascinating study of the role of statistics in bureaucracies shows the utility of this form of documentation in the control of complex organizations.[30] If you know what goes on, have a way of finding out, and are presumed to be omniscient; any further control is largely unnecessary. Foucault made the general point. Surveillance can become power and is indeed best conceived of as a form of power.[31]

7) You should engage the full capacity of the officials in your bureaucracy. In practice, you know achieving this control will be difficult, but you also know that the closer you come to it, the better. An official who works for you will then not have occasion for deviousness, nor will he or she fritter away time.

8) You should govern your bureaucracy through universal rules, among which is promotion through expertise. It is in your interest that progress through the ranks of your bureaucracy is reasonably unbiased and acknowledges expertise. Other procedures may incur rancor. You would not have created a bureaucracy had you the time or inclination to bother with individual cases. The best bureaucracy is one that works for you without you.

9) You should establish a system that precludes quibbles. Since you do not have the time to settle each individual case and will seldom engage the people in your bureaucracy individually, the best you can do is make some statistical estimate of their potential contribution. Such statistical discrimination will hire and promote people according to average skill. To the extent that your bureaucracy precludes quibbles, it breeds belonging.

10) You should construct your bureaucracy so that it proceeds according to established rules, builds relationships through hierarchy, and shows its power by the form of the bureaucracy rather than entrusts it to the relations of the people within it. But you are not so naïve as to think that other power relationships will not exist. You certainly would not have gotten as far as you have in life if you had been so naïve. Violations of rules or exercises in private power and accommodation are not dangerous to your bureaucracy but rather, in moderation, helpful. Nevertheless, you will want general rules to govern your bureaucracy at the limits.

11) You should expect imperfections in your bureaucracy. It is not surprising that a bureaucracy works in the domain of people as a factory works in the domain of things. After all, you may have had some experience with factories. There are imperfections in any real-world

organization. As a prudent elite, you would hardly expect or even want it otherwise.

12) You should remind yourself that complete control, even where possible, is counterproductive. But you are equally aware that it is possible to construct an organization that will conduct the business that needs to be done in your absence more or less as it would have been done if you had been present. That is all you can ask for in an imperfect world.

Weber's "rules" read like the uncommonly common sense of any elite constructing any organization. What is their consequence when they are realized in the world and then analyzed? First, intelligibility. Second, ensconced in domination, durability.

Weber's study of bureaucracy occurred in the context of a wider project. That wider project was the study of domination, which of course includes the domination of people with disabilities, if they are not excluded from a bureaucracy altogether. Weber understood that the study of bureaucracy was an important chapter in any project concerned with domination.

If the realization that bureaucracy is a structure of domination was an important measure of Weber's vision, an important measure of his scholarship was to check insight against historical record. The Prussian bureaucracy of the eighteenth century closed its higher ranks to the bourgeoisie.[32] This specific feature of the Prussian bureaucracy had to do with the response of a Kaiser to a pressing situation. While there are certain principles in building any house, gothic arches, or even cellars, are not necessary to all houses. Weber chose those features necessary to all bureaucratic houses, not those that are contingent.

People make many things made in the world. Some endure. Endurance is a result of nurturing, economic viability, and politics. Elites construct bureaucracies and their power renders them actual out of a subset of possible artifacts. Bureaucracies endure not only through perceptive design but also through social selection. There may be odd characteristics injected into a bureaucracy to make it suitable for a certain place and time where and when it was created or to fulfill the idiosyncratic nature of its creator. Such idiosyncrasies are not likely to persist. Idiosyncrasies that do persist do so because of social selection. Modern bureaucracies require not only written documents but also telephones, computers, and other modern technologies. Bureaucracies may evolve, indeed have. In the personal mode into which Weber was translated, does the common sense of elites change or does that common sense become socially unfit?

The modern American corporate bureaucracy is neither natural nor invariant. Rather, it emerged from the pre-bureaucratic structures of the nineteenth century, fashioned by entrepreneurs who wanted to conserve, preserve, and extend the products of their entrepreneurship. At other times, bureaucracies were established to perform a task that needed doing, such as the TVA or Manhattan Project.[33]

Rosabeth Moss Kanter claims that the main issue at the start of bureaucracies was that of trust.[34] There are ways of exacting trust and insuring predictability that supplement the ways of bureaucracies, particularly at the elite level. As Kanter observed, elites in American corporations are likely to be of one class, one race, one sex, and dress and behave in a similar fashion. Elites are also likely to engage each other socially. Similarity ensures the reliability and trust central to the concerns of the original entrepreneurs, who are more likely to allow people like themselves to run their creations. Bureaucracies ensure other qualities that are meant to exact trust in an otherwise untrustworthy situation. People of diversity, including people with disabilities, may be considered untrustworthy.[35]

Both Weber and Taylor codify common sense, refine it, and sift it. One operates at the level of the worker, the other at the level of elites. One is more concerned with submission and economy, the other with domination. They complement each other.

In these reflections, I have redirected the problem of bureaucracy from discovering certain characteristics of existing bureaucracies to isolating rules for elites to use in constructing bureaucracies. This redirection has implications for the connection of knowledge and power. Knowledge about the social world is a result of the power of small groups of people to implement their blueprints on the world after their own design. Other propositions in social science, ostensibly about the social world, may in fact be propositions about individuals and groups of individuals with the power to realize their social visions.

Is bureaucracy necessary? According to what has been said, bureaucracy is necessary to the degree that elites think that way, that elites are able to realize their visions in the world, and that those visions are selected through social processes largely constructed by other elites. The question is in the builder rather than in what is built. I have said little about the possibility of non-elite organizational development that would honor diversity. Such bureaucratic equivalents might not look much like bureaucracies. Complex organizations where people with disabilities could work without bending or breaking might not look like bureaucracies at all.

In 1995, IBM dispensed with certain sartorial expectations. Earlier, American automakers started emulating some of the organizational techniques of their Japanese competitors. Bill Gates can contact anyone directly at Microsoft without going through intermediaries. Do such developments signal the end of bureaucracy in favor of some new form of organization? Or, are they rather changes in bureaucracy reflective of new technologies, global markets, and changing lifestyles? The second is correct. The essential structure of bureaucracy—never mind the domination and submission that are part of it—persists.

Bureaucracies are rapidly replacing professionalism, information understanding, and quantity quality. Bureaucracies do not oppose markets but work very well with markets. Weber foresaw this compatibility. He also foresaw the increasing rationalization of society that has occurred through the combination of bureaucracies and markets. Today, it is obvious that the business of America is business. This may also be true of the globe, ever more dominated by markets and bureaucracies. Do people with disabilities fit into this brave new world?

If bureaucracies deliver their goods efficiently, what is wrong with bureaucracy? There may be more right than wrong in isolated institutions that are not beneficial to those involved in them if they nonetheless render services to the larger society. The issue is the degree to which bureaucracies not only serve society but also expand to cover so much of society that virtually everyone works for, is part of, or is controlled by a bureaucracy. People with disabilities are or ought to be candidates for work in bureaucracies along with everyone else. That was one of the intentions of the ADA. But the bodies of people with disabilities are less likely to be interchangeable and more likely to be implacable. Their bodies do not fit or only fit with extreme pain. There is only so far that their bodies can be normalized without being broken. In short, they are more likely to be at odds with bureaucracy.

Increasingly, whether or not one joins a bureaucracy amounts to whether or not one survives. Most people work in bureaucracies; almost everyone works for someone else. Whether or not one works decides survival, which is figured ever more by the wages one earns. People have little choice about whether or not they work. To the extent that society is uniformly bureaucratized, people have little choice about whether or not they work in bureaucracies. The effect of a bureaucracy on those who work for it becomes as much of a standard by which to judge it as its efficiency.

As Kanter demonstrated, a bureaucracy also affects the lives of people well beyond its impact on those formally engaged in it.[36] Bureaucracies then have to be judged not only by their products and by what happens within them but also by their external effects. This issue is a pressing one in a present and future world that is and will remain largely bureaucratized.[37] All people dominated by bureaucracies have bodies. Many of these people have disabilities.

Democracy beyond bureaucracy

Many years ago I participated in a meeting of people with disabilities in the Boston area. There is a problem and humor in many such meetings. How does one get everybody together in the same place? Disabled people may live in residences figured by their physical and financial accessibility, and, therefore, located in otherwise strange places. I do not drive; hence, I am wary of suburbs. This meeting was in a suburban apartment building to which four of us were driven by a person whose disability did not interfere with her driving. Of course, we got lost, and, of course, we made a time of it by talking in the car.

When we got to our destination, we faced the problem of getting everybody out of the car. I was reasonably strong but poorly coordinated. The driver of the car had a powerful upper body, but the braces on her lower body did not provide her with sufficient stability. The third person was missing two forearms. The fourth person was floppy, too much so to exit the car himself. Instead of what usually happens when four people exit a car, really rather prosaic, we had a glorious time of it, interrupted by much laughter, trial and error, and open dialogue about who could do what. Leaving the car was less an act of four individuals than it was a communal democratic act.

Many situations among people with disabilities are democratically communal. Community and democracy come naturally to people with disabilities, unless, of course, the environment is a formal outing, a school function, bureaucratically organized work, or other similarly structured environments. But when people with disabilities can act in freedom they often embody the possibility of communal democracy.

Are people with disabilities exemplary of the possibilities of community, democracy, and freedom? I think they are. Do people with disabilities mesh well with pre-existing empowered bureaucratic environments? I think not. The same could be said of other people, if less obviously.

Modern power is often transmitted through the intermediary of environments, ever more constructed by human beings. Rarely is our species now confronted by the naked power of nature or God. Typically people exist in environments constructed, manipulated, and dominated by other people. Presumably constructed for the benefit of all people, these environments are usually constructed to benefit some people at the expense of other people. Is it even possible to construct environments that benefit all or almost all people?

Our species constructs, controls, and dominates its environments through elaborate technologies. Our species also dominates and even modifies its environments through supposedly free markets. The market is a self-evident arbiter of the worth of people and goods, also of humanity and the good. We also comfortably endow other environments, such as bureaucracies, assembly lines, and schools, with a morality and goodness, if not smugness. The easy morality of environmental manipulation and domination holds human beings superior to dinosaurs because they have survived while dinosaurs are extinct. Such assertions of superiority, of might makes right, and of moralizing the survival of a species, ignore the endurance of birds, bees, and bacteria. Non-self-regarding qualities, such as love of the young, may actually enhance the survival of a species.

One only need consider the child who, until a certain age, cannot survive in the natural environment or even in most environments dominated by human manipulation. We are told that the family provides a human

"*Haven in a Heartless World.*"[38] We are also told that it is "*Here to Stay,*" even though the "*World Changes,*" and yet to be concerned about "*The Politics of the Family,*" "*The Policing of Families,*" and, especially, "*Families on the Fault Line.*"[39] But other powerful, manipulated environments, such as schools, television, medicine, law, markets, and bureaucracies, whether "*Maid in the U.S.A.*" or elsewhere, influence and dominate this human environment of families.[40] One way or the other, children need tailored human environments to make it into adulthood. Why? And why are they usually provided (more or less)?

Parents have an interest not only in the survival of their children but also in the survival of their children's children. One lesson of family life is learning to become a parent. Evolutionary biologists find this interest congenial to their own way of thinking, according to which a member of any species has an interest in the perpetuation of his or her gene, as might be expected with *The Selfish Gene.*[41] They even find this interest moral and, to that degree, find morality natural. Though this assertion of morality from within is questionable, it is not self-evidently silly. Indeed, it may provide a foundation for what is commonly referred to as natural law.

Human beings are the same in most respects but different in other respects. For example, no non-twins have exactly the same genome. Even twins are biologically different, since their experiences are bound to be different. (Perhaps one has a trivial scar from an accident.) Such instances of diversity among human beings underlie morality.

There are, however, other differences of deeper consequence. Usually, these differences issue from some interaction of environments and people, of society and biology. The cut according to age is largely social and environmental, perhaps having to do with who works and how. Men and women are different biologically. (Women can bear children, men cannot.) But their differences are overwhelmingly social. (Men have access to more social resources than women do.) With race, an amazing social ruckus is made over aspects of diversity that are biologically trivial. Able-bodied and disabled people are different and differently so, and people with disabilities are differently different as well.

People in wheelchairs require ramps instead of stairs. (Interestingly, when a ramp is placed next to stairs about half the people who ambulate use the ramp, and everybody pushing a baby carriage or cart and wheeling a bicycle or other wheels does. The ramp is an architecturally unexpected viable solution to changes in elevation.) Suppose the wheelchair rider is a worker and the building he or she is attempting to enter is a workplace, productivity without the ramp is zero; productivity with the ramp is probably more or less the same as for the pedestrian.

People with visual impairments have other requirements of the environment. Among these are cues to navigate the environment. One such cue is the curb, which informs many visually impaired people of the vital distinction between people traffic and automobile traffic. Over three decades ago in Berkeley, visually impaired people had a conflict with wheelchair riders. The wheelchair riders wanted curb cuts, miniature ramps through the curbs. Visually impaired people wanted curbs to warn them of the street.

In Berkeley, people with disabilities were organized in this country's first independent living center, the only reason that curb cuts were even considered. After democratic discussion, a solution was reached. The curb cuts would lead diagonally off the corner of the sidewalk. It is hard to be certain if this environmental modification was a solution or a compromise, but it appears more of a solution. Are such solutions always possible between two sorts of people and, more generally, among all people?

I must clarify some of what I mean by democracy and some of what I do not mean. Democracy does not consist in inconsequential choices, whether in a supermarket or in a vote between the lesser of two evils. Democracy is not defined by the American experience; rather, America is democratic to the degree that it honors democracy. (Of course, the same holds true of the newly emerging democracies around the globe.) Democracy cannot be confined to the interstices of life. For life to be democratic, work must be democratic, living conditions must be decent, and morality must be human rather than organizational. Whether we live in such a country, in a country requiring modification, or in one requiring transformation is a serious question.

The human manipulations of environments that have occurred in this country and around the globe do not often show the characteristics of democracy. Instead, the polity, as it has evolved, dominates the human body through an artificial body called the corporation. This form of polity is organizationally rational, bureaucratic, utilitarian, and distributes its resources with gross and increasing inequality. I denote it a "corpocracy." The existence of a corpocracy makes the practice of democracy more diffi-cult, for a corpocracy sacrifices human freedom to organizational efficiency. Yet, democracy is the most effective and least dangerous way to pursue freedom for people in general and for people with disabilities in particular.

Few people ask for an infinite or even a very large number of environ-mental modifications for a very large number of people. That is unfortu-nate, because it may be necessary for a truly human approach to people with disabilities, children, indeed, all human beings. Social theorists from Karl Marx to Karl Polanyi have critiqued the consequences of not asking for it.[42] Both would find current human environments extremely problematic from a democratic perspective.

Such critiques of human environments are, however, surprisingly rare. Many people accept, rationalize, or rejoice in current human environments and look forward, more or less uncritically, to what the future holds. They say that anything else is dreaming, futile, or destructive. Often they question the ability and wisdom of people, or at least most people, to change their environments, which is effectively to deny the ability of people to be meaningfully democratic. Some people view powerfully manipulated human environments as given, even natural, which is effectively to deny that human nature is capable of democracy. In fact, there is no basis for such assertions, which stand more as rationalizations of power than of human nature.

What is might be otherwise, indeed might be changeable by a human race that has in the past changed environments to the significant point of not requiring natural selection. There is ample reason to critique aspects of the environment, including the media, bureaucracy, markets, technology, and more, not only abstractly but also through the lived experiences of populations of people, including those with disabilities. Such critiques recognize that disability is often defined by the negation of the able-bodied, an implicit definition of diversity by negation in the tradition of discourses of deviance, deficiency, domination, and discipline.

In practice, the voiced critiques of existing human environments by those different or thought different are often modest. This modesty is understandable, for the goals of assimilation, mainstreaming, and integration are honorable for members of such groups, who may understandably yearn to be part of the dominant culture. Such modern environments as the media, bureaucracy, markets, technology, and more not only beckon but also sometimes coerce. *The Man in the Gray Flannel Suit* of the 1950s and *The Brady Bunch* of the 1970s may have morphed in this "Information Age" but most people still desire to conform to the dominant culture, despite some protestations to the contrary.

Those who embody critiques may not be about to voice them. The effects of this disposition on people of diversity are profound. Rather than risk breaking, they may bend, sometimes over backwards. The women who revel in their biological diversity, extol sisterhood, and affirm the wrongness of patriarchy form one exception. They have greatly influenced the dialogue among women and between women and men. Since some of these women are mothers, children have been affected as well. People with disabilities find living in a time where partriarchy is being challenged felicitous—if disabled men because patriarchy often excludes them; if disabled women because patriarchy often diminishes them.

The ADA's reasonable-accommodations and undue-hardship language holds that reasonable accommodations for people with disabilities are desirable if they do not impose undue hardship on the organization. A reasonable accommodation is one that does not impose undue hardship increasingly in relation to the difference between its cost and the increased productivity of the organization. One can immediately recognize this calculus as a corruption of cost–benefit analysis because its focus is the organization and not the society. If it is any consolation, the legal system has become permeated with economics, efficiency, and cost–benefit analysis. But that should be no consolation. Rather, it shows the increasingly *de jure* relevance of utilitarianism in an empowered society, where utilitarianism is already largely the *de facto* ethic.

Of course, a reasonable accommodation is better than no accommodation. But are there no occasions when environments should be changed fundamentally? And do not the requirements of people with disabilities offer valuable indications about the directions that those changes might take? Instead of modifying an assembly line, might the assembly line not be in some radical sense dehumanizing, degrading, dominating, even disabling? And what of bureaucracy and its need for interchangeable people? In this context, reasonable accommodations might suggest a mere restructuring of jobs. But are people interchangeable? And what about the media that excludes people with disabilities because they do not conform to some ideal that no one else does either? Should reasonable accommodation include young handsome people in wheelchairs? Or, ought the media to be changed in more fundamental ways? One could clearly go on at some justified length.

The significance of the ADA is not diminished by the existence of environments requiring it to achieve some measure of justice toward people with disabilities. Nor is the consummate political skill involved in its construction and passage anything but a monument to the possibilities of political maneuver within a system of powerful organizational realities. People with disabilities surely have the same rights as people without disabilities, which is what the ADA was all about. Nevertheless, the justice of the act confirms the existence of an unjust system that requires it.

How much change is possible, for whom and at what cost? Is it possible to solve environmental problems always, or even usually, as neatly as in the Berkeley sidewalk example? Is it possible to accommodate the individual needs of many people or even many different sorts of people? If there had been a person or set of people who legitimately could not abide with angled curb cuts, it would have thrown Berkeley's solution into an arena of conflict. There were also financial costs associated with making angled curb cuts. It is likely that taxpayers included a sufficient number of friends of people with disabilities, bicycles, and baby carriages to make what looked like an additional burden a universal design that was at least acceptable, if not also enjoyable, to most people Yet surely at some point modification challenges uniformity, the exception challenges the norm, and the lived body challenges the assembly line, bureaucracy, and the other powerfully manipulated environments of a *status quo* that is too often regarded as given or even natural.

People with disabilities may often be too oppressed to push for or even seriously envisage more than modifications to oppressive environments. However, the difficulties that people with disabilities face in conforming to existing environments may indicate that many other people also have difficulties with these environments. The bodily diversity of the disabled person is a moral signal of what environmental change should be.

Living in manipulated environments may be frustrating, depressing, stressful, and painful. Sigmund Freud found civilization to be in conflict with many of the most powerful urges of the human psyche.[43] Weber found bureaucracy inevitable, powerful, efficient, and yet oppressive.[44] We remember Franz Kafka more for his writings, in which bureaucracy is soulless and mindless, than for his efforts as a talented bureaucrat to make bureaucracy less intolerable. Indeed, many critiques of bureaucracy use art, as Kurt Vonnegut and Joseph Heller did.

Many disabling accidents are iatrogenic to work. Not only are farm implements and assembly lines dangerous but so is our friendly manipulated environment of automobile transportation. The human body offers an unspoken critique of many manipulated environments of power. The validity of such critiques depends on the higher moral status of human bodies and unique human identities than organizational environments. Holding human beings to be of more value than organizational environments is certainly a plausible human morality.

Manipulated environments of power have their own morality, nonsentient, nonhuman, undemocratic, and uncaring. Often, one group of people exercises its power over another mediated by the environments it has created. Although a human being can recognize more immediate human oppression, exploitation, and domination, transmitting such qualities through environments renders them less obvious.

In business schools, "job analysis" is the study of how people fit into environments. Usually, some job analysis exists tacitly. In its more primitive forms, job analysis allowed for no bending of the organization after the needs of the people in it. Modern job analysis allows for some bending, so long as the bending is consistent with the higher morality of the organization.[45] The ADA is consistent with modern job analysis.

According to Jai V. Ghorpade, "modern job analysis is a managerial activity performed within organizations, and directed at gathering, analyzing and synthesizing information about jobs, which information serves as the foundation for organizational planning and design, human resource management and other managerial functions." Ghorpade provided four basic reasons for job analysis: jobs serve as the building blocks of organizations; jobs are consciously created in the modern enterprise; jobs are often created by people who do not perform them; and modern organizations constantly face rapid changes in their products, clienteles, and supply markets.[46]

Each of these four reasons for job analysis, while stated in comfortable abstractions, requires significant power in practice. It requires power to dissect an organization into building blocks. As there are generally many ways to perform this dissection, it also requires power to realize one particular way. That jobs are created shows the use of power, even if the word is not attached. That people who do not hold jobs create jobs for others is an act of power established by the difference between managers and managed. In fact, there are many ways to break down jobs. Arguably, job analysis is, or at least tries to be, part of the very environments that should be open to criticism, hence incapable of criticizing them. Job analysis that holds the projects of human beings as the ultimate arbiters of morality is simply not done.

One need only consider the job analysis of the members of a family. The traditional breakdown into breadwinner, housewife, and small friendly parasite obviously serves the interests of the adults, specifically the adult male, and the interests of external environments, such as the organization of work. A seemingly more modern version would be female and/or male human resource and resources for the future. Yet, it is possible to perform still more human job analyses. These might include such categories as affectionate, nurturing, and communicative female and/or male and frisky, developing, and responsive child.

Douglas C. Lummis described the organization of garment makers among a group of Filipino women.[47] Their sewing machines arranged in a circle, they talk to each other about job-related and non-job-related matters, and have control over what they do. This form of organization is different from the assembly line, with a different morality that holds the needs of its human members first. Its job analysis is correspondingly different, including such categories as person who sews, story teller, friend, and fixer. Lummis cited this case as an example of the democratic organization of work in opposition to the assembly line, most reasonably regarded as undemocratic, indeed dictatorial and dominating.

People with disabilities who are not evident—the common term is "hidden"—have a choice or others around them have a choice. A school system may, for example, get more funds by labeling its students disabled. The existence of public money for people with disabilities has caused many people who once abused substances of one sort or another to claim disability. There may also be incentives for people who are mentally ill to claim a disability status.

Part of the reason that more people are claiming such a status is that significant changes in public law as well as in social norms have reduced the stigma of being disabled. Given the diversity among human beings, it is possible to envisage everyone calling themselves disabled, or, as the euphemism goes, "differently abled." Many people are differently abled, probably all people, and a law providing for this diversity is one that could easily be abused according to organizational morality. But among the Filipino garment makers, a person with a disability would be given a different sort of job as a matter of course. In families, this is also usually true; although since families are part of a broader organizational framework, disability can be distressing even to the point of breaking them apart.

A common complaint against the ADA is that it goes too far, includes too many, and differs too much from traditional ways of doing things. Another way of looking at the act is that it does not go far enough.

Ultimately, it makes modifications according to organizational rather than human morality. This shortcoming does not lessen its progressive nature. A politics of freedom is advanced variously, particularly for people who are oppressed, as people with disabilities are.

What about human morality? Would the ADA even be necessary if human morality were honored? Is such a situation possible? Is there an inevitable conflict between human morality and instrumental ends? Is it possible to create environments that reconcile the two? Does every combination of human diversity have a job analytic solution?

As to the last question, the answer is no. Imagine that a solution has been arrived at for any finite set of diverse human beings. It is always possible to add another person or group for whom the initial solution does not work. Still, proximate solutions are always possible once we reckon with the human capacities for communication, creativity, and cooperation. An unsolved problem becomes open to discussion of people working together democratically, which discussion itself becomes part of their productive work.

People with disabilities embody the necessity and possibility of this democratic project, which is largely beyond the scope of the ADA to accomplish. They embody the conflict between human and organizational morality. If we fully respected and honored human morality, the ADA would be unnecessary. But it is necessary because we do not respect and honor human morality but rather allow organizational morality to dominate it. The ADA is thus necessary to provide a measure of decency to the work lives of people with disabilities. If, on the other hand, we held human morality above organizational morality in the collision between people with disabilities and organizational morality, where the collision is so obvious, it would provide valuable lessons for everyone. Human diversity is often the incarnation of an aspiration toward democratic organization, such as what Lummis reported on in the Philippines and what others have called for in other contexts.

To be political does not mean to cast a usually pathetic vote. Nor does it mean strengthening the parts of an empire that are evil and think of themselves as good, though that is the version of politics practiced by policy wonks and people in corporate power, not to mention the representatives of patriarchy, racism, and other forms of oppression who direct their power to oppress those who are different from themselves. At best, the social science on which public policy is based is descriptive, at worst misleading, and at any rate more sorcery than science. Public policy is at least partially and often largely applied utilitarianism. It dominates and normalizes. It is anti-political and its numbers trivialize. It is in the armies of the diverse and oppressed that an authentic politics appropriate to this postmodern age has emerged.

This politics is most developed among feminists who have perceived the inevitably political nature of much that was previously regarded as private, where power, oppression, and the subjugation of diversity fester. In collapsing traditional empowered boundaries between the public and private, between what was and was not political, modern feminism has offered another answer to Lenin's question, "What Is to Be Done?"[48]

We should never underestimate the significance of localized resistance. Frequently, resistance against local power, oppression, and subjugation is appropriate, cumulative, and possible. Localized resistance can precipitate massive political change with more efficacy and less danger than the vote or violence can. This approach proclaims a sensible answer, more accurately, many sensible mini-answers, to power, oppression, and the subjugation of diversity.

It is wise to conduct such a politics of freedom simply and unburdened from the shackles of hope, fear, and threat. Already it may be impossible to act in freedom while afraid of death. Such a politics must issue from courage, heroism, and love, not the abstract love of masculine heritage, but the concrete love of family, friends, parents, and children. In this respect, feminism's contribution has been decisive.

Disability and diversity figure prominently in a politics of freedom, which must continually question existing power. Disability and diversity are also often channels through which existing power flows. Existing power is not abstract; it is the subject of everyday life. It is for us to challenge power and to affirm diversity, not once and for some but for all and always. Only then might we create a truly inclusive body politic in which public policies such as the ADA will no longer be necessary.

Notes

1 See Jean Paul Sartre, *Anti-Semite and Jew* (New York: Schocken Books, 1995).

2 See William Roth, "Handicap as a Social Construct," *Society* 20, no. 3 (March 1993): 56–61.

3 See Irving K. Zola, "Self, Identify and the Naming Question: Reflections on the Language of Disability,' in 2nd edn, *Perspectives on Disability: Texts and Readings,* ed. Mark Nagler (Palo Alto: Health Markets Research, 1993), 15–23.

4 See John Gliedman and William Roth, *The Unexpected Minority: Handicapped Children in America* (New York: Harcourt Brace Jovanovich, 1980).

5 See Deborah A. Stone, *The Disabled State* (Philadelphia: Temple University Press, 1984).

6 See James E. Ysseldyke and Bob Algozzine, *Introduction to Special Education* (Boston: Houghton Mifflin, 1984).

7 *The Ragged Edge,* formerly *The Disability Rag*; www.ragged-edge-mag.com.

8 See Gliedman and Roth, *Unexpected Minority*, chap. 1; Harlan Hahn, "Civil Rights for Disabled Americans: The Foundation of a Political Agenda," in *Images of the Disabled, Disabling Images*, eds Alan Gartner and Tom Joe (New York: Praeger, 1987), 181–203; Roth, "Handicap as a Social Construct," 56–61.

9 See Harlan Hahn, "Can Disability Be Beautiful?" *Social Policy* 18, no. 3 (Winter 1988): 26–32; Paul K. Longmore, "Conspicuous Contribution and American Cultural Dilemmas: Telethon Rituals of Cleansing and Renewal," in *The Body and Physical Difference: Discourses of Disability*, eds David T. Mitchell and Sharon L. Snyder (Ann Arbor: University of Michigan Press, 1997), 134–58.

10 See David T. Mitchell and Sharon L. Snyder, "Introduction: Disability Studies and the Double Bind of Representation," in *Body and Physical Difference*, 1–31; Lennard J. Davis, ed., *The Disability Studies Reader* (New York: Routledge, 1997), esp., Rosemarie Garland Thompson's essay, "Integrating Disability Studies into the Existing Curriculum: The Example of 'Women and Literature' at Howard University."

11 See William Roth and Richard Sugerman, "Experience," in *Encyclopedia of Disability*, ed. Gary L. Albrecht (Thousand Oaks, CA: Sage Publications, 2006), II: 647–54.

12 See Lisa Walker, "Procedural Rights in the Wrong System: Special Education is Not Enough," in *Images of the Disabled*, 97–115.

13 See Michel Foucault, *Discipline and Punish: The Birth of the Prison* (New York: Vintage Books, 1995). Willowbrook was a state-run school for children with intellectual disabilities located on Staten Island. The school was closed in 1987, fifteen years after it had been the subject of a Geraldo Rivera exposé for child abuse.

14 See Michel Foucault, *The History of Sexuality*, vol. 1, *An Introduction* (New York: Vintage, 1980), 93.

15 See Isaiah Berlin, *Four Essays on Liberty* (New York: Oxford University Press, 1969).

16 This section of the essay is based on extensive personal communications, observations, and interviews.

17 Modern inquiries into the philosophy of science, however, call into question the autonomy of even the natural sciences. See, for example, Norwood Russell Hanson, *Patterns of Discovery* (Cambridge, UK: Cambridge University Press, 1961).

18 The 2010 Supreme Court decision in *Citizens United v. Federal Election Commission* overturning campaign finance restrictions on "corporate speech" exemplifies this appropriation.

19 See Seymour B. Sarason and John Doris, *Education Handicap, Public Policy, and Social History: A Broadened Perspective on Mental Retardation* (New York: Free Press, 1997).

20 See Mitchell and Snyder, "Introduction," 4.

21 See Ralph P. Hummel, *The Bureaucratic Experience* (New York: St Martin's Press, 1981).

22 See Zola, "Naming Question," 20–21; Marcia Rious, "Rights, Justice, Power: An Agenda for Change, a Culture of Diversity, Rights-Based Technology," in *Perspectives on Disability*, 515–23.

23 See Michel Foucault and Colin Gordon, eds, *Power/Knowledge: Selected Interviews and Other Writings, 1972–1977* (Brighton, UK: Harvester Press, 1980); Joseph Rouse, "Power/Knowledge," in *The Cambridge Companion to Foucault*, ed. Gary Gutting (New York: Cambridge University Press, 1994), 92–114.

24 See Max Weber, "Science as a Vocation," in *From Max Weber: Essays in Sociology*, eds and trans. Hans Gerth and C. Wright Mills (New York: Oxford University Press, 1946), 129–56.

25 See Gary Becker, *Human Capital: A Theoretical and Empirical Analysis, with Special Reference to Education* (Chicago: University of Chicago Press, 1980).

26 See Alex Carey, "The Hawthorne Studies. A Radical Criticism," *American Sociological Review* 32, no. 3 (June 1967): 403–16.

27 See Foucault, *Discipline and Punish*, 295–96.

28 See Robert Michels, *Political Parties* (New York: Free Press, 1966).

29 This discussion relies on Max Weber, 4th edn, *Economics and Society*, eds G. Roth and C. Wittich (New York: Irvington Publications, 1968), chap. 11; Max Weber, *Essays in Sociology*, chap. 8.

30 See Peter Blau, 2nd rev. edn, *The Dynamics of Bureaucracy* (Chicago: University of Chicago Press, 1963), chap. 3.

31 See Foucault, *Discipline and Punish*, 201–2, 206–7.

32 See Walter Dorn, "The Prussian Bureaucracy in the Eighteenth Century I," *Political Science Quarterly* 46, no. 3 (September 1931): 403–23; "The Prussian Bureaucracy in the Eighteenth Century II," *Political Science Quarterly* 46, no. 4 (December 1931): 259–73; "The Prussian Bureaucracy in the Eighteenth Century III," *Political Science Quarterly* 47, no. 1 (March 1932): 75–94.

33 See Anthony Downs, *Inside Bureaucracy* (Boston: Little, Brown, 1967).

34 See Rosabeth Moss Kanter, *Men and Women of the Corporation* (New York: Basic Books, 1977), 48–54.

35 See Erving Goffman, *Stigma: Notes on the Management of Spoiled Identity* (Englewood Cliffs, NJ: Prentice Hall, 1963); Kanter, *Men and Women of the Corporation*, 54–55.

36 See Kanter, *Men and Women of the Corporation*, 7–8, 250–51.

37 For one such vision, see Simone Weil, *Oppression and Liberty* (Amherst: University of Massachusetts Press, 1973).

38 See Christopher Lasch, *Haven in a Heartless World: The Family Besieged* (New York: Basic Books, 1977).

39 See Mary Jo Bane, *Here to Stay: American Families in the Twentieth Century* (New York: Basic Books, 1976); William Josiah Goode, *World Changes in Divorce Patterns* (New Haven, CT: Yale University Press, 1993); Ronald David Laing, *The Politics of the Family and Other Essays* (New York: Vintage Book, 1972); Jacques Donzelot, *The Policing of Families* (New York: Pantheon Books, 1979); Lillian Rubin, *Families on the Fault Line: America's Working Class Speaks About the Family, the Economy, Race, and Ethnicity* (New York: Harper Collins, 1994).

40 See Mary Romero, *Maid in the U.S.A.* (New York: Routledge, 1992).

41 See Richard Dawkins, *The Selfish Gene* (Oxford, UK: Oxford University Press, 1989).

42 See Karl Marx, *Dialectical Materialism* (Oxford: Basil Blackwell, 1979); Karl Polanyi, *The Great Transformation* (Boston: Beacon Press, 1985).

43 See Sigmund Freud, *Civilization and Its Discontents* (New York: W. W. Norton, 1962).

44 See, again, Weber, *Economics and Society*, chap. 11; Weber, *Essays in Sociology*, chap. 8.

45 See Richard Morfopoulos and William Roth, "Job Analysis and the American with Disabilities Act," *Business Horizons* 39, no. 6 (November–December 1996): 68–72.

46 See Jai V. Ghorpade, *Job Analysis: A Handbook for the Human Resource Director* (Englewood Cliffs, NJ: Prentice Hall, 1988), 2–3. See also Wayne F. Cascio, "Whither Industrial and Organizational Psychology in a Changing World of Work?" *American Psychologist* 50, no. 11 (November 1995): 928–39.

47 See Douglas C. Lummis, *Radical Democracy* (Ithaca, NY: Cornell University Press, 1996).

48 See Vladimir Ilyich Lenin, "What Is to Be Done? Burning Questions of Our Movement," *Collected Works* (Moscow: Foreign Languages Publishing House, 1961), V: 347–530.

10 The Conservative Attack on Affirmative Action

Toward a Legal Genealogy of Color Blindness

Julie Novkov

It's time for a change! The government should stop categorizing its citizens by color and ancestry, and create a society in which our children and grandchildren can just think of themselves as *Americans* and individuals. The colorblind ideal—judging others by the content of their character rather than the color of their skin—is more than a dream in California; it is central to the definition of who we are as a people, because, in California, we don't just dream; we *do* what others dream of doing.[1]

In 2003, Californians voted to reject Proposition 54, a measure that would have barred the state from recognizing race at all except in a few limited areas. This measure, promoted heavily by black California conservative and racial gadfly Ward Connerly, lost by a resounding margin of 64 percent to 36 percent. Its supporters must have been somewhat dismayed, as it came on the heels of three successful initiatives around racial issues in 1994, 1996, and 1998.[2] Nonetheless, the lessons learned through the Proposition 54 campaign served colorblind advocates well as they reconfigured their policy goals and strategies. The American Civil Rights Institute, founded largely to support the 1996 California initiative that barred racial affirmative action in California and had supported Proposition 54, moved to extend its agenda beyond the Golden State and replicate its less radical successes elsewhere. By the end of the 2008 election cycle, Nebraska had joined Washington, Michigan, and California in adding a ban on affirmative action in a variety of contexts to its state constitution. While Colorado narrowly rejected such a ban, Arizona will take up the question in this year's general election, and similar efforts have recently been undertaken in Oklahoma, Missouri, and Utah under Connerly's leadership.

What is the link between discursive practices and policy outcomes in these campaigns? In Michigan in 2006, the American Civil Rights Coalition, working in conjunction with the American Civil Rights Institute, provided strategic and institutional support for the Michigan Civil Rights Initiative. The polished campaign literature promoting the initiative featured photographs of a happy, integrated crowd of school children, a studious, integrated cluster of college students perusing a laptop, and a preschool-aged African American girl and blond white boy sharing an ice cream cone. The coalition fighting for the initiative received crucial support from the Center for Equal Opportunity, which describes its mission as "the promotion of colorblind equal opportunity and racial harmony."[3]

The initiative, which passed with 58 percent of the vote, banned affirmative action in Michigan. The coalition supporting it followed the rhetorical and organizational strategies that had proven successful in California in 1996 and Washington in 1998, and then were used again in Nebraska in 2008. In Arizona, which will vote on a similar constitutional amendment this November, the same image of the preschoolers sharing an ice cream cone appears on the banner of its supporters' website.[4] The initiation of a campaign against affirmative action also prompted Florida Governor Jeb Bush in 1999 to introduce the One Florida plan, which severely limited the state's capacity to engage in race-conscious remediation in education, contracting, and hiring. The primary advocates for these measures have been political and social conservatives, individuals and groups who reject the idea that attitudinal and institutional racism still require state correction, and who generally oppose efforts to ground anti-subordination policies and practices in any state institution. As Thomas Keck has shown, the rhetorical trope of colorblindness is now associated strongly with racial conservatism, if not outright racism, due to its widespread use in efforts to render the state impotent in addressing racial discrimination.[5]

The election of Barack Obama has heightened the salience of political rhetoric about colorblindness with discussions of whether America can now be considered a post-racial society. The aim of this chapter is to explore the roots of contemporary colorblindness and understand how this rhetorical trope has become a policy tool favoring conservative shifts in racial policies in the United States. To understand this development, I will explore the genesis of colorblindness as an aspirational racial policy for liberals at the end of the nineteenth century and its transformation into a policy argument during the struggles over desegregation in the early 1960s. I will also trace the appropriation of colorblindness as a conservative ideal, something that happened at a far earlier point than most scholars have recognized. This recovered history demonstrates the extent to which racial hierarchy is both hardwired into the structure of governance in the United States and highly malleable in linguistic terms. Without an underlying commitment to substantive racial equality that recognizes the history of institutionally embedded forms of racial hierarchy, racialized arguments are readily unmoored from their political implications and redeployed for other purposes.

Contemporary colorblind rhetoric harkens back to two iconic sources. The first is Supreme Court Justice John Harlan's dissent in *Plessy v. Ferguson* (1896), which marked the public initiation of the phrase itself. Harlan, objecting to the majority's adoption of the separate but equal standard for reviewing state actions that differentiated between individuals on the basis of race, wrote "[o]ur Constitution is color-blind, and neither knows nor tolerates classes among citizens. In respect of civil rights, all citizens are equal before the law."[6] The second source is Martin Luther King, Jr.'s "I Have a Dream" speech delivered at the March on Washington in 1963. King stated "I have a dream that my four little children will one day live in a nation where they will not be judged by the color of their skin but by the content of their character."[7]

While the logic of the claims for using colorblindness to oppose racial reform is clear, the use of the words of Harlan and King to ground this standpoint is interesting. Other scholars have concluded that both men would see the contemporary uses of their words as illegitimate appropriations that ill fit their own theories of the connection between racial subordination and state action. How, then, did colorblindness become the banner of a particular brand of racial conservatives who use it to promote retrenchment and retreat from what Reva Siegel termed the anti-subordination principle rooted in constitutional doctrine, most famously by *Brown v. Board of Education* (1954)?[8]

How appears at first glance to be the crucial question in this inquiry. This chapter will argue that *when* is equally important. The *when* of the rise of colorblindness as a malleable concept available for appropriation turns out to be highly significant in situating the term as a legal avenue for resistance to egalitarian reform. The association of colorblindness with affirmative action has, I shall argue, made it difficult for contemporary scholars to grasp its full significance as an ideology, an ordering device, and a constitutional principle.

Answering this question illuminates related questions about the New Right's mobilization of a racial agenda to generate cultural and political change in response to the legal dismantling of the white supremacist regimes of the early- to mid-twentieth century. Tracing colorblindness back to its early sources and uses generates two significant insights. First, it explains how racial discourse interacts with institutional change by focusing on the legal system as a crucial point of contact between state and culture. Michael Omi and Howard Winant have described the ideological nature of racialized change as a process of *racial formation* driven by social movements.[9] My analysis focuses on how racial formation occurs on the state's, as opposed to the movement's, side of the coin. The case of color-blindness demonstrates how racial formation can begin as a project that is simultaneously statist and cultural. It also more clearly shows how racial orders are constructed through the building of discursive associations facilitated through the exploitation of nodes of conflict in the courts.

Second, it indicates that, contrary to common beliefs about the rise of colorblind conservatism, the building blocks of these arguments were assembled in the 1960s. They were already available before the first legal controversies emerged over affirmative action and have remained largely invisible (except for Siegel's work) because they were built in the state courts. The use of colorblindness as a rhetorical and ideological challenge to affirmative action was not the result of growing conservative discomfort with racial progress that resulted in a political backlash.[10] Rather, it reflected a conscious strategy having its genesis in legal struggles over desegregation and the efforts of white supremacists to generate an ideological standpoint with sufficient legitimacy to resist change.

This chapter first situates contemporary colorblindness historically in the late-nineteenth and then mid-twentieth centuries. I argue that an investigation of the early struggles over colorblindness produces insights into the relationship between the building of racial ideologies and the development of legal norms and principles. In setting up this approach, I draw on Siegel's work on the shift from anti-subordination principles to colorblindness as well as on Omi and Winant's work concerning racial formation. Tracing the genealogy of colorblindness reinforces the latter's analysis of the dynamic processes of racial formation, but suggests that the state and social movements are not monolithic entities acting upon and responding to each other. In my own analysis, I review early uses of colorblindness in the courts, showing that it began to appear much earlier than most scholars have recognized. This genealogy lays bare a conflict over colorblindness that, when properly situated in its historical context, can explain how this concept became linked with conservatism in the late 1960s, several years before the affirmative-action battles reached the federal courts. The chapter closes with a discussion of how these developments came together to ground a full-blown legal- and state-based conception of colorblindness, which could then be mobilized for racial retrenchment. I also suggest the existence of an alternative, more progressive path not taken.

The early genealogy of colorblindness

As Justice Harlan's analysis is the source of the principle of colorblindness, it is worth investigating his use of the term. Constitutional scholars have generally seen *Plessy* as placing the final seal on the Supreme Court's abandonment of blacks, a process begun almost as soon as the Reconstruction Amendments were ratified. But recent work by Pamela Brandwein calls this narrative of consistent and progressive judicial abandonment into question.[11] Rereading Harlan's dissent through her lens provokes a reassessment of the initial meaning of colorblindness, rendering its contemporary uses for race unconsciousness deeply questionable.

Rewriting this history requires beginning with the *Slaughter-House Cases* (1872), the traditional place for starting such a narrative. While *Slaughter-House* is best known for limiting the potential breadth of the thirteenth and fourteenth amendments, it also initiated a debate over how the racial genesis of these amendments would play into their interpretation. Attorneys

John Campbell and J.Q.A. Fellows, arguing for the butchers seeking protection under the amendments, claimed that the scope and language of the amendments belied their origins. As the court reporter summarized their argument before the justices, "[f]rom whatever cause originating, or with whatever special and present or pressing purpose passed, the fourteenth amendment is not confined to the population that had been servile, or to that which had any of the disabilities or disqualifications arising from race or from contract."[12] This framing presented the language as having a neutral but extensive impact on all groups.

In interpreting the amendments, the Waite Court rejected this understanding. The thirteenth amendment, explained the Court, was aimed at a particular understanding of servitude that relied upon the experience of racial slavery.

> The word servitude is of larger meaning than slavery, as the latter is popularly understood in this country, and the obvious purpose was to forbid all shades and conditions of African slavery. It was very well understood that in the form of apprenticeship for long terms, as it had been practiced in the West India Islands, on the abolition of slavery by the English government, or by reducing the slaves to the condition of serfs attached to the plantation, the purpose of the article might have been evaded, if only the word slavery had been used.[13]

Likewise, the Court interpreted the addition of the fourteenth amendment as explicitly racial in its inception. It read the amendment as an attempt to address the freedmen's dilemma. "It was said that their lives were at the mercy of bad men, either because the laws for their protection were insufficient or were not enforced." Due to this state neglect, the federal government realized that "something more was necessary in the way of constitutional protection to the unfortunate race who had suffered so much. They accordingly passed through Congress the proposition for the fourteenth amendment."[14]

The Court summarized its interpretation of the Reconstruction Amendments with a reference to the Civil War and emancipation as events so recent as to barely warrant identification as history. Nonetheless, the majority stated that it was worth laying out "the one pervading purpose found in them all, lying at the foundation of each." This purpose was threefold: "the freedom of the slave race, the security and firm establishment of that freedom, and the protection of the newly-made freeman and citizen from the oppressions of those who had formerly exercised unlimited dominion over him." While only the fifteenth amendment directly invoked race, "each of the other articles was addressed to the grievances of that race, and designed to remedy them."[15]

Scholars have generally taken this racialized reading of the amendments as the Court's effort to limit the parameters for federal intervention into state governance, thereby grounding its interpretation of the privileges or immunities clause as not applying to the butchers. This interpretation of the Court's questionable motives is strengthened by analyses that then criticize its circular view of privileges and immunities as being subject to state-level definition rather than heralding a new era of federal intervention to protect civil rights on the ground.

Brandwein challenged this view. To be sure, the Waite Court was not pressing a vision of racial egalitarianism and it specifically denied the implications of national citizenship. But the Waite Court did not engage in an immediate, wholesale abandonment of blacks. Brandwein argued that the first justices to interpret the Reconstruction Amendments did so with an aim toward protecting the "civil freedom" of blacks and guaranteeing the backstop of federal intervention in instances where the states failed to protect the basic rights that the constitution now protected.[16]

With this reorientation, the Court's otherwise paradoxical interpretation of the privileges and immunities clause in *Slaughter-House* looks more coherent. Yes, the Court did consider and reject the adoption of a national standard for privileges or immunities. But the endorsement of state conceptions of privileges and immunities generated specific protections for freedmen if read as a conjunction of the state neglect doctrine and its analysis of the racial roots of the Reconstruction Amendments.

Indeed, the Court laid out its first interpretation of the equal protection clause in almost precisely these terms. The majority wrote that the equal-protection clause clearly invalidated the black codes that the Southern states had passed in the wake of emancipation. Even more, if the states did not take equal protection into account in framing future laws, "then by the fifth section of the article of amendment Congress was authorized to enforce it by suitable legislation." The Court expressed doubt that the equal-protection clause would ever extend to address "any action of a State not directed by way of discrimination against the negroes as a class, or on account of their race." Why? Because the equal-protection clause was "so clearly a provision for that race and that emergency, that a strong case would be necessary for its application to any other." Nonetheless, the Court left room for its forceful application either in the event of Congress's exercise of its enforcement powers under section five or in the case of state neglect whenever "some case of State oppression, by denial of equal justice in its courts, shall have claimed a decision at our hands."[17]

Through Brandwein's reinterpretation of state neglect, the racial significance of the fourteenth amendment becomes salient in the notorious *Cruikshank* case. The case arose from one of the most violent incidents of Southern resistance to racial reform, when whites in Colfax, Louisiana, surrounded and massacred about 200 black Republicans, many of whom were state militia members who had surrendered their weapons to the mob. Federal agents arrested the ringleaders, some of whom were indicted and convicted under the federal Enforcement Act of 1870. When they appealed to the United States Supreme Court, the Court overturned their convictions on the ground that the charges were improperly framed. While the case has been read as a core piece of the abandonment narrative, Brandwein noted that the Court's ruling rested upon technical objections to the charges. The justices felt that

> [t]here is no allegation that this was done because of the race or color of the persons conspired against. When stripped of its verbiage, the case as presented amounts to nothing more than that the defendants conspired to prevent certain citizens of the United States ... from enjoying the equal protection of the laws of the State and of the United States.[18]

While the fourteenth amendment prohibited the states from denying equal protection, the Court reasoned that it did not add to the rights that citizens held against each other, nor obligate the states to protect the equal enjoyment of those rights. The legislation "is intended for the protection of citizens of the United States in the enjoyment of certain rights, without discrimination on account of race, color, or previous condition of servitude." Absent a specific allegation that the deprivation of rights that the citizens of Colfax suffered "was on account of their race or color," no prosecution could be sustained.[19]

Brandwin's analysis of *Slaughter-House* and *Cruikshank* set up a reinterpretation of *Strauder* in which the Supreme Court invalidated a West Virginia statute barring blacks from jury service. The latter case's references to *Slaughter-House* now appear uncontradictory and clear, as an extension of this race-conscious interpretation on the part of the Court rather than as an ungainly lurch toward a more proactive interpretation of the Reconstruction Amendments. In *Strauder*, the Court invoked *Slaughter-House* to support the principle that the Reconstruction Amendments "cannot be understood without keeping in view the history of the times when they were adopted and the general objects they plainly sought to accomplish." The Court viewed the African American race as

> abject and ignorant. ... Their training had left them mere children, and as such they needed the protection which a wise government extends to those unable to protect themselves. They especially needed protection against unfriendly action in the States where they were resident.

The Court situated white rights as the yardstick, declaring that the purpose of the fourteenth amendment was

> to assure to the colored race the enjoyment of all the civil rights that under the law are enjoyed by white persons, and to give to that race

the protection of the general government, in that enjoyment, whenever it should be denied by the states.[20]

Without this context, *Strauder* appears to be a preliminary framing of the principle of colorblindness. The Court explained that the fourteenth amendment's general meaning was "that the law in the States shall be the same for the black as for the white; that all persons, whether colored or white, shall stand equal before the laws of the States."[21] But the Court qualified this neutral framing, explaining that the fourteenth amendment was primarily designed to protect blacks from racial discrimination. As the Court phrased it,

> [t]he words of the amendment ... contain a necessary implication of a positive immunity, or right, most valuable to the colored race—the right to exemption from unfriendly legislation against them distinctively as colored—exemption from legal discriminations, implying inferiority in civil society, lessening the security of their enjoyment of the rights which others enjoy, and discrimination which are steps towards reducing them to the condition of a subject race.[22]

The Court then rejected the West Virginia statute as discriminatory.

In invalidating the statute, the Court noted that it would reach the same result if those excluded were white men or "all naturalized Celtic Irishmen," which would seem to support a principle of colorblindness. But the Court clarified that it was not the simple fact of racial differentiation, but rather the message it sends, that renders such statutes invalid. Singling a group out in this way

> is practically a brand upon them, affixed by the law, an assertion of their inferiority, and a stimulant to that race prejudice which is an impediment to securing to individuals of the race that equal justice which the law aims to secure to all others.[23]

The Court condemned discriminatory laws not because they violated a principle of neutrality but because they themselves generated racial prejudice.

Harlan wrote his famous words in 1896 against this nuanced historical backdrop. By this time, Southern whites had finally triumphed in their insurgent campaign against the Northern imposition of black equality. The groundwork for the analysis in *Plessy* was laid through the turn toward a thinner analysis of equality grounded in state-level analyses of anti-miscegenation laws and their validation by the United States Supreme Court in *Pace v. Alabama* (1883). In *Plessy* itself, the Court, ignoring the principle of state neglect, claimed that the thirteenth amendment's elimination of badges of slavery did not apply to "every act of discrimination."

The principle of segregating public transportation did not threaten legal equality, as it was

> a statute which implies merely a legal distinction between the white and colored races—a distinction which is founded in the color of the two races, and which must always exist so long as white men are distinguished from the other race by color.[24]

With regard to the fourteenth amendment, the Court comprehensively reinterpreted the *Civil Rights Cases* (1883), setting aside the principle of state neglect and the historical rooting of the amendment in racial subordination. Rather, the Court claimed that the amendment secured "positive rights and privileges," but only "by way of prohibition against state laws and state proceedings affecting those rights and privileges."[25] Far from dismissing colorblindness, the majority insisted that legislation could not effectively break down racial consciousness.

> If the civil and political rights [which the Court defined in the most cramped fashion possible] of both races be equal, one cannot be inferior to the other civilly or politically. If one race be inferior to the other socially [which the Court defined broadly], the constitution of the United States cannot put them upon the same plane.[26]

Harlan's dissent reversed the polarity of this claim. He did not deny the reality of social inequality between the races, and readily acknowledged the dominance of the white race. But in his view legislation had the potential to send negative cultural messages, and segregation laws did just that.

> What can more certainly arouse race hate, what more certainly create and perpetuate a feeling of distrust between these races, than state enactments which, in fact, proceed on the ground that colored citizens are so inferior and degraded that they cannot be allowed to sit in public coaches occupied by white citizens?

In fact, Harlan argued, segregation laws went so far as to "defeat legitimate results of the war … and can have no other result than to render permanent peace impossible."[27]

This historically and politically engaged analysis led Harlan to conclude that "our constitution is color-blind." The idea of colorblindness did not originate with Harlan. He seems to have taken it from the brief filed on Homer Plessy's behalf. Plessy's representative before the Court, novelist and attorney Albion Tourgée, had been an abolitionist before the Civil War and an advocate for African American equality afterward. In his brief, Tourgée wrote

[i]nstead of being intended to promote the *general* comfort and moral well-being, this act is plainly and evidently intended to promote the happiness of one class by asserting its supremacy and inferiority of another class. Justice is pictured blind and her daughter, the Law, ought at least to be color-blind.[28]

Harlan's adoption of the phrase situated it in a related context, using it to deny the existence of a "superior, dominant, ruling class of citizens." Harlan's explication presented the proposition that "all citizens are equal before the law" and chided the majority for allowing the states "to regulate the enjoyment by citizens of their civil rights solely upon the basis of race." While this language could be taken as insisting that the state ignore race for all purposes, one is well advised to read Harlan's next words, which correctly predicted that "the judgment this day rendered will, in time, prove to be quite as pernicious as the decision made by this tribunal in the *Dred Scott Case*."[29] As Aleinikoff noted, the reference to *Dred Scott* underlined Harlan's point that the Reconstruction Amendments fundamentally sought to generate durable institutional change that would both guarantee access to full citizenship rights to African Americans and empower the national government to defend that access.[30]

Situating contemporary colorblindness

The phrase "colorblind" went relatively unrecognized until, as Siegel observed, the NAACP picked up the concept and included it in their brief before the Court in *Brown*. The Court declined the invitation to rest their ruling on that basis, instead going with a context-sensitive analysis of the message sent by segregation, in effect echoing and augmenting Harlan's analysis in his *Plessy* dissent. Both Kull and Siegel found scattered uses of colorblind principles to ground various elements of the judicial campaign to dismantle Jim Crow in the 1960s.[31] But the major public debates over the use of colorblindness took place around the United States Supreme Court's affirmative-action jurisprudence, beginning with *Bakke* in 1978. By the time of its use in these cases, it had emerged as a doctrinal principle largely used to counter affirmative-action plans. Advocates for state-level referenda and initiatives against affirmative action have generally used it in this way. This history suggests that the critical transformation of colorblindness into conservative ideology took place in the early 1970s.

King's "I Have a Dream" speech occurred before the struggles over affirmative action had erupted. King hoped to spur Congress to pass the first major round of legislation targeting racial discrimination since Reconstruction. His speech, taken in the context of the March on Washington, presented an image of an integrated and egalitarian community based in common brotherhood and situated against separatism and gradualism.[32] The original plan for the march emphasized economic and social issues, but the involvement of the NAACP, the Southern Christian Leadership Conference (under King's aegis), and the Student Nonviolent Coordinating Committee shifted civil rights to the forefront. King "primed the pump" for the speech with the widely disseminated "Letter from a Birmingham Jail," which introduced many of the themes of "I Have a Dream" to a broader, national audience.[33] While much of the language and structure of the *Letter* previewed "I Have a Dream," the language of character content did not. When King referred to his children in the *Letter*, it was to describe the pain of explaining racial segregation to them and seeing them incur bitterness and resentment toward whites for the practice.[34]

King's dream that his children be judged not by the color of their skin but by the content of their character came in the climactic dream sequence of the speech. As David Bobbitt noted, this section of the speech corresponds with redemption, "an elevated plane of meaning in which images of dreams and mountains are used to communicate a transcendent vision of equality, fulfillment of national promise, and secular/spiritual redemption."[35] The dream sequence presents six individual dreams, one of which includes the language of character content. That dream comes between two dreams of historical transcendence that refer specifically to the struggle against segregation and state-sponsored mass resistance to that struggle.

> I have a dream that one day even the state of Mississippi, a state sweltering with the heat of injustice, sweltering with the heat of oppression, will be transformed into an oasis of freedom and justice. ... I have a dream that one day, down in Alabama, with its vicious racists, with its governor having his lips dripping with the words of "interposition" and "nullification"—one day right there in Alabama little black boys and black girls will be able to join hands with little white boys and white girls as sisters and brothers.[36]

The speech then proceeds to the mountain imagery that closes it.[37] The context and the mixed references to public subordination and private violence against African Americans and their allies link black victimization to white guilt in a way that belies later uses of the speech to support a transcendent vision that forgets this history.

The trip from "I Have a Dream" to conservative invocations of color-blindness was not one that King or his allies would willingly have taken. The King who condemned "vicious racists" was also the King who demanded remediation and transformation for the ultimate cause of justice, not merely to perform the third act of a redemptive play designed to make whole the American body politic.[38] But the dream sequence's transcendental and partially timeless nature made it accessible as the core for a new national consensus legitimizing and taming the black struggle for a historically situated justice. This process transformed the black struggle for situated justice (what Siegel terms anti-subordination) into a universalized struggle for equality in which all can participate and which is broadly malleable in the absence of its context. These factors contributed to the identification of the dream sequence with the speech itself, the stripping away of the historical and political critique of racism in King's expression of the dream, and the simultaneous identification of the dream with the civil rights struggle and its rise to prominence as a new racial hegemony. Bobbitt emphasized how the dream sequence, both in its form and context as delivered in 1963 in Washington and in its received and mythologized presence afterward, excluded alternative, more radical visions of racial justice.[39]

The legal and cultural worlds operated on parallel tracks, but intersected at times. King could be seen as the moderate liberal center of the civil rights movement, soon to generate a national consensus around the dismantling of Jim Crow. The NAACP represented the moderate liberal legal center of the movement, promoting equality but still selecting cases carefully to avoid issues that, in its lawyers' perceptions, might ultimately derail the movement. Just as King rejected black nationalism and separatism, the NAACP steadfastly refused to litigate the question of anti-miscegenation laws in the 1940s and 1950s.[40] Likewise, the NAACP held off on litigating against overt racism among labor unions until fairly late in the game, working persistently to mediate and resolve conflicts over race through engagement with union leaders.[41] It is thus not coincidental that the NAACP Legal Defense Fund's principal brief in *Anderson v. Martin*, filed two days before the March on Washington, which argued for the invalidation of a Louisiana statute requiring the public racial identification of political candidates, relied extensively upon the principle of colorblindness and invoked Harlan's language.[42]

Given these starting points, we can see how it might be useful to explain the transformation of Harlan's and King's words from criticisms of the concrete racial subordination embedded in law and culture in the 1890s and 1960s to an endorsement of a thinly neutral conception of equality that repulses efforts toward racial remediation. This explanation will situate the rise of colorblindness as a rhetorical and political strategy for the New Right through its mobilization in the courts in the 1960s.

Making racial change: theory and method

Scholars across disciplines have sought to understand how state actors and institutions become invested in particular understandings of race. A full discussion of this topic is beyond the scope of this chapter, but, within political science, this project has been pursued primarily through the approach of American political development. This literature views race as a constructed phenomenon and addresses how race functions as an ideology. It also emphasizes how racial construction and the implementation of racial ideologies happen over time through the actions of state institutions and those working within them. The literature often incorporates the role of social movements as catalysts in this process.

Omi and Winant's work on racial formation provides a useful starting point for this inquiry. They presented a general model of racial formation, but focused on the transition between the civil rights movement and the rise of a racially based conservatism. They showed how the politics of the civil rights movement contributed to cultural transformations that ultimately resulted in the state's endorsement of new racial hegemonies. Their theory of racial formation laid out a cycling process of movement mobilization, engagement with the state, and institutionalization. Social movements, in their theory, generate new ideological conceptions of race that challenge the dominant racial hegemony embedded in culture and expressed through state institutions. Through engagement with the rest of society and state, social movements challenge the existing hegemonic structure, which may bend to allow access or ultimately transformation. When the state responds by adopting pieces of the movement's ideology, it transforms the hegemonic conception of race. The movement's ideological interventions are then woven into new practices and expressions that establish a new, and at least temporarily stable, racial hegemony.[43]

Omi and Winant explain the rise of conservative racial retrenchment through this model. In their view, the state adopted a normative position favoring equality through the pressure of the civil rights movement that contributed to the elimination of formal *de jure* racial discrimination in state practices and policies. This consensus solution closed down overt appeals to racism as well as the reintroduction of segregation and the black power movement as legitimate alternatives to mainstream civil rights. It also sparked the articulation of a new racial project on the right to challenge it. The result, again achieved through the politics of a social movement, was colorblind conservatism. In Omi and Winant's terms, colorblind conservatism has not yet fully transformed the state but it has become a significant limiting factor on the scope of egalitarian racial reform and has sometimes even been successful in attaining state retrenchments.[44]

These insights speak to the political science literature on race and political development. For one thing, they complicate Desmond King and Rogers Smith's racial orders thesis. King and Smith mapped political struggles over race through two competing racial orders, one seeking movement toward a substantively egalitarian ideal and the other supporting racial ascription in some form. These orders structure major swaths of political controversy, even when the controversies do not directly involve race. King and Smith then traced the competition between these orders through American history, noting the moments of transformative change when the orders themselves were in flux.[45] They attributed change in the orders to the shifting nature of racial coalitions and the configurations of particular groups of institutional stakeholders within the competing orders.

In the contemporary era, they identify the competing orders as a racially transformative egalitarian order and an anti-transformative order. The transformative order seeks change to address the material inequalities among the races in the United States, and mobilizes state actors and institutions to promote such change. The anti-transformative order opposes explicit efforts to reduce racial inequality and resists the use of state-based resources to promote equality.[46] The anti-transformative order, King and Smith explain, incorporates the civil rights consensus even while using the rhetoric of colorblindness to resist further racial equalization.

One common benefit of both theories is that they understand color-blindness and other racial ideologies as ideologies subject to processes of construction and change. This understanding distinguishes them from theories arising primarily from legal scholars who argue over the significance and meaning of colorblindness detached from its articulation as a historical phenomenon. Kull's controversial book, *The Color-Blind Constitution*, endorses colorblindness as the core principle of the equal protection clause's jurisprudence on race and describes what he sees as a continuous history of the principle's use for achieving racial justice. Colorblindness, in his analysis, is a fixed and universal practice that averts the dangers of judicial activism or, alternatively, inappropriate judicial acquiescence to legislative recognitions of race.[47] This analysis necessarily relies upon a static, universal, and ahistorical conception of race in back of the color to which the law should supposedly be blind. Such a conception of race ignores the historical relationship between the state and race as a dynamic co-constructive process.

But how does the process of racial formation work in dialogue with the state, and how do racial orders change over time? King and Smith's theory does not explain how change occurs beyond noting that racial coalitions can be destabilized through defections to the opposing order. Furthermore, the duality of the orders, though useful in understanding partisan competition, allows little room for understanding the influences of broader cultural phenomena (for instance, black power) that do not map readily into the binary.[48] Omi and Winant's theory does seek to explain racial transformation but their account does not adequately interrogate the role of the state, which appears as a passive and undifferentiated target for social movements. They thus ignore the interpenetration of social movements and the state.

We can understand how cultural struggles over race translate into political agendas for change by considering the law as a site of discursive development. This approach helps to explain racial transformation in the post-*Brown* era to the degree that *Brown* has come to serve as an aspirational icon of the constitutional principle of racial egalitarianism. As Siegel argued, *Brown* itself can most readily be read as rooting the constitutional principle of anti-subordination as the core of the equal protection clause.[49] Like "I Have a Dream," *Brown* has, however, been persistently subject to interpretations moving it away from this core. Because of the impact of *Brown* both legally and culturally—its instant emergence as a challenge to the edifice of Jim Crow and its provocation of wide-ranging strategies of mass resistance—race relations became simultaneously a legal and cultural battle in the post-*Brown* years.

Tracing the development of racial ideology through published opinions in court cases helps to show how social actors contending primarily over the scope and nature of state action sought to advance racial projects. This approach also reveals how and when particular discursive strategies began to break through into state discourse. Lawyers actively linked racial projects expressed in carefully chosen language to constitutional principle. The courts that adjudicated the resulting legal disputes advanced, rejected, or transformed those racial projects through their opinions. Judicial opinions then sparked further argumentative, ultimately ideological, efforts toward the advancement of racial projects. Considering this process closely can illuminate how racial transformation occurred at the specific discursive interface of state and culture that constitutional law provides.

The emergence of colorblindness as a legal strategy

Colorblindness remained dormant as a legal strategy or broadly employed trope after its debut in *Plessy*. Rather, the phrase lingered invisibly in constitutional law for several decades, in significant part because the announcement of the decision and the wave of state-level institutionalization of structural forms of racial ascription placed agendas of egalitarian transformation in retreat. While the courts largely hewed to the principle that the law had to pay lip service to equality, abstracted, decontextualized, and thin versions of equality were sufficient to pass constitutional muster on both the state and federal levels. Only the most egregious forms of overt racial discrimination provoked direct action on the part of the courts. Beginning in the 1930s, the NAACP's litigation strategy mounted a multilayered attack on *Plessy's* minimalist vision of equality. This attack emphasized both the need for a more robust analytic vision of equality that considered the state's complicity in sustaining racial discrimination and the need to consider the substantive, concrete, and vast inequalities existing under these practices. The NAACP strategy culminated in direct challenges to *Plessy* in *Sweatt v. Painter* (1950) and *Brown*, finally achieving the desired abandonment of separate but equal in the latter on both substantive and analytic grounds.

When *Brown* was announced, the outcome was less controversial among legal scholars than the reasoning, particularly its reliance on social science evidence. As Siegel observed, the controversy of the 1950s underlined *Brown's* roots in anti-subordination principles that did not directly address the question of racial classification. Herbert Wechsler's famous critique of *Brown*'s reasoning stressed its failure to articulate a neutral basis for invalidating segregation.[50] Siegel showed that resistant Southern activists and judges, faced with *Brown*'s analysis of the factual psychological harms of segregation, generated legal responses based on claims of psychological harm arising from forced integration. Wechsler's claim that neutral principles could not ground the outcome in *Brown*, taken in the context of the Southern legal argumentation challenging the real harm of segregation, generated a range of responses from legal scholars seeking to revise the reasoning and place it upon less controversial, and manipulable, constitutional ground.

Siegel argued that this dynamic sparked the rise of anti-racial classification justifications in the 1960s among academics supporting the assault on segregation. She identified Owen Fiss's pathbreaking article in the *Harvard Law Review* in 1965 and respected federal justice John Minor Wisdom's 1966 opinion upholding the Department of Health, Education, and Welfare's efforts to enforce the Civil Rights Act of 1964 as significant public turning points. She also identified the incentives for this shift among liberals, explaining that "a constitutional regime that treated racial classification as presumptively irrational would legitimate *Brown* by deflecting attention away from social struggle over the kinds of injury to which equal protection doctrine ought to be responsive."[51] This mode of reasoning began to take hold as a "cooler" means of justifying the invalidation of Jim Crow policies than the "hot" allegations concerning the status harms of segregation.[52] Siegel noted that when the Court finally confronted the explosive question of laws barring interracial sexual intimacy (first in *McLaughlin v. Florida* in 1964 and then in *Loving v. Virginia* in 1967), the justices sidestepped the status or dignitary harms communicated by these statutes in favor of invoking a rule against racial classification.[53]

Siegel claimed that the arguments against racial classification effectively challenged *de jure* segregation in the South and, as judges began to express these arguments in terms of colorblindness, they supported an agenda of racial equalization through federal court decision-making. She emphasized that anti-classification primarily served as a tool to dismantle state-based efforts to support racial hierarchies placing people of color at the bottom, while the federal courts consistently allowed state and local governments to act against segregation, even if these actions required the direct recognition of race. She summarized the developments of the 1960s as generating a liberal—in King and Smith's terms, racially egalitarian—form of colorblindness, replacing the Supreme Court's jurisprudence of the 1950s based in the psychic and status harms of segregation.[54] This practice enabled federal and state courts to uphold race-conscious plans designed to address *de facto* racial discrimination in public school pupil placements outside of the South. Federal courts in New York, New Jersey, and Oklahoma, and a state court in Illinois all upheld race-conscious plans against the anti-classification claims of white parents in the mid- and late 1960s.[55] By 1965, federal justice Skelly Wright, a leading architect of school desegregation in the North, had written a law review article objecting strenuously to white plaintiffs' citation of Harlan's dissent and efforts to connect it to *Brown* to generate an anti-classification principle to use against desegregation plans.[56]

These arguments, however, could ultimately be detached from the desegregation context and moved elsewhere. Siegel argued that such efforts began to gain traction in the context of Nixon's election as president in 1968. This space was opened in part because Nixon ran against the Warren Court on issues of race, initially by appealing to Northern whites opposed to school desegregation as well as through a coded racial language of law and order. While Nixon provided equivocal support for several desegregation measures during his first term, in 1972 he campaigned, to quote Siegel, "on opposition to welfare, busing, quotas, and affirmative action—even against programs begun in his own administration."[57] His federal court appointments reflected these sentiments, creating additional space for change. Siegel thus viewed the late 1960s as the initiation of institutional change through the courts and claimed that the pressures on courts to adopt conservative colorblindness were not effective until the cultural and political context had shifted in that direction.[58]

Siegel's analysis complements Omi and Winant's. She focused on the efforts to achieve desegregation on the part of legal strategists for the civil rights movement. She contended that in the early years following *Brown*, these strategists promoted a racial project of reform based on anti-subordination rhetoric, linking this rhetoric to constitutional principle. As the state began to acknowledge and assimilate the reformist language, elite members of the legal community, both within and outside of state institutions, articulated fallback justifications. By the late 1960s, these justifications had been fully assimilated by the state through the legal system, as judges regularly invoked anti-classification language to invalidate stigmatizing racial regulations and practices while rejecting this language as a basis for denying ameliorative race consciousness. The principle of anti-classification as a norm for state behavior grounded the civil rights racial hegemony in the center of American culture and politics in the late 1960s and early 1970s.

In Omi and Winant's terms, this hegemony posed a target for an oppositional right-wing racial project. Siegel's research suggests that opponents of the civil rights consensus recognized by the mid-1960s that they would not be able to return to the previous racially conscious and overtly ascriptive regime, and made a considered choice to build out from the new consensus. Appropriating the language of anti-classification and linking it to colorblindness in their legal arguments, these advocates pushed back against race-conscious remedies for discrimination by invoking neutral constitutional principles. But as Omi and Winant had suggested, Siegal was able to demonstrate that these legal arguments could not gain significant enough traction to influence the state until the cultural and political conditions were hospitable.

In considering litigation in the federal courts, this analysis largely resonates. The explicit use of colorblindness as a legal principle supporting desegregation emerged in the early 1960s. The Fifth Circuit Court of Appeals first raised it in a Texas desegregation case decided in 1960. *Boson v. Rippey* invalidated a plan devised to avert desegregation in the Dallas public schools by "grouping ... the schools into white, Negro, and mixed schools, and ... canvassing parents and pupils in order to learn 'who does and who does not want integration, and thereby give all concerned what they prefer'."[59] The court's opinion rejected alternative frameworks for its ruling in favor of colorblindness. "Negro children have no constitutional right to the attendance of white children with them in the public schools. Their constitutional right ... is the right to ... be treated simply as individuals without regard to race or color."[60] The first time the United States Supreme Court used the phrase after 1896 was in 1961 in *Garner v. Louisiana*, where the Court reversed the convictions of seven defendants engaged in a sit-in at an all-white lunch counter for disturbing the public peace. Justice Felix Frankfurter quoted Harlan's language approvingly in his concurrence.[61]

The Fifth Circuit followed the Supreme Court into the realm of criminal justice in a 1964 case involving a black man who was sentenced to death for raping a white woman in Louisiana. The case came out of Jefferson Davis Parish, which was approximately 25 percent black and 75 percent white. The jury commission had ensured that blacks were included in each grand jury. The grand jury for Collins's case had apparently been subject to particularly careful selection methods, as six blacks were purposely included in the pool of twenty from which the grand jury of twelve, which only heard this particular case, was selected.[62] The Fifth Circuit condemned this process on colorblind grounds, explaining

> [a] Negro is entitled to the equal protection of the laws, no less and no more. He stands equal before the law, and is viewed by the law as a person, not a Negro. ... An accused cannot demand a mixed grand jury, some of which shall be of his same race.[63]

When the case was re-argued due to allegations of factual errors in the circuit court's ruling, the majority reached the same outcome. Nonetheless, a concurrence and a dissent distinguished analytically between the permissibility of excluding jurors on the basis of race and making an effort to include minorities in jury pools, thus implicitly criticizing a blanket rule of colorblindness.[64] These early critiques of colorblindness did not prevail against the framing device, however, as the Fifth Circuit again relied on colorblindness, citing Judge Richard Rives's endorsement of the principle in his majority opinion in *Collins*, to push forward a 1968 suit challenging long-standing Georgia practices of discrimination against blacks in jury service.[65]

The phrase made scattered appearances in federal district court opinions as well. In 1962, the district court for the Southern District of New York endorsed colorblindness as a constitutional principle in a case challenging the racialized drawing of congressional district lines in New York City. The plaintiffs alleged that three districts had been drawn to "pack" non-white citizens and citizens of Puerto Rican ancestry, while a fourth district had been drawn to over-represent whites.[66] The district court, in dismissing the suit, claimed that creating districts that took racial proportions into account "would indeed be to indulge in practices verging upon the unconstitutional."[67] In his concurrence, Justice Wilfred Feinberg rejected the claim that "under the Constitution there can be 'good' segregation along racial lines as against 'bad' segregation," invoking colorblindness as the appropriate principle for congressional redistricting.[68]

The other cases addressing colorblindness all involved school desegregation plans and mostly involved judges who were confronting arguments from whites that state-initiated desegregation measures constituted unconstitutional recognition of color. In early 1961, the district court for the Southern District of New York supported a desegregation suit in *Taylor v. Board of Education*.[69] The New Rochelle school board argued that if permissive zoning privileges were to be mandated for blacks, the law would also require the extension of the same privileges to other ethnic and racial minorities, and that this would place too great a burden on the district. The court quickly brushed aside this concern, explaining that "the Constitution is not this color-blind. The *Brown* decision dealt only with Negroes."[70] The NAACP's struggles to desegregate the Oklahoma City School District bore fruit in 1965 as the federal district court approved a rezoning plan. The court stated that

> [c]learly, defendants may consider race in disestablishing their segregated schools ... *Brown* ... did not convert Justice Harlan's metaphor into constitutional dogma barring affirmative action to accomplish the purposes of the Fourteenth Amendment. Thus, racial classifications which effect invidious discrimination are forbidden but may be upheld if deemed necessary to accomplish an overriding governmental purpose.[71]

In the same year, a New York federal district court admonished white plaintiffs challenging a desegregation plan in Buffalo, characterizing their argument as a "so-called 'colorblind' standard" and noting that "the Fourteenth Amendment, while prohibiting any form of invidious discrimination, does not bar cognizance of race in a proper effort to eliminate racial imbalance in a school system."[72]

One case foreshadowed arguments we associate more readily with the late 1970s. In adjudicating a Virginia case allowing a freedom-of-choice plan to stand in 1966, Justice Thomas J. Michie quoted the language of the Oklahoma school district decision approvingly in insisting that the plan had to promote the integration of the teaching staff. This portion of his opinion highlighted the significance of history, explaining that the consideration of racial factors in assigning teaching staff was appropriate in the context of the Augusta County school district's past discriminatory practices. He approved this plan as a specific measure to address previous faculty segregation and emphasized that his order "envisions no ... permanent race consciousness."[73] The insistence on using race consciousness only to address previous discrimination and to ameliorate the specific wrongs caused by it, alongside the implication that race consciousness itself was a dangerous tool, presaged the debate over affirmative action. Not coincidentally, this ruling also dealt a partial loss to the foes of segregation through Michie's approval of the conservative freedom-of-choice plan in lieu of mandatory desegregation.[74] His analysis of the specific history of racially discriminatory practices did not fully interrogate Virginia's troubled racial past nor justify addressing it through measures that privileged group remediation over individual associative choice.

Despite this case, federal court justices generally used colorblindness fairly lightly, and usually as a simple quotation of the Harlan principle in support of some action taken to dismantle segregation. This history bolsters the commonly accepted view that colorblindness in the 1960s was primarily an anti-racist principle.

The picture on the state court level is somewhat more complex. It suggests that conservative appropriations of colorblindness *by state actors* began well before the first lawsuits were filed challenging affirmative action plans. As on the federal level, colorblindness made its emergence in the early 1960s, first appearing in a North Carolina case in 1961. However, the concept was not initially used to invalidate or question the state-sponsored implementation of racially discriminatory policies. Seven defendants, five black students from North Carolina College for Negroes and two white students from Duke, challenged their convictions for trespass at a segregated Durham luncheonette. The court rejected their claims, resting its ruling upon the principle that a private operator of a restaurant "has the right to select the clientele he will serve, and to make such selection based on color, race, or White people in company with Negroes."[75] The only place that the court looked for discrimination was in the trespass statutes themselves. It concluded that both statutes under which the defendants had been charged were "color blind." The main purpose of the statutes "is to protect people from trespassers on their blinds" and the only proper form of inquiry was to establish possession, intentional entry, and denial of permission to enter by the person in possession.[76] The high court of South Carolina cited this language approvingly in 1961 in reaching a similar decision to uphold the convictions of several black high school students who refused to leave a segregated lunch counter.[77]

Michigan's high court cited Harlan's *Plessy* dissent more equivocally in a 1962 case that overturned an administrative regulation targeting racial discrimination in the real estate business. The court agreed that Harlan's view was an appropriate statement of "constitutional faith" even as it was using the state action doctrine to invalidate a regulation seeking to move closer toward that "faith."[78] In this sense, colorblindness appeared as a liberal ideal rather than a principle, as it did not provide sufficient authority for the court to find a state action appropriate for redress.

The first appearance of colorblindness in a state court ruling against racial discrimination affecting a person of color was in Delaware in 1963, where the high court considered a challenge to the Delaware Alcoholic Beverage Control Commission's denial of a license to a black man. Diverting from the central issue in the case, the court provided a wide-ranging analysis of the history, politics, and practices of racial discrimination in the region as well as a broad look at the racial and geographic elements of the market for alcohol. Citing sources ranging from United States Supreme Court cases on discrimination to anthropologist Ruth Benedict, the court demolished the Delaware commission's claim that they had not known the plaintiff's race when they had denied his license and that the neutrality of the stated policy was sufficient to save it. Color-blindness appeared near the end of the opinion as an aspiration, rather than a rule of law or principle, when the court quoted Lyndon Johnson. "Until justice is blind to color, until education is unaware of race, until opportunity is unconcerned with the color of men's skins, emancipation will be a proclamation but not a fact."[79]

Liberal uses of colorblindness to dismantle racism predominantly pre-vailed on the state level in the 1960s in school desegregation cases. New Jersey, Illinois, Michigan, and New York courts all endorsed color-blindness in desegregation lawsuits that upheld plans for closing segre-gated schools or otherwise tackling the problem of school segregation. In New Jersey, the high court rejected a claim that the school board had taken inappropriate notice of race by citing colorblindness as an ideal but relying factually on the long history of inimical race consciousness in state policies and practices.[80] In Michigan, the high court pointed out that colorblindness need not prevent the recognition of the historical sig-nificance of race in state practice, especially in the organization of public schools.[81]

However, even in the realm of school desegregation, colorblindness was not solely a liberal or anti-racist concept in the 1960s. A dissent in a 1964 New York Court of Appeals case presented a full-blown endorsement of colorblindness in arguing that a school desegregation plan should have been rejected. Justice John Van Voorhis argued that the school board had clearly used race as the dominant factor in redrawing school district boundary lines and attacked this practice as violating the principle of equality. He identified the bedrock of anti-discrimination as "that each person shall be treaded without regard to race, religion or national origin" and claimed that "if school children ... can be admitted because they are Negroes, they can also be admitted because they are Aryans."[82] This understanding of colorblindness also grounded a 1964 New York trial court ruling that invalidated the busing of black pupils to white schools. The court labeled the program a form of "preferential treatment" and condemned it as "a departure from the ideal which judges individuals by their own merits rather than by affiliations."[83] Likewise, another dissenting justice on the New York Court of Appeals in a different school desegregation case commented the next year that "in striving for the desired color-blind society, we should avoid creating an increasingly color-conscious one."[84]

Another dissent criticized a 1968 Illinois ruling upholding a state statute that mandated the regular review and redrawing of school district boundaries to promote integration in language reminiscent of 1990s critiques of affirmative action. Justice Byron House complained that the act told school authorities, "for the first time in the history of this State ... to make decisions based upon race and nationality."[85] Quoting *Brown*, House's dissent defined racial discrimination as "the act of making distinctions based on race" and identified the principle of anti-discrimination at the heart of *Brown* as a neutral principle. He suggested that targeting policies based on class rather than race would be a more acceptable constitutional basis for ameliorating inequality, citing Paul Freund's famous analysis of the limits of civil rights law.[86]

The phrase also appeared in two more Southern state cases before the 1970s. In both cases, the court rejected challenges to racist practices. The location of colorblindness in these cases was, however, quite different. In 1965, a Georgia appellate court took a position that fit more comfortably in the standard story that colorblindness was an anti-racist principle in the 1960s by rejecting a black defendant's challenge of his conviction on the ground that blacks had been excluded from his jury. The court cautioned that a strong invocation of colorblindness would strip away discretion in jury selection. The interests of justice, implied the court, rested upon a process that would secure higher-quality jurors than "random selection."[87] While the court in this case did not issue an anti-racist ruling, it did view colorblindness as a commitment to (inappropriate) racial equalization.

In the other case, an Alabama appellate court considered whether the arrest and conviction of six black defendants for trespass at a Talladega soda fountain constituted sufficient state action to trigger an equal protection claim. The facts of this case looked significantly like *State v. Avent*, the 1961 case where the North Carolina high court upheld the convictions of seven participants in a Durham lunch counter sit-in. The Alabama court asserted that, in this case, the state was not disingenuously claiming to be colorblind because it had not drawn an explicit color line in passing the criminal statute under which the defendants were prosecuted.[88] Since the sheriff and criminal court had simply been enforcing the law, reasoned the court, the racial motives of the complaining drugstore owner could be read out of the narrative. This 1964 case mobilized colorblindness in support of a racist outcome.

Ultimately, these cases show that the process of appropriating color-blindness to support racialized subordination began almost as soon as the phrase began to show up in court opinions again in the 1960s. This process involved the direct engagement between private opponents of deseg-regation and supporters of Jim Crow, on the one hand, and judges seeking to slow or reverse the pace of racial change, on the other. It took place quietly alongside what Siegel identified as the articulation of color-blindness as a potential alternative justification for outcomes supporting racial liberalization. The existence of this largely unnoticed engagement that began in the early 1960s undercuts any reading of colorblindness as a neutral principle that worked for people of color in the 1960s when the agenda was to dismantle state-supported discrimination but against people of color in the 1990s when the agenda was to give people of color special assistance from the state. It also undercuts the idea that conservatives began to appropriate the language of abstract liberal equality in the 1970s as part of a backlash against the racial advances of the 1950s and 1960s.[89] Even before local conflicts over schooling busing became nationally salient through the United States Supreme Court's ruling in *Swann* in 1971 and the racial violence in Boston in 1974, the argument that colorblindness should be embraced to block legislation or court orders mandating racial remediation was present and available not just among private white opponents to desegregation and state defenders of Southern restrictive laws but in judicial discourse itself. The tools of colorblind conservatism were already fully assembled and ready when the cultural struggles over affirmative action broke out.

The significance of the genealogy of colorblindness: genealogy as generative

Tracing the uses of colorblindness and finding the roots of its conservative appropriation in the early 1960s shows how colorblindness was able to emerge so quickly and dominantly as an ideological tool in the 1990s to be deployed against affirmative action and other race-conscious practices designed to remedy the long investment of both the federal and state governments in institutionalizing racism. By the late 1960s, while con-servative colorblindness was not yet dominant, significant groundwork had been laid, and its ideological coherence had been cemented through a series of fairly invisible court cases. The arguments for using color-blindness were coming both from private individuals challenging anti-racist changes in state practices as well as from state officials seeking to sustain racially subordinating practices. When judges adopted those arguments, they encouraged their continued use in future cases.

These judicial endorsements were significant even if not widespread. Straightforward judicial uses of colorblindness to push back against racial reform encouraged those sharing such an agenda that this tactic could work effectively by assimilating the new constitutional language of substantive racial equality and turning it around to reinforce the *status quo* by denying the legitimacy of state ameliorative action. The more ambiguous uses were helpful, too, as some judges endorsed a colorblind society as an ideal. Even if they went on to rule that this ideal had not yet been reached, the linkage of colorblind discourse with a vision of the nation's liberal ideals generated normative principles cabining state action by questioning its legitimacy and requiring justification for state recognition of race. This analytic move rendered history invisible and outside the realm of judicial access, unless it was a specific and individually based history, such as that recited by Michie in his ruling upholding a freedom-of-choice plan to desegregate local schools. Other judges who endorsed colorblindness recognized its risks and sought to limit the scope of the principle or else establish criteria through which it would operate as a general rule while still being subject to exceptions.

Genealogical analysis also underlines the significance of discourse and its mobilization through the interaction of political activists and state actors capable of institutionalizing it. Colorblindness was neither inherently liberal nor conservative, but could be mobilized to serve either agenda. A liberal/conservative distinction misses the ambiguity and complexity of the rhetoric in the critical period following its reintroduction when its meaning and political impact were being contested.

Ultimately, the conservative appropriation of colorblindness won out over the efforts of those who attempted to use it to facilitate the dismantling of ascriptive racial hierarchies. Purveyors of the conservative version of colorblindness that triumphed legally and culturally linked it to liberal values of justice and fairness as abstract principles.[90] This linkage facilitated the triumph of their particular understanding of colorblindness over alternative conceptions of the concept. It also enabled conservatives to articulate their vision of colorblindness as a legitimate interpretation of widely shared American values.

The ability of conservatives to link their vision of colorblindness both to the cultural iconography of King's "I Have a Dream" speech and to the United States Constitution likely helped their cause. While conservatives did not directly cite King in embracing colorblindness until later, they nonetheless used the concept to generate ideological challenges from within the fragile civil rights consensus in the hopes of ultimately dismantling it.

The embrace of colorblindness as a policy of retrenchment by some judges created a legal script that facilitated the later appropriation of

King's rhetoric. By linking the legal language of colorblindness to King's encompassing vision and rendering that vision compatible with their own political goals, conservatives, working both within and outside of state institutions, were able to create an effective legal and cultural response to liberal egalitarianism. In their vision, national redemption for past racist practices could only be reached through the embrace of conservative colorblindness as a foundational norm. This form of redemption would make existing institutional and structural forms of racism invisible by insisting upon the state's incapacity to see race while simultaneously defining racism as an uncontrollable individual attitude not subject to regulation.

Genealogy enriches our understanding of both political and legal development. American political development tends to view state institutions as the starting and ending points of change, and the metric of change is the transformation of institutions. Focusing on the genealogy of a racial ideology highlights the interface between state and culture through the mechanism of legal discourse. As work on legal mobilization has shown, legal discourse provides a point of contact between social movements and state institutions. Once the production of legal discourse is endorsed by multiple state actors in the form of judicial discourse, it reflects back out through case law, which, in turn, can shape the trajectories of social movements. An obvious example of this phenomenon is the significance of the discourse of choice in liberal feminist arguments for abortion rights. The legalization of the right to choose abortion through the means of identifying choice as a constitutionally protected liberty had implications beyond the courthouse door, ultimately generating the common cultural identifier for liberal feminists who favor the protection of abortion rights as pro-choice.

The example of colorblindness, while rendered more complex by the initial struggle over ownership of the word, illustrates this process as well. In the end, colorblindness as a constitutional discourse provided the grounding for the rise of the rights-based conservatism that Keck identified. It wrote the cultural script that enabled the New Right to succeed in both legislative and legal forums.[91]

Siegel suggested that liberal defenders of black rights struggling for advances in the 1960s made a crucial mistake in abandoning the anti-subordination talk of *Brown* in favor of colorblindness. Her mistake story could be enhanced by pushing the timeline back and showing that the initial liberal embrace of colorblindness had a conservative counterpart from the outset. My point is, however, somewhat different and turns to political science's recent engagement with history. Siegel's lost tradition of anti-subordination, while valuable, overlooks the potential of historical analysis as a mode of egalitarian constitutional analysis. Given the intensive process of construction and doctrinal production that has taken place during the last four decades, a straightforward return to her anti-subordination tradition also seems impossible.

In other work, I used this approach to consider two cases, both addressing the same constitutional question and reaching the same result, but doing so through very different argumentative mechanisms.[92] These cases were *Loving*, which Siegel and I both criticize for the United States Supreme Court's reliance upon a constrained and abstract use of equal protection and due process to invalidate the Virginia law barring interracial marriage, and *Perez v. Sharp* (1948), where the California Supreme Court generated a deep historical and deconstructive attack on the purposes and outcomes of California's anti-miscegenation statute in invalidating it. Recognizing the significance of a state actor's adopting this approach not only demonstrates how racial projects (in Omi and Winant's terminology) are advanced, but also underlines how state agents can be active participants in the reconfiguration of racial hegemony.

Justice Roger J. Traynor's approach in *Perez* employed the equal-protection methodology of 1948. Rather than first inquiring as to the nature of the distinction and determining the level of scrutiny, he directly considered the state interests at stake in generating and maintaining a policy against interracial marriage. Working through the interests articulated in legislative debates and in the state's briefs, he systematically demonstrated that those interests masked a state desire to establish and maintain racial hierarchy. Like the ruling in *Brown*, Traynor relied upon social science evidence. (He turned to anthropology more than sociology.) Nonetheless, the primary mode of reasoning was tracing the historical generation of the statute and its concrete purposes and effects over time.[93] Unlike *Brown* and *Loving*, which both considered history but lightly and focused on the tangled debates over the fourteenth amendment, *Perez* focused closely upon the history of discriminatory state practices as the root of racist attitudes and institutionalized racism in the present. The links between individual racist attitudes and embedded institutional racism were tightly enough woven to render it the state's responsibility to act affirmatively to address the problem in Traynor's view. As a state agent himself, he actively contributed to the generation of a new racial project rooted in a historicized vision of equality and participated on the ground level in initiating new racial formations that social movements would soon advance.[94]

Eventually, these attempts at carving out new racial projects were only temporarily dominant within social movements and never fully commanded the endorsement of most state agents. Rather, the interplay between movement activists and state agents reinforced another path, this one a dehistoricized embrace of a more universal and neutral vision of racial equality.

Such critics as Robert Gordon might reply that the generation of yet another lost tradition of interpretation misses the main point. To him, the point is the conservative focus on vulnerable sites of power relations and manipulations of constitutional and common law doctrines in order to rebalance the deep structure of the legal system to privilege New Right agendas.[95] This criticism, however, overlooks the opportunity genealogical analysis affords to deconstruct that process and identify nodes for advancing more progressive racial formations. One such node is Judge Traynor's in *Perez*, a historically sensitive analysis that questions the generation of the group distinction at stake in a statute undergoing equal protection review and the state interests that it was intended to serve.

Notes

1 See "Vote 'YES' on Proposition 54, Argument in Favor of Proposition 54," in *Voter Information Guide* (Sacramento: State of California, 2003); http://vote2003.sos.ca.gov/propositions/2-3-2-arguments.html [accessed April 14, 2010].
2 Proposition 187 (1994) limited undocumented immigrants' access to state services; Proposition 209 (1996) barred the use of race or ethnicity in admissions, employment, or contracting by any public institution; and Proposition 227 (1998) severely limited bilingual education. See Gary Segura and Luis Fraga, "Race and Recall: Racial and Ethnic Polarization in the California Recall Election," *American Journal of Political Science* 52 (2008): 421–35.
3 See Center for Equal Opportunity; www.ceousa.org [accessed March 27, 2007].
4 See Arizona Civil Rights Initiative; www.arizonacri.org [accessed April 15, 2010].
5 See Thomas Keck, *The Most Activist Supreme Court in History* (Chicago: University of Chicago Press, 2004).
6 See *Plessy v. Ferguson*, 163 U.S. 537 (1896), at 559 (Harlan dissenting).
7 See Martin Luther King, Jr., "I Have a Dream"; http://gvctermp01.virtualclassroom.org/rights/mlk/speech.html [accessed April 15, 2010].
8 See Reva Siegel, "Equality Talk: Antisubordination and Anticlassification Values in Constitutional Struggles over *Brown*," *Harvard Law Review* 117 (2004): 1470–1547. See also Reva Siegel, "Discrimination in the Eyes of the Law: How 'Color Blindness' Discourse Disrupts and Rationalizes Social Stratification," *California Law Review* 88 (2000): 77–117.
9 See Michael Omi and Howard Winant, *Racial Formation in the United States: From the 1960s to the 1990s*, 2nd edn (New York: Routledge, 1994).
10 Joseph Lowndes has critiqued this commonly held view. See Joseph Lowndes, *From the New Deal to the New Right: Race and the Southern Origins of Modern Conservatism, 1945–1976* (New Haven, CT: Yale University Press, 2008).
11 See Pamela Brandwein, "A Judicial Abandonment of Blacks? Rethinking the 'State Action' Cases of the Waite Court," *Law and Society Review* 41 (2007): 343–86.
12 See *Slaughter-House Cases*, 83 U S 36 (1873), at 35 ("Brief for the Plaintiff in Error").
13 See *Slaughter-House* at 62.
14 See *Slaughter-House* at 70.
15 See *Slaughter-House* at 71–72.
16 See Brandwein, "Judicial Abandonment," 347.
17 See *Slaughter-House* at 81.
18 See *United States v. Cruikshank*, 92 U.S. 542 (1875), at 554.
19 See *Cruikshank* at 555.
20 See *Strauder v. West Virginia*, 100 U.S. 303 (1879), at 306.
21 See *Strauder* at 307.
22 See *Strauder* at 307–8.
23 See *Strauder* at 308.
24 See *Plessy* at 543.
25 See *Plessy* at 547.
26 See *Plessy* at 552.

27 See *Plessy* at 560–61 (Harlan dissenting).

28 See Alexander T. Aleinikoff, "Re-reading Justice Harlan's Dissent in *Plessy v. Ferguson*: Freedom, Antiracism, and Citizenship," *University of Illinois Law Review* 1992 (1992): 961–77; Andrew Kull, *The Color-Blind Constitution* (Cambridge: Harvard University Press, 1992), 119–21.

29 See *Plessy* at 559 (Harlan dissenting).

30 See Aleinikoff, "Re-reading Harlan's Dissent," 970.

31 See Kull, *Color-Blind Constitution*, 160–81; Siegel, "Equality Talk," 1480.

32 See Mark Vail, "The Integrative Rhetoric of 'I Have a Dream'," *Rhetoric and Public Affairs* 9 (2006): 57.

33 See Vail, "Integrative Rhetoric," 59–60.

34 See Martin Luther King, Jr., "Letter from a Birmingham Jail," *Why We Can't Wait* (New York, NY: Penguin, 2000), 64–84.

35 See David Bobbitt, *The Rhetoric of Redemption: Kenneth Burke's Redemption Drama and Martin Luther King, Jr.'s "I Have a Dream" Speech* (Lanham, MD: Rowman & Littlefield, 2004), 83–84.

36 See King, "I Have a Dream."

37 Bobbitt read this section as "mov[ing] out of historical time and the sociopolitical realm and into mythic time and the supernatural realm." See Bobbitt, *Rhetoric of Redemption*, 83. One should note, however, that when King turns from exhorting freedom to ring from the mountains of the north and west to the south, he specifically mentions Lookout Mountain in Tennessee and Stone Mountain in Georgia, the birthplaces of the first and second Ku Klux Klan respectively.

38 Derrick Bell and other critical race theorists have suggested that the focus of the speech was upon assuaging white guilt, not achieving racial justice. See Derrick Bell, *Faces at the Bottom of the Well: The Permanence of Racism* (New York: Basic Books, 1992).

39 See Bobbitt, *Rhetoric of Redemption*, 111.

40 The ACLU, not the NAACP, provided primary support for the suit resulting in the legitimation of interracial marriage in *Loving v. Virginia* (1967). See Peter Wallerstein, *Tell the Court I Love My Wife: Race, Marriage, and Law—An American History* (New York: Palgrave, 2003).

41 See Paul Frymer, *Black and Blue: African Americans, the Labor Movement, and the Decline of the Democratic Party* (Princeton, NJ: Princeton University Press, 2008).

42 See Kull, *Color-Blind Constitution*, 166.

43 See Omi and Winant, *Racial Formation*, 48–53.

44 See Omi and Winant, *Racial Formation*, 95–136.

45 See Desmond King and Rogers Smith, "Racial Orders in American Political Development," *American Political Science Review* 99 (2005): 1–17.

46 See King and Smith, "Racial Orders," 9.

47 See Kull, *Color-Blind Constitution*, 182–225.

48 See Nikhil Singh, *Black is a Country: Race and the Unfinished Struggle for Democracy* (Cambridge, MA: Harvard University Press, 2005).

49 See Siegel, "Equality Talk," 1470–78.

50 See Siegel, "Equality Talk," 1476.

51 See Siegel, "Equality Talk," 1499.

52 See Siegel, "Equality Talk," 1502–3.

53 See Siegel, "Equality Talk," 1503–4.

54 See Siegel, "Equality Talk," 1518.

55 See Siegel, "Equality Talk," 1517, n. 162, 1519, n. 168.

56 See Siegel, "Equality Talk," 1519, n. 170.

57 See Siegel, "Equality Talk," 1523.

58 See Siegel, "Equality Talk," 1521.

59 See *Boson v. Rippey*, 285 F.2d 43 (5th Cir. 1960), at 45.

60 See *Boson* at 45.

61 See *Garner v. Louisiana*, 368 U.S. 157 (1961), at 263 (Frankfurter concurring).

62 The Circuit Court's opinion gives few details about the full background of the case and process of jury selection; however, the opinion states that the blacks put on the grand jury were known to parish officials and implied that they were selected for that reason.

63 See *Collins v. Walker*, 329 F.2d 100 (5th Cir. 1964), at 105.

64 See *Collins v. Walker*, 335 F.2d 417 (5th Cir. 1964).

65 See *Pullum v. Greene*, 396 F.2d 251 (5th Cir.1968). The Middle District of Alabama also quoted Rives's language in invalidating the jury selection processes in Macon County, Alabama. See *Mitchell v. Johnson*, 250 F.Supp. 117 (M.D. Ala. 1966).

66 The case was complicated by the intervention of Democratic Party elites, including Congressman Adam Clayton Powell, who claimed that the real injury was partisan rather than racial, as the Republican-controlled New York legislature had drawn district lines to dilute Democratic voting strength. See *Wright v. Rockefeller*, 211 F.Supp. 460 (S.D.N.Y. 1962).

67 See *Wright v. Rockefeller*, 211 F.Supp. 460 (S.D.N.Y. 1962), at 467.

68 See *Wright* at 468 (Feinberg concurring).

69 See *Taylor v. Board of Education*, 191 F.Supp. 181 (S.D.N.Y. 1961).

70 See *Taylor* at 196.

71 See *Dowell v. School Board of Oklahoma City*, 244 F.Supp. 971 (D. Okla. 1965), at 980.

72 See *Offermann v. Nitowski*, 248 F. Supp. 129 (W.D.N.Y. 1965), at 129.

73 See *Kier v. County School Board of Augusta County*, 249 F. Supp. 239 (W.D. Va. 1966), at 247.

74 Freedom-of-choice plans, often advanced by opponents of desegregation, allowed some latitude for parents to select the schools their children were to attend. While plans that were clearly designed to evade the mandate of *Brown* were universally invalidated, plans with more modest scopes in districts with smaller proportions of black students sometimes made it through constitutional review.

75 See *State v. Avent*, 253 N.C. 580 (1961), at 586.

76 See *Avent* at 589.

77 See *City of Charleston v. Mitchell*, 239 S.C. 376 (1961), at 387.

78 See *McKibbin v. Corporation & Securities Comm.*, 369 Mich. 69 (1962), at 90.

79 See *Mitchell v. Delaware ABC Comm.*, 193 A.2d 294 (Del. 1963), at 371.

80 See *Morean v. Board of Education*, 200 A.2d 97, 99 (N.J. 1964).

81 See *Jipping v. Lansing Board of Education*, 166 N.W.2d 472 (Mich. 1968), at 474.

82 See *Balaban v. Rubin*, 199 N.E.2d 375 (NY 1964), at 378.

83 See *Strippoli v. Bickal*, 248 N.Y.S.2d 588 (SC NY 1964), at 603–4.

84 See *Van Blerkom v. Donovan*, 207 N.E.2d 503 (NY 1965), at 506.

85 See *Tometz v. Board of Education*, 237 N.E.2d 498 (Ill. 1968), at 506 (House dissenting).

86 See *Tometz* at 507 (House dissenting).

87 See *Brookins v. State*, 144 S.E.2d 83 (Ga. 1965), at 89.

88 See *Banks v. State*, 170 So.2d 417 (Ala. App. 1964), at 421.

89 See, again, Lowndes, *New Deal to New Right*.

90 Interestingly, John Rawls's celebrated abstract theory of justice as fairness, which he developed analytically through a heuristic device imagining individuals (not groups) lacking any markers of identity as the fundamental subjects of justice and law, was first published in 1971. See John Rawls, *A Theory of Justice* (Cambridge, MA: Belknap Press, 1971).

91 See Thomas Keck, "From *Bakke* to *Grutter*: The Rise of Rights-Based Conservatism," in *The Supreme Court and American Political Development*, eds Ronald Kahn and Kenneth Kersch (Lawrence: University Press of Kansas, 2006), 414–42.

92 See Julie Novkov, *Racial Union: Law, Intimacy, and the White State in Alabama* (Ann Arbor: University of Michigan Press, 2008). In this work, I benefited greatly from the insights of historian Peggy Pascoe. See Peggy Pascoe, "Miscegenation Law, Court

Cases, and Ideologies of 'Race' in Twentieth-Century America," *Journal of American History* 83 (1996): 44–69; Peggy Pascoe, *What Comes Naturally: Miscegenation Law and the Making of Race in America* (New York: Oxford University Press, 2009).

93 See *Perez v. Sharp*, 32 Cal.2d 711 (1948).
94 This approach was also used in the Delaware liquor commission case considered above.
95 See Robert Gordon, "The Struggle Over the Past," *Cleveland Law Review* 44 (1996): 123–43.

Index

For Product Safety Concerns and Information please contact our EU
representative GPSR@taylorandfrancis.com
Taylor & Francis Verlag GmbH, Kaufingerstraße 24, 80331 München, Germany